LAUREN HELLIS

DELICIOUS *Potato* COOKBOOK

*350 quick and wholesome homemade recipes
to celebrate the beauty of potato*

TABLE OF CONTENT

INTRODUCTION

Research on nutritional and medical-related issues has taken several decades, and is still in process. Although there are many articles about the nutritional quality of the potato, most of them deal only with specialized areas of research (Woolfe 1987). Reviews covering all nutritive aspects of the potato are very rare, and none so far has dealt with theeffects of the potato on human health by looking at both the nutritive, medical and toxicological issues associated with the potato. This review will bring together the nutritional, medical and toxicological characteristics and studies of the potato, addressing issues of relevancein each of these specific aspects.

Basic information about the potato

The potato is grown in 80% of the countries of the world (FAO 1999). It is second only to maizein terms of the number of producer countries, and fourth in global tonnage, after wheat, maize and rice. Its importancein the United States, Canada, Europe, Australia, the countries of the former Soviet Union and Latin America is well known. Much less well known is the rapid growth rate of potato production in most other underdeveloped or developing countries.

During the past 20 years, the rate of increasein potato production in under developed or developing countries has outpaced growth rates of most other major food crops. Today, the potato is produced in 132 of 167 independent countries of the world and more than three and a half billion people, about 80% of the world's population, inhabit underdeveloped or developing countries that produce potatoes (Woolfe 1987).

Potatoes are one of the most efficient crops for converting natural resources, labor and capital into a high-quality food. They can yield more nutritious food material more quickly on less land and in harsher climates than most other major crops. In addition, theedible food material can be harvested after only about 60 days (Valdes 1998).

A potato plant is 50-100 cm high. Leaf arrangements are spiral, with 20-30 compound leaves consisting of a terminal leaflet and two to four leaflet each 6-10 cm long. The underground parts may enlarge to form from a few to about 20 tubers, varying in size and shape round to long. Tuber skin varies from brownish white to deep purple, with a flesh of white to yellow, along with purple. Genetic alteration of desired characteristics has produced a great variety of cultivars.

One serving of potatoes is usually one potato, which has about 148 grams, 100 calories, zero cholesterol, no fat, and contains Vitamins A, C, B, riboflavin and thiamin.

It also has minor nutrients such as protein, amino acids and nicotinic acid (Oguntuna and Bender 1986).

The potato contains high nutritive value. Its chief food component is starch, but also has protein of high biological value. As the potato is alkaline, it is very helpful in maintaining the alkali reserves of the body and preventing acidosis. Besides containing a substantial amount of alkaline salts, it is rich in soda, potash and vitamins A and B (Valdes 1998). The most important contribution of the potato is probably its Vitamin C content. Scurvy in Europe has become uncommon with theincreased use of the potato.

Common misconceptions about potatoes

There are many misconceptions about the nutritional value of potatoes. Potatoes are usually regarded as a ritual food or a garnish for other major meal components. Where consumed as a complementary vegetable with staple food items, potatoes are usually believed to make a negligible contribution to the nutritive value of a meal. Even where the potato is regarded as a staple food, it is usually seen only as an energy source and thereis little awareness of its vitamin or protein content (Bakel 1986).

Obtaining factual information to correct these misunderstanding is difficult. Reviews covering all aspects of the subject areextremely rare, and most treat the topic in a superficial manner. In addition, the journals in which many of these articles appear address mostly theinterests of the processing industry (Bakel 1986).

Potatoes areindigenous to Central and South America, and were probably first domesticated in Chile. Europeans discovered them when Pizarro destroyed theInca Empirein Peru and they were brought back to Europe around 1570 (Schmiedieche 1983; Hawkes 1998; Valdes 1998). From Spain, the potatoes moved to England and Ireland, probably in 1586 by Sir Walter Raleigh, but they were already popular by 1610. Some people, however, resisted them as food for a long time: until 1780, they were vigorously excluded from French tables, because they were thought to cause leprosy.

In France, they were finally established during the famine that followed the Seven Years' War (1756-1763). Frenchman Antoine August Parmentier, who was fed potatoes in a prisoner-of-war camp in Germany, returned to France to find his people starving. He set up potato-soup kitchens throughout Paris to assist the poor, and Louis XVI recognized his work by saying "France will thank you some day for having found bread for the poor" (Schmiedieche 1983). In fact, heis recognized in a most appropriate way by the famous potato soup Parmentier. Interestingly, Ben Franklin dined at Parmentier's home and was treated to course after course of potato-based dishes, up to and including a potato-based after-dinner liqueur (Schmiedieche 1983).

Devout Scotch Presbyterians refused to eat potatoes for some time because they were not mentioned in the Bible. However, Ireland was the first to adopt the potato, and even madeit the foundation of its national diet, a fact that was to have terrible repercussions in 1845 when a late blight attacked the potato crop and caused the famine that was to send Irish émigrés all over the world seeking a better life (Hawkes 1998; Valdes 1998).

In Prussia, King Frederick William I liked potatoes so much that he threatened to cut the noses and ears of all the peasants who refused to plant potatoes. Russian peasants considered potatoes unclean and un-Christian, calling them "Devil's apples". In colonial Massachusetts, they were considered the spoor of witches (Valdes 1998).

NUTRITIONAL VALUE OF POTATOES

Nutrients are classified as essential or nonessential. Essential nutrients are obtained from food sources because the body does not produce them or produces them in amounts too small to maintain growth and health. Essential nutrients include water, proteins, fats, vitamins and minerals. Nonessential nutrients are those manufactured by the body and do not need to be obtained from food, such as cholesterol.

Carbohydrates

Carbohydrates are the most abundant organic compounds found in nature. They are produced by green plants and by bacteria using the process known as photosynthesis, in which carbon dioxideis taken from the air by means of solar energy to yield the carbohydrates as well as all the other chemicals needed by the organisms to survive and grow. Carbohydrates are the human body's key source of energy, providing four calories of energy per gram (Smith 1988; Valdes 1998). When carbohydrates are broken down by the body, the sugar glucoseis produced, which is critical to help maintain tissue protein, metabolize fat, and fuel the central nervous system.

Potato carbohydrates may be classified as starch, non-starch, polysaccharides, and sugars. Starch is present in the form of granules, consisting of amylopectin and amylosein a fairly constant ratio of 3:1. Amylopectin is a large, highly ramified molecule containing about 105 glucose residues. The amylose moleculeis smaller, containing about 5000 glucose residues. There are small amounts of phosphorus, combined chemically with starch, mostly in the amylopectin fraction (Smith 1988).

When potatoes are subjected to heat during cooking or processing, the water they contain is absorbed into the starch granules, and the starch is gelatinized at temperatures of 70° C and above. The resulting gel usually remains inside the potato cells unless these are ruptured during cooking or other processing treatments such as mashing, in which case the release of starch from the cells makes cooked potato very sticky (Smith 1988; Niederhauser 1993).

The high starch content has made manufacture of potato starch economically feasiblein developed countries. Potato starch is used in the manufacture of adhesives, in the textileindustry, in the food industry and for the production of derived substances such as alcohol and glucose. Such starch gels set rapidly and has a high pot-paste viscosity, unlike those from cereal starches (Smith 1988). The non-starch polysaccharides are only a small part of the tuber dry matter. Non-starch polysaccharides have an important rolein the final texture of the cooked potato, because during cooking the pectins are solubilized, and to someextent degraded, causing separation, and occasionally rupture, of the cell walls. Non-starch polysaccharides contribute to the nutritional value of the potato because of its characteristic as dietary fiber (Smith 1988; Niederhauser 1993).

The major sugars in the white potato are sucrose, fructose and glucose, although traces of some minor sugars are also found. Sugars are of considerableimportancein the potato flavor, and also in giving a characteristic color to French fries and chips (Smith 1988).

Lipids

The lipid content of potato is low. Galliard (1983) found 0.08 to 0.13% fresh weight bases in 23 varieties (Augustin et al. 1988). This rangeis too low to have any nutritional significance but contributes toward potato flavor, enhances tuber cellular integrity and resistance to bruising, and plays a part in reducing enzymic darkening in tuber flesh.

The greater importance of the lipids lies in their susceptibility to enzymic degradation and non-enzymic auto-oxidation, which cause "off" flavor and rancidity in dehydrated and "instant" potato products. Galliard (1983) also has described the fatty acid composition of the lipid, and studied the lipid-degrading enzymes in 23 varieties of potatoes. He found that about 75 percent of the total fatty acids of the lipids are the polyunsaturated linoleic and linoleic acids.

These contribute to production of both desirable flavor characteristics in cooked tubers and undesirable "off" flavors in processed products. The polyunsaturated acids are rapidly converted to free fatty acids and other compounds by lipid-degrading enzymes during tuber processing, and are also extremely susceptible to auto-oxidation (Galliard 1983).Proteins   Protein is needed by humans, particularly infants, for growth, maintenance of tissues, restoration of losses caused by damage or disease, and pregnancy and lactation. Different proportions of amino acids are required for maintenance and for growth, and a particular protein may be moreeffective for one purpose than for another (Smith 1988; Werge 1989).

Proteins are powerful compounds that build and repair body tissues, from hair and fingernails to muscles. In addition to maintaining the body's structure, proteins speed up chemical reactions in the body, serve as chemical messengers, fight infection, and transport oxygen from the lungs to the body's tissues (Wolfe 1987; Smith 1988; Werge 1989). They are the predominant ingredients of cells, making up more than 50 percent of the dry weight of humans. Humans have an estimated 30,000 different proteins, of which only about two percent have been adequately described (Wolfe 1987). Although proteins provide four calories of energy per gram, the body uses protein for energy only if carbohydrates and fat intakeis insufficient. When tapped as an energy source, protein is diverted from the many critical functions it performs in our bodies.

Proteins are made of smaller units called amino acids. Of the more than 20 amino acids our bodies require, eight (ninein some older adults and young children) cannot be made by the body in sufficient quantities to maintain health. These amino acids are considered essential and must be obtained from food.

Crude potato protein at about 2% fresh weight basis is comparable to that of most other root and tuber staples, with theexception of cassava, which has only half this amount. It is also comparable, on a dry basis, with that of the cereals and, on a cooked basis, with that of boiled rice (Werge 1989).

One advantage of the potato has over the cereal staples is its high lysine content. However, it contains lower concentrations of the sulfur-containing amino acids, (such as methionine and cystine/cysteine) than the cereals. In combination with other foods, potatoes can supplement diets that are limiting in lysine, such as rice accompanying potatoes, which provides a better quality protein. In some developing countries, meals are frequently served with mixtures of boiled potatoes and rice or pasta. However, such mixtures are often wrongly assumed by developed-country consumers to provide nothing more than large quantities of carbohydrateenergy (Werge 1989).

It has been suggested that the comparative advantage of the potato as a foodstuff in the tropics, on a unit weight basis, lies in its ability to supply high-quality protein. Using the latest figures for energy and protein requirements (FAO 1999), it can be calculated that 100 grams (one small tuber) of potato can supply 7%, 6%, and 5% of the daily energy, and 12%, 11% and 10% of the daily protein needs of children aged 1-2, 2-3, and 3-5 years respectively. For adults, depending on body weight and sex, 100 grams of potatoes can supply from 3% to 6% of the daily protein requirements. In a study in England in 1983, potato contributed 3.5% of the total household protein intake. The protein contribution of some other foods are the following: fruit, 1.3%, eggs, 4.6%, fish 4.8%, cheese 5.8%, beef 5.7%, white bread 9.8% and milk 14.6% (Werge 1989).

For infants and children, an energetically adequate diet cannot support growth if its protein content is inferior to the recommended daily requirement. On the other hand, with an energetically inadequate diet, protein is metabolized as an energy source, rather than being used for growth. Therefore, it is essential to consider the quality of a food or diet in terms of both protein and energy, for example, by the percentage of the total energy supplied by protein.

Regional food availability, costs, food preferences, preparation times, and cooking fuel costs might also be considered on a local basis when determining the relative utility of the mixes. Potato requires less of theexpensive protein-rich supplements than do other root, tuber and fruit staples, due to the high quality of its protein. (Werge 1989).

The only published work evaluating the quality of potato protein in infant diets is that by Lopes de Romana et al. (1991) in Peru. Studies with infants and young children recovering from malnutrition demonstrated that potatoes can supply all the daily dietary requirement of protein, and a substantial part of that for energy (Lopez de Romana et al. 1991).

Potato protein is of sufficient high quality for maintenance purposes in adult men, and for growth of infants and children. The relatively low digestibility of potato protein is a disadvantage when potatoes are used for feeding children because the potatoes have to be consumed in large quantities to satisfy protein and energy requirements, a characteristic that potatoes share with other root and tuber staples. Potatoes are rarely consumed as the sole source of nitrogen in the diets of either adults or children, but they can make a valuable contribution to the protein content and the quality of a mixed diet (Desborough and Lauer 1987). Plant breeders should not overlook the maintenance of protein levels in potatoes when searching for higher-yielding varieties.

Nitrogen

Potatoes are rarely eaten alone as the sole source of nitrogen and there are supplementary or synergistic effects as a result of mixing potatoes with other foods. Potato is not a rich source of energy, supplying approximately 80 kilocalories per 100 grams, but it supplies high-quality protein (Herrera 1989). This is of considerable importancein developing countries, whereenergy supplies tend to be more readily available than protein. The nitrogenous content of the potato tuber has a high nutritional value compared with many other vegetable crops, and thereis a rich literature devoted to the subject.

Variations in total nitrogen of potato tubers are attributable not only to differences in the varieties, but also to cultivation practices, climatic effects, growing season, and location. Theincrease of total nitrogen with increasing levels of applied nitrogen is well-documented (International Potato Center 1991). Total nitrogen was increased significantly also by applications of phosphorus of 56 kilograms per hectare. A study of theeffects of moderate temperatures on tuber protein metabolism (22° C and 18 ° C for day and night, and 11° C and 7° C for day and night), showed that, in general, lower temperatures stimulated an increasein the percentage of tuber nitrogen. Marked differences in total nitrogen were between varieties and between crops from different years and locations. Breeding-program selections for increased nitrogen content should take place preferably in conditions representative of theintended area of production (International Potato Center 1991).Distribution of nitrogen within the tuber is not homogeneous (Herrera 1989), being highest in the skin, decreasing in the cortex and rising again toward the pith. Desborough and Weiser (1974) reported that protein content was similar in the cortical, medullar and pith regions, whilethe pith area has significantly more non-protein nitrogen than the cortex tissue (Ponnampalam and Mondy 1993).

The total nitrogen of potato tubers includes: (a) soluble, coagulable (true) protein; (b) insoluble protein; and (c) soluble non-protein nitrogen, which is composed of free amino acids, the amides asparagine and glutamine, and small amounts of nitrate nitrogen and basic nitrogen compounds including nucleic acids and alkaloids. Theinsoluble protein fraction occurs mainly in the peel (Chang and Avery 1979). It is only about four percent of total nitrogen. The proportion of soluble protein nitrogen to  total nitrogen, considered to average about 50%, can range widely. A range of 29.5% to 51.2% was noted among 11 different S. tuberosum varieties, and of 40% to 74% in 50 clone samples of S. tuberosum group andigena (Bakel 1986).

Thereis a brief review of adult human feeding experiments with potatoes by Knorr (1989). In contrast to animal feeding trials, work with human adults has consistently shown that men or women can bemaintained in nitrogen equilibrium and good health on diets in which all the nitrogen, or almost all, was supplied by potatoes (Knorr 1989).

Herrera (1989) reported that Rose and Cooper (1917) maintained a young woman in nitrogen balance for seven days on an intake of 0.096 grams of nitrogen from potato per each kilogram of body weight, and that Kon and Klein (1928) kept a man and a woman in nitrogen equilibrium and good health for almost six months on a diet in which all the nitrogen required was supplied by potatoes.

The authors found that the daily need for potato protein was 36 grams for the man and 24 grams for the woman on a 70-kilogram body weight basis (Herrera 1989). Kofranyi and Jekat (1987) are cited by various authors (Herrera 1989; Knorr 1989) as having determined that the average amount of protein necessary for the maintenance of nitrogen balancein the case of three healthy college students was 0.545 grams per kilogram of body weight for potato, and 0.505 grams per kilogram of body weight for egg protein. In addition, the protein of potatoes has better nutritive value than the protein of beef, tuna fish, wheat flour, soybean, corn, beans or seaweed in terms of the quantities required to maintain nitrogen balancein adult human beings (Herrera 1989; Knorr 1989).

Amino acids

Amino acids are an important class of organic compounds. Of these, 20 serve as the building block for proteins and as raw materials for the manufacture of many other cellular products, including hormones and pigments. In addition, several amino acids are key intermediaries in cellular metabolism.

There are few complete amino acid analyses of potato tubers in the literature. Kaldy and Markavis (1982) and Knorr (1989) provide tables of previous analyses by several authors, and report the amino acid compositions of several North American varieties grown in different locations. Knorr determined the amino acid compositions of potato samples with varying levels of nitrogen in their dry matter (Knorr 1989). The usual method of reporting tuber amino acid composition has been used to evaluate the nutritive value of the potato. The protein scores of six potato varieties varied from 60 to 78, on the basis of the sulfur-containing amino acids (Kaldy and Markakis 1982).

The latest estimates of patterns of amino acid requirements for various age groups were published by FA0 in 1999. Potato protein does not satisfy most of the amino acid requirements for infants, but has a very high average amino acid score of 90 for the pre-school child, and scores of over 100 for all other age groups (Woolfe 1987). Potato protein has a particularly favorable lysine content in comparison with cereal proteins, whose amino acid scores are much lower (Mudambi and Rajagopal 1990).

Concentrations of potato amino acids have been reported in the literature, although thereis a need for standardization to avoid confusion, and to facilitate comparisons of the nutritive value of the different samples. Meaningful comparisons of the capacity of different potato samples to satisfy protein needs must be made on the basis of the amino acid concentrations in the food as eaten, which will depend on the composition and on the content of tuber nitrogen (Kaldy and Markakis, 1982).

Enzymes

Enzymes are one of the many specialized organic substances, composed of polymers of amino acids that act as catalysts to regulate the speed of many chemical reactions involved in the metabolism of living organisms. There are more than 700 enzymes identified, which are classified as hydrolytic, oxidizing, and reducing, depending on the type of reaction that they control (Valdes 1998). Hydrolytic enzymes accelerate reactions in which a substanceis broken down into simpler compounds through reaction with water molecules. Oxidizing enzymes, known as oxidases, accelerate oxidation reactions; reducing enzymes speed up reduction reactions, in which oxygen is removed (Valdes 1998). Other enzymes catalyze other types of reactions.

The potato contains numerous enzyme systems that constitute a considerable proportion of the total protein. The mechanism of low-temperature sweetening during storage occurs because of the relative activities of enzymes and enzymeinhibitors (Linnemann et al. 1995). Phosphorylase (the action of which may be reduced by an inhibitor at higher temperatures) breaks down starch to glucose-1-phosphate. Some of this is converted to sucrose by sucrose phosphate synthetase (Linnemann et al. 1995).

Of the lipid-degrading enzymes, oneis a lipolytic acyl hydrolase, which liberates free fatty acids from phospholipids and glycolipids, and the other is a lipoxygenase that converts linoleic and linolenic acids to their 9-hydroperoxide derivatives (Horton 1992). Theimportance of theseenzymes in food processing is their probableinvolvement in the formation of flavor and "off" flavor compounds (Horton 1992).

Another enzyme system, important during the preparation of both home-cooked and industrially processed potatoes, causes enzymic discoloration or blackening of peeled or cut tubers. When tuber cells areinjured, polyphenoloxidase (tyrosinase) gains access to tyrosine and other orthodihydric phenols, which are oxidized to dark or black compounds (melanins). Since this reaction is initiated when cells areinjured, some purchased potatoes may already haveenzymic blackening as part of the flesh because of rough handling or mechanical damage.

This results in wastage when these tubers are prepared for cooking (or after cooking in skins), because the blackened parts are normally discarded. Also, high rates of enzymic darkening are undesirable for industrial processing especially for producers of pre-peeled potatoes. Smith (1988) briefly reviewed the factors affecting the susceptibility of the potatoes to enzymic discoloration. Theseincluded variety, cultural practices, and climatic conditions. The same author also reviewed the methods of inhibition of enzymic discoloration caused by peeling (Smith 1988).

Fiber

In recent years there has been increasing interest in dietary fiber, as a result of suggestions that it gives protection against diverticulosis, cardiovascular disease, colon cancer, and diabetes. Trowell (1960) defined dietary fiber as "the plant polysaccharides and lignin that are resistant to hydrolysis by the digestiveenzymes of man" (Liechsenring 1971). Dietary fiber is not, however, a precise term, and opinions vary on its exact composition.Methods of determining dietary fiber are continually being modified and improved. Dietary fiber analyses utilize physiologically activeenzymes to break down non-fiber components, whileearlier chemical determinations of crude fiber used acid or alkali. Crude fiber analyses have largely been abandoned because they measure only a small and variable fraction of the dietary fiber (Liechsenring 1971).

Raw potato dietary fiber content ranges between one and two grams per 100 grams of fresh weight (Paul and Southgate 1988; Finglas and Faulks 1994). In addition, part of the dietary fiber may be starch that is resistant to hydrolysis by theenzymes used to remove starch prior to dietary fiber determination. This "resistant starch" is produced by subjecting the foods to heat or dehydration, which confers a more ordered structure on the starch molecules, and renders them less susceptible to enzymatic digestion. Mudambi and Rajagopal (1990) found that there was little "resistant starch" in raw potato, but that it formed from 20% to 50% by weight of the total dietary fiber of cooked potato (Mudambi and Rajagopal 1990). However, it is unknown whether this resistant starch is digested in the human intestine. If it is not, then it should be considered part of the dietary fiber because, like other types of fiber, may benefit health by helping the colon function (Mudambi and Rajagopal 1990).

Various types of dietary fiber have different physiological effects. Insoluble cereal fiber affects transit time and fecal weight, while soluble gel-forming fiber reduces serum cholesterol levels, and blood glucose and insulin response to meals containing carbohydrates (Meuser and Smolnik 1989). A chemical characterization of the dietary fibers in various foods, including potatoes, revealed that cereal brans have the highest lignin values, are rich in arabinoxylans and cellulose, but are low in uronic acids, while various vegetables, including potatoes, have higher cellulose content and more peptic and pectin-associated substances than the brans. The significance of the findings in terms of the nutritional properties of different dietary fiber sources has not been determined (Meuser and Smolnik 1989).

Compared with other raw items, the fresh potato has dietary fiber content similar to sweet potatoes, but somewhat lower than that of other roots and tubers and much lower than most cereals and dry Phaseolus beans, although, on a dry basis, potatoes and cereals are similar. Dietary fiber determinations have been conducted mainly on raw rather than on cooked foods.

Boiled potato flesh has dietary fiber content similar to cooked white rice and a much lower content than boiled green plantains or boiled Phaseolus beans. Potatoes, cooked as French fries or chips, are a more concentrated source of fiber. It has been calculated that 100 grams of boiled potatoes supply 1.0, 0.7 and 0.56 times the fiber than can be found in a 35-gram "medium" slice of white, brown or whole-meal bread, respectively, and that a 25-gram packet of chips supplies 1.9, 1.4 and 1.0 times the respective bread fiber content (Meuser and Smolnik 1989).

Thereis no recommended daily allowance for dietary fiber at the present time. However, it has been suggested that about 40 grams per day should be consumed to maintain correct colon function (Chappell 1978). When potatoes are consumed on a regular basis, they make a significant contribution to dietary fiber intake. It has been estimated that fresh potatoes contribute about 15% of the dietary fiber intakein British households (Finglas and Faulks 1995).

Consumption of the whole tuber, rather than the flesh alone, may increase dietary fiber intake. Jones et al (1985) found a higher dietary fiber content in unpeeled than in peeled raw or boiled potatoes (Anderson et al. 1974). There have been investigations into whether peel, as a by-product of the potato-processing industry in developed countries, could beincorporated into bread to increase fiber in the diet (Toma et al. 1989; Orr et al. 1992).

Minerals and traceelements

Minerals and traceelements are needed by the body in very small amounts to trigger the thousands of chemical reactions necessary to maintain good health. Many of these chemical reactions are linked, with one triggering another. If thereis a missing or deficient mineral anywherein the chain, the process may break down, with potentially devastating health effects. Minerals are vital for the healthy growth of teeth and bones, and they also help in such cellular activity as enzyme reaction, muscle contraction, nerve reaction, and blood clotting (Wolfe 1997). Mineral nutrients are classified as major elements (calcium, chlorine, magnesium, phosphorus, potassium, sodium, and sulfur) and traceelements (chromium, copper, fluoride, iodine, iron, selenium and zinc).

The ash content of potatoes is about 1% fresh weight basis, and contains someimportant minerals and traceelements essential to various human body structures and functions. The determinations of the major minerals and traceelements in raw potatoes have been carried out by various researchers (Trueet al. 1989; Finglas and Faulks 1994). However, although wide ranges have been found in the contents of many minerals and traceelements in potatoes, thereis littleinformation about what determines these levels. Trueet al. (1989) in a brief review, cite work attributing variations in mineral content to soil type, location of growth, and the application of phosphorus (Trueet al. 1989).

In addition, there are great differences in the contents of calcium, phosphorus, and iron in 13 varieties grown in the same location (Leichsenring et al. 1977). Wide ranges in some mineral elements, such as calcium, phosphorus, sodium, potassium, selenium and aluminum, were observed in nine varieties grown at five locations, and were attributed to location of growth rather than to variety. However, it was noted that these differences could be due to other factors, including themineral content of the soil, cultivation practices or even sampling procedures (Liechsenring et al. 1977).

Nitrogen fertilization had littleeffect on magnesium, calcium, potassium, sodium and phosphorus levels in "Russet Burbank" tubers, although theiron content was increased somewhat (Augustin 1985). Augustin also reported that potatoes grown on sandy soils had lower quantities of magnesium than those that were grown on loamy soils, but he concluded that the higher iron content in tubers from sandy soil was a result of theiron content of the soil rather than of the soil type.

In potato, theiron content is about the same as in other roots and tubers, or some vegetables, and is comparable on a dry weight basis to cereals. It is higher than theiron levels found in white rice, on either a dry or cooked basis. Although not an outstanding source of iron, 100 grams of cooked potatoes can supply between 6% and 12% of the daily iron requirements for children or adult men (Smith 1988). The percentage contributions are lower in women of child-bearing age, due to the greater demand for iron caused by menstruation, pregnancy, and lactation.

The availability of iron may beenhanced by the presence of ascorbic acid ingested at the same time as theiron source. Potato ascorbic acid contributes towards the level needed to influenceiron absorption from a meal. A positive correlation was found between the content of ascorbic acid of potatoes and the amount of iron solubilized from potatoes by gastric juicein vitro (Fairweather-Tait 1993).

However, a much higher proportion of theiron from potato was solubilized in vitro than from other vegetable foods such as kidney beans, wheat flour and bread. It has been suggested that iron solubilization is the first step in determining iron availability from a food or meal. Therefore, potato appears to have a moderateiron availability that is superior to other vegetable foods (Trueet al. 1993; Fairweather-Tait 1993). In England, potatoes have been shown to supply 6% of the total household dietary iron intake, ranking third of all individual foods as a dietary source (Poats and Woolfe 1992). Trueet al. (1979) found that 160 grams of potato could supply from 2.3% to 19.3% of the United States recommended daily allowance (Trueet al. 1979). This relatively large rangeis due to variation in theiron content found by the authors among varieties that were grown in several different locations. Also, it should be noted that the United States recommended daily allowance for iron is considered very high. If we use the more realistic recommended daily allowance given by both FAO and WHO, potato makes a significant contribution (Trueet al. 1979).

Potatoes are a good source of phosphorus, being similar, in this respect, to roots and tubers and most cereals on a cooked basis. Tortillas, bread and boiled P. vulgaris beans are richer sources of phosphorus than potatoes. However, 100 grams of boiled potato supplies 7% of the United States recommended daily allowance for phosphorus for both children and adults (Quick and Li 1986).

A relatively small percentage of the total phosphorus in potatoes occurs in the form of phytic acid. Phytic acid is insoluble and cannot be absorbed in the human intestines. It also binds calcium, iron, and zinc in the form of phytates, rendering them unavailable for absorption into the body. About 25% of the total phosphorus was found in the form of phytic acid in seven commercial North American potato varieties (Quick and Li 1986).

The same authors quoted two sources that found that at least 80% of the phosphorus in potatoes was non-phytic (Swaminathan and Pushkarnath 1982). In contrast, other plant foods contain much higher levels of phytic acid. In samples of field beans (Vicia faba), 40% to 60% of the total phosphorus was in the form of phytate phosphorus (Rhoades 1992). The lower phytic acid content of potatoes may beadvantageous in allowing greater availability of the phosphorus, calcium, iron, and zinc which may be present in a meal which includes potatoes.

This is especially important in the case of calcium. Potato is a poor source of calcium, a characteristic that cooked potatoes share with other cooked staples, with theexception of lime-treated tortillas, P. vulgaris beans, and other legumes. With theexception of okra, no other vegetableis a particularly good source of calcium (Quick and Li 1986). Magnesium is another important dietary mineral. For raw potatoes, 150 grams were found to provide between 6% and 10% of the United States recommended daily allowance for magnesium, and this rangeis likely to be the same for cooked potatoes, because thereis almost 100% retention of the mineral in potatoes boiled in their skin (Bretzloff 1981).

In the United States, recommended daily allowances have been established for only two of the traceelements found in potatoes: zinc and iodine. Comparing figures for levels of zinc and iodinein potatoes with the United States recommended daily allowance levels, 100 grams of potato should provide 13% of adult, and up to 30% of child requirements of iodine, and 2% and 4% of adult and child requirements respectively of zinc. Labib (1982) has noted that biological availability of zinc is generally lower in vegetables than in foods derived from animals (Labib 1982).

Other, less extensively investigated traceelements reported to have beneficial effects in humans include copper, chromium, manganese, selenium and molybdenum (Meikejohn 1973). It has been shown that 100 grams of potatoes can supply at least part of the daily requirement for copper, manganese, molybdenum and chromium (Labib 1982; Espinola 1989). Trueet al. (1989) found that a 150-gram serving of potatoes supplies 8% of the United States recommended daily allowance for cooper (Trueet al. 1989). The same authors determined that the manganese content of potatoes ranged from 0.7 to 1.9 mg/kg, and that it made a partial contribution to the 15% of daily intake provided by all fruits and vegetables in the British diet. According to a study made by Spring et al. (1979), potatoes provided 10% of the magnesium, 11% of the copper and 3% of the zinc of the British diet. A more recent analysis revised these contributions to 8.4% and 4.3% for copper and zinc, respectively (Finglas and Faulks 1994). Lastly, potatoes are not a good source of selenium, containing less than 0.01 mg/kg. (Espinola 1989)

Other traceelements, for which no requirements have been established, but in which someinterest has been shown, include cobalt, nickel, fluoride, and vanadium. Potato is not an outstanding source of fluoride and in this respect is similar to most other foods (Davies 1987). The content of vanadium is less than 1 ng/g (Joseph et al. 1983).

Organic acids

The major organic acids identified in the potato are citric and malic acids. Other organic acids present in smaller amounts in the potato are oxalic and fumaric, chlorogenic and phosphoric as well as ascorbic, nicotinic, and phytic acids, amino acids and fatty acids. All these contribute to flavor. The level of malic acid can be used as an indication of tuber maturity. Ascorbic acid and nicotinic acids influence directly, and phytic acid indirectly, the nutritional value of the potato (Schwartz et al. 1982).

Chlorogenic acid can react with ferric ions during cooking to produce a dark-colored complex. This phenomenon, known as post-cooking or non-enzymatic blackening, may occur morein the "heel" than in the "rose" end of the potatoes, in which caseit is called stem-end blackening. Citric acids in tubers prevent this by sequestering theiron present and making it unavailable for forming a complex with chlorogenic acid. The susceptibility of potatoes to post-cooking blackening depends on the relative concentrations of iron and of chlorogenic and citric acids (Augustin et al. 1988).

Pigments

Potato flesh may be white or various shades of yellow, depending on the variety. Yellow coloration is generally due to the presence of carotenoid pigments. The major carotenoid identified in a study of 13 German varieties of potatoes was violaxanthin, followed by lutein and lutein-5, 6-epoxide, and, in lower concentrations, neoxanthin A and neoxantin. B-carotene was detected only in trace amounts or was totally absent (Augustin 1985). Anthocyanin pigments in the periderm and peripheral cortex produce totally or partly pigmented skins in potatoes. In some South American varieties, the pigment is so dark that some tubers may appear black and others dark purple. Another type of pigmentation occurs because of chlorophyll. When harvested, potato tubers exposed to light form chlorophyll forms in the superficial parts of the skin, giving it a green color (Augustin 1985). Very littleis known about the nutritional value of the different potato pigments (Woolfe 1997).

It is possible that, in some varieties, the yellow color may be due to other, unidentified pigments as well as to carotenoids. In some places, such as Peru, yellow-fleshed varieties of potatoes are highly prized and command higher prices than potatoes with white flesh.

Vitamins

Among many other functions, vitamins enhance the body's use of carbohydrates, proteins, and fats. They are critical in the formation of blood cells, hormones, nervous system chemicals known as neurotransmitters, and the genetic material deoxyribonucleic acid (DNA). Vitamins are classified into two groups: fat soluble, and water soluble. Fat-soluble vitamins, which include vitamins A, D, E, and K, are usually absorbed with the help of foods that contain fat. Fat containing these vitamins is broken down by bile, a liquid released by the liver, and the body then absorbs the breakdown products and vitamins. Water-soluble vitamins, which include vitamin C (ascorbic acid), B1 (thiamine), B2 (riboflavin), B3 (niacin), B6, B12, and folic acid, cannot be stored and rapidly leave the body in urineif taken in greater quantities than the body can use (Page and Hanning 1983; Smith 1988; Valdes 1998). Foods that contain water soluble vitamins need to beeaten daily to replenish the body's needs.

Potatoes are substantial sources of several vitamins: ascorbic acid (vitamin C), and the B vitamins: thiamin (B1), pyridoxine (B6), and niacin. Riboflavin (B2), folic acid and pantothenic acid are also present, as well as small amounts of vitamin E. Biotin is present only in traces (Meikejohn 1973). Vitamin C exists in the tuber in both the reduced and oxidized forms. In the freshly harvested raw tuber the reduced form L-ascorbic acid is quantitatively the most important, although dehydroascorbic acid is also present. In the stored, cooked or processed potatoes, only the L-ascorbic acid is generally present (Page and Hanning 1983). This vitamin is important in the formation and maintenance of collagen, the protein that supports many body structures and plays a major rolein the formation of bones and teeth. It also enhances the absorption of iron from foods of vegetable origin.

Red Garlic Mashed Potatoes

Ingredients

- 8 medium red potatoes, cubed
- 2 teaspoons crushed garlic
- 1/2 cup butter or margarine
- 1/4 cup half-and-half cream
- 2 tablespoons white sugar
- 1/4 teaspoon steak seasoning
- 1/4 teaspoon garlic powder

Directions

- Place the potatoes into a large pot, and fill with enough water to cover. Add 1 teaspoon of the crushed garlic to the water for flavor. Bring to a boil, and cook for about 10 minutes, or until easilypierced with a fork.

- Drain the potatoes, and add the butter. Mash until the butter is melted. Mix in the half-and-half, sugar, steak seasoning, garlic powder and remaining garlic. Mix potatoes with an electric mixer until smooth.

Wine Baked Potato

Ingredients

- 1 medium baking potato
- 1/2 medium onion, sliced
- 1/4 teaspoon butter
- 1/4 cup cooking sherry

Directions

- Preheat the oven to 450 degrees F (230 degrees C).Make several cuts crosswise across the potato, about 1/2 inch apart and not quite all the way through. Place half of an onion slice, and a piece of butter into each cut.

➤ Place the potato onto a sheet of aluminum foil, and form a bowl. Pour the cooking wine over the potato, and fold the foil around to seal, turning theends up like a boat to keep the wine from spilling out.

➤ Place the potato onto a baking sheet, and bake for 50 to 60 minutes, depending on the size of the potato. When done, cutthrough foil, and top with your favorite potato toppings or just salt and pepper.

Badische Schupfnudeln (Potato Noodles)

Ingredients

* 1 1/2 pounds russet potatoes
* 1/2 cup all-purpose flour
* 1 egg
* 1 tablespoon chopped fresh parsley
* 1/2 teaspoon salt
* 1/4 teaspoon freshly ground nutmeg
* 1/4 cup lard or other cooking fat

Directions

➤ Place whole potatoes in their skins into a large pot of boiling water; boil for 25 to 30 minutes. Remove potatoes, and discard water.

➤ When cool enough to handle, peel potatoes, and place on a lightly floured surface. Mash potatoes with a rolling pin.

➤ Place mashed potatoes into a large bowl. Stir in flour, egg, parsley, salt, and nutmeg. Knead well to form a smooth dough. Then roll out the dough to a thickness of about 1/2 inch.

➤ Cut flattened dough into thin strips, about 1 1/2 inches long. Gently roll out the strips, orstretch them until theends taper. Set aside for 15 minutes.

> In a large skillet, heat lard over medium heat. Place the potato strips into the skillet, and fry until golden brown on both sides.

Mexican Potato Stew

Ingredients

- ❀ 1 pound ground beef
- ❀ 1 (10 ounce) can diced tomatoes with green chile peppers
- ❀ 1 (15 ounce) can ranch-style beans
- ❀ garlic salt to taste
- ❀ 4 potatoes, sliced
- ❀ salt and ground black pepper to taste

Directions

> Heat a large skillet over medium-high heat and stir in the ground beef. Cook and stir until the beef is crumbly, evenly browned, andno longer pink.

> Drain. Stir in the diced tomatoes, ranch-style beans, and garlic salt. Bring to a boil; reduce the heat to low.

> Layer the sliced potatoes evenly over the ground beef mixture; season with salt and black pepper. Cover; simmer until potatoes aretender, about 30 minutes.

Candied Sweet Potatoes

Ingredients

- ❀ 4 pounds sweet potatoes, quartered

- ❀ 1 1/4 cups margarine
- ❀ 1 1/4 cups brown sugar
- ❀ 3 cups miniature marshmallows, divided
- ❀ ground cinnamon to taste ground nutmeg to taste

Directions

- ➤ Preheat oven to 400 degrees F (200 degrees C). Grease a 9x13 inch baking dish.Bring a large pot of water to a boil. Add potatoes and boil until slightly underdone, about 15 minutes. Drain, cool and peel.

- ➤ In a large saucepan over medium heat, combine margarine, brown sugar, 2 cups marshmallows, cinna-mon and nutmeg. Cook, stirring occasionally, until marshmallows are melted.

- ➤ Stir potatoes into marshmallow sauce. While stirring mash about half of the potatoes, and break the others into bite-sized chunks. Transfer to prepared dish.

- ➤ Bake in preheated oven for 15 minutes. Remove from oven and cover top evenly with remaining marsh-mallows. Return to oven and bake until marsh-mallows are golden brown.

Fantastic Grilled Potatoes

Ingredients

- ❀ 2 large baking potatoes, thinly sliced
- ❀ 1 onion, thinly sliced
- ❀ 1 green bell pepper, diced
- ❀ 1 red bell pepper, diced
- ❀ 6 button mushrooms, sliced
- ❀ Salt and black pepper to taste
- ❀ 1 pinch mixed vegetable flakes, or to taste
- ❀ 1 pinch paprika, or to taste

* 2 tablespoons reduced fat spread (such as Brummel & Brown®), or to taste

Directions

> Preheat an outdoor grill for medium-high heat; lightly oil the grate.Cut two 12x18-inch pieces of aluminum foil and fold them in half to create two 12x9-inch rectangles. Spray one side of each piece with cooking spray.

> Arrange the potatoes over one sheet of prepared foil in an overlapping pattern, leaving 2 inches free on all sides. Sprinklewith the onion, green bell pepper, red bell pepper, and slicemushrooms.

> Season with salt, pepper, vegetable flakes, andpaprika to taste. Dot with the reduced fat spread. Place the second piece of foil over the potatoes with the greased side down.

> Seal theedges by creating several folds; poke 4 to 6 holes in the top to allow steam to escape.Cook on the preheated grill until the potatoes are tender, 20 to 30 minutes.

Broccoli Mac and Cheese with Bacon and Potato

Ingredients

* 1 (16 ounce) packageelbow macaroni
* 6 slices bacon
* 2 teaspoons butter
* 1 head broccoli, cut into florets
* 1 small onion, chopped
* 3 eggs
* 2 cups milk
* salt and pepper to taste
* 1/4 teaspoon adobo seasoning
* 2 cups shredded Cheddar cheese, divided
* 2 cups shredded mozzarella cheese, divided

* 20 frozen bite-size potato nuggets (such as Tater Tots®)

Directions

> Fill a large pot with lightly salted water and bring to a rolling boilover high heat. Once the water is boiling, stir in the macaroni, and return to a boil.

> Cook the pasta uncovered, stirring occasionally,until the pasta has cooked through, but is still firm to the bite, about8 minutes. Drain well in a colander set in the sink.

> Preheat an oven to 350 degrees F (175 degrees C). Grease a 9x13 inch baking dish.Place the bacon in a large, deep skillet, and cook over medium-high heat, turning occasionally, until evenly browned, about 10 minutes.

> Drain the bacon slices on a paper towel-lined plate. Crumble thebacon and set aside. Heat 1 teaspoon of butter in a skillet over medium heat. Stir in the broccoli and onion; cook and stir until theonion has softened and turned translucent, about 5 minutes.

> Whisk together theeggs, the remaining 1 teaspoon of butter, and milk in a large bowl. Season with salt, pepper, and adoboseaso-ning. Stir in 1 cup of Cheddar cheese, 1 cup of mozzarella cheese, the broccoli mixture and half of the potato nuggets.

> Placemacaroni into the baking dish and pour the cheese mixture over thepasta, mixing well. Top with the remaining 1 cup of Cheddarcheese, 1 cup of mozzarella, bacon, and potato nuggets. Cover with aluminum foil.Bake in the preheated oven until golden brown, 40 to 45 minutes

Lamb and Potato Skillet

Ingredients

* 1 tablespoon vegetable oil
* 1 leek, chopped
* 1 cup chopped fresh mushrooms
* 1 pound ground lamb
* 1 clove garlic, minced

- 3/4 cup beef broth
- 1 tablespoon chopped fresh dill
- 1/2 teaspoon garlic and herb seasoning blend
- 1/4 teaspoon ground black pepper
- 1/4 teaspoon onion powder
- 1 bay leaf
- 3 cups chopped potatoes
- 1 (6.5 ounce) can tomato sauce
- 1/2 head cabbage, cored and shredded

Directions

> Heat oil in a skillet over medium heat. Stir in leeks and mushrooms until they begin to soften, about 8 minutes.

> Crumble lamb intoskillet, add garlic, and cook, stirring occasionally, until lamb loses its pink color, about 8 minutes. Drain liquid from pan.

> Stir in broth, dill, garlic and herb seasoning blend, pepper, onion powder, bay leaf, and potatoes. Bring to a boil, then reduce heat to low. Cover and simmer until potatoes are almost tender, about 12 minutes.

> Add tomato sauce and shredded cabbage.Increaseheat to medium and simmer, covered, until cabbage is cooked andpotatoes are tender, 5 to 7 minutes.Remove bay leaf and serve.

Baked Yam and Potato Casserole

Ingredients
- 1 large sweet potato, thinly sliced
- 1 large potato, thinly sliced
- 1 onion, thinly sliced
- 4 tablespoons butter, divided salt and pepper to taste

- 2 tablespoons all-purpose flour
- 3/4 cup vegetable broth
- 1 cup shredded mozzarella cheese
- 2 tablespoons dry bread crumbs
- 1 tablespoon dried parsley (optional)

Directions

- ➤ Preheat oven to 350 degrees F (175 degrees C). Grease a 9x13 inch baking dish.In the prepared dish, make a single layer of sweet potato slices.

- ➤ Place a few onion slices on top, dot with butter, and sprinkle with salt and pepper. Repeat, alternating layers of white and sweetpotatoes.

- ➤ In a small bowl, or measuring cup, combine flour and broth. Pour over potatoes.Sprinkle cheese, bread crumbs and parsley over the potatoes. Dot with remaining butter. Cover.Bake in preheated oven for 1 hour, or until potatoes and onions aresoft.

Twice-Baked Sweet Potatoes With Mini

Ingredients

- 4 medium sweet potatoes
- 1/4 teaspoon salt
- Freshly ground black pepper, to taste
- 1/3 cup buttermilk
- 1/3 cup milk
- 4 tablespoons butter
- 1/2 cup miniature marshmallows

Directions

- Adjust oven rack to low position and heat oven to 400 degrees. Place potatoes on a baking sheet lined with parchment paper or foil. Bake until fork tender, about 45 to 60 minutes. Let cool slightly.

- Handling the potatoes with a potholder, sliceeach in half lengthwiseand scoop potato flesh into a blender or food processor - for anespecially silky texture, use the blender - leaving a 14-inch border of flesh to support the potato skin.

- Puree scooped-out flesh, alongwith salt and pepper, until smooth. With machine motor running, gradually add both milks through feeder tube. Stop machine, add butter, then process until potatoes are silky smooth. (Puree and potato shells can be cooled, then refrigerated in an airtightcontainer, up to 2 days.

- Return to roomtemp-erature before proceeding.) Spoon puree back into each shell. Just before baking, press marshmallows intopotatoes. Bake at 400 degrees until potatoes are hot and marshmallows aregolden brown, 10 to 12 minutes.

Bacon-Roasted Chicken with Potatoes

Ingredients

- 6 chicken thighs
- 6 chicken drumsticks
- 12 slices center-cut bacon
- salt and black pepper to taste
- 1 onion, coarsely chopped
- 1 1/2 pounds baby Dutch yellow potatoes
- Seasoning Mix:
- 2 tablespoons dried chives
- 2 tablespoons dried basil
- 1 tablespoon garlic powder
- 1 tablespoon adobo seasoning

* 1 tablespoon ground black pepper
* 1 teaspoon salt, or to taste

Directions

> Preheat oven to 400 degrees F (200 degrees C).Wrap each chicken piece in a slice of bacon, trying to cover as much of the chicken as possible.

> Place the wrapped chicken pieces in a 9x13 inch baking dish, season with salt and pepper, and sprinkle theonion over the chicken. Push potatoes down into the spaces between the chicken pieces and around theedge of thedish.

> Combine the chives, basil, garlic powder, adobo seasoning, and black pepper in a small bowl, and sprinkle the seasoning to tasteover the chicken and potatoes.

> Bake in the preheated oven for 1 hour, until the bacon is crisp and brown and the potatoes are tender. Sprinkle with salt, if desired, and serve hot.

Sweet Potato Casserole VI

Ingredients

* 4 cups mashed sweet potatoes
* 1 cup white sugar
* 2eggs ,beaten
* 1/2 cup milk
* 1/2 teaspoon salt
* 1/3 cup butter, melted
* 1 teaspoon vanilla extract
* 1 cup packed brown sugar
* 1/2 cup all-purpose flour
* 1/3 cup butter, melted
* 1 cup chopped pecans

Directions

- ➢ In a mixing bowl, combine the sweet potatoes, sugar, eggs, milk, salt, 1/3 cup butter and vanilla. Mix together and pour into agreased 13x9 inch baking dish.

- ➢ To prepare the topping, combine in a separate bowl the brown sugar, flour, 1/3 cup melted butter and pecans.

- ➢ Mix together andcrumble over sweet potato mixture. Bake uncovered at 350 degrees F (175 degrees C) for 35 to 45 minutes.

Twice Baked Potatoes II

Ingredients

- ❀ 6 large baking potatoes
- ❀ 1 (16 ounce) container sour cream
- ❀ 1/4 cup shredded Cheddar
- ❀ cheese
- ❀ 3/4 cup butter
- ❀ salt and pepper to taste
- ❀ 3 slices American cheese

Directions

- ➢ Preheat oven to 350 degrees F (175 degrees C). Bake potatoes for 1 hour or until soft.Cut enough of the skin off the top of each potato to be able to scoop the potato out of the skin and into a mixing bowl.

- ➢ Add butter, sour cream, grated cheese and mix together well. Add salt and pepper to taste.Fill the skins with the mix and top with 1/2 slice American cheese. Bake for 20 to 25 minutes just until heated through.

Mom's Brown Potatoes

Ingredients

- 1 tablespoon driedparsley
- garlic salt to taste
- 5 medium potatoes, cut into small
- 2 cups oil for frying cubes

Directions

- potatoes from the oil, sprinkle them generously with garlic salt andparsley. Deep fry the potatoes until golden brown. As you remove theHeat the oil in a deep fryer or large, heavy sauce-pan to 350 degreesF (175 degrees C).

Make-Ahead Mashed Potatoes

Ingredients

- 5 pounds Yukon Gold potatoes, cooked and mashed
- 2 (3 ounce) packages cream cheese
- 8 ounces sour cream
- 1/2 cup milk
- 2 teaspoons onion salt ground black pepper to taste

Directions

- Combine mashed potatoes, cream cheese, sour cream, milk, onion salt, and pepper to taste.

> Mix well and place in a large casserole.Cover and bake at 325 degrees F (165 degrees C) for 50 minutes.

Lilley Mashed Potato Casserole

Ingredients

- 3 cups mashed potatoes
- 2 green onions, chopped
- 3 slices American cheese

Directions

> Preheat oven to 350 degrees F (175 degrees C).Mix the mashed potatoes with the green onions and spoon into one8 inch square casserole dish.

> Bake for 30 minutes. Spread slices of cheese over the top of the casserole for the last 5 minutes of baking.

Red Skinned Potato Salad

Ingredients

- 2 pounds clean, scrubbed new red potatoes
- 6 eggs
- 1 pound bacon
- 1 onion, finely chopped
- 1 stalk celery, finely chopped
- 2 cups mayonnaise
- salt and pepper to taste

Directions

- ➢ Bring a large pot of salted water to a boil. Add potatoes and cook until tender but still firm, about 15 minutes. Drain and set in therefrigerator to cool.

- ➢ Placeeggs in a saucepan and cover with cold water. Bring water to a boil and immediately remove from heat.

- ➢ Cover and let eggs stand in hot water for 10 to 12 minutes. Remove from hot water, cool, peel and chop.

- ➢ Place bacon in a large, deep skillet. Cook over medium high heat until evenly brown. Drain, crumble and set aside.Chop the cooled potatoes, leaving skin on.

- ➢ Add to a large bowl, along with theeggs, bacon, onion and celery. Add mayonnaise, salt and pepper to taste. Chill for an hour before serving.

Potato Salad with Cream

Ingredients

- ❀ 2 1/2 pounds potatoes
- ❀ 1/2 cup vinegar, boiling
- ❀ 4 eggs, beaten
- ❀ 1 tablespoon butter
- ❀ 1 cup heavy cream
- ❀ 4 tablespoons chopped fresh parsley
- ❀ 2 tablespoons chopped onion
- ❀ 2 teaspoons dry mustard
- ❀ 1 teaspoon salt
- ❀ 1/2 teaspoon ground black pepper
- ❀ 1 pinch ground cayenne pepper

Directions

> Peel the potatoes and add to a large pot of boiling salted water. Cook until tender but still firm, about 15 minutes. Drain, cool and cube. Place into a large bowl and set aside.

> In a double boiler, bring vinegar to a boil. Gradually beat in eggs and cook over simmering water until thickened.

> Stir in butter and cook 1 minute. Whisk in cream, parsley, onion, mustard, salt,pepper and cayenne. Pour over hot potatoes and combine. Cool, sprinkle with parsley and refrigerate until serving time.

Italian Vegetable Potato Topper

Ingredients

* 1 (10.75 ounce) can
* Campbell'sB® Condensed Cream of Mushroom Soup (Regular or
* 98% Fat Free)
* 1 dash ground black pepper
* 2 cups frozen Italian vegetablecombination
* 1/4 cup grated Parmesan cheese
* 4 hot baked potatoes , split Chopped tomato

Directions

> Heat the soup, black pepper, vegetables and cheese in a 3-quartsauce-pan over medium heat to a boil, stirring occasion-nally. Reducethe heat to low.

> Cover and cook for 5 minutes or until thevege-tables are tender, stirring occasionally.Spoon the vegetable mixture over the potatoes. Top with thetomato.

Special Sweet Potatoes

Ingredients

- ❀ 2 small sweet potatoes, peeled and cut into 1/2 inch cubes
- ❀ 2 tablespoons brown sugar
- ❀ 1/4 teaspoon ground cinnamon
- ❀ 1/8 teaspoon salt
- ❀ 1/4 cup orange juice
- ❀ 2 tablespoons butter or margarine
- ❀ 1/2 cup miniature marshmallows

Directions

➤ In a saucepan, cook sweet potatoes in boiling salted water for 10 minutes or until tender; drain. Transfer to a greased 1-qt. baking dish. Sprinkle with brown sugar, cinnamon and salt.

➤ Drizzle withorange juice and dot with butter. Bake, uncovered, at 450 degrees F for 15 minutes. Top with marshmallows. Bake 2 minutes longer or until marshmallows are puffed and golden brown.

Potato Curry

Ingredients

- ❀ 3 tablespoons ghee
- ❀ 1 teaspoon cumin seeds
- ❀ 1 teaspoon turmeric
- ❀ 1 teaspoon ground coriander
- ❀ 1 teaspoon salt

- 1/2 teaspoon mustard seed

- 1/2 teaspoon ground cayennepepper

- 6 medium potatoes, peeled and diced

- 2 cups water

- 1 cup yogurt

- 2/3 cup frozen green peas

Directions

> Heat the ghee in a skillet over medium heat, and mix in the cumin, turmeric, coriander, salt, mustard seed, and cayenne pepper.

> Placepotatoes in the skillet, and stir to evenly coat with the ghee. Cook10 minutes, stirring often. Pour water into the skillet. Reduce heat to low, and simmer 30 minutes, until potatoes are tender. Mix the yogurt and peas into the saucepan. Continue cooking until heated through

Garbage Fried Potatoes

Ingredients

- 2 tablespoons vegetable oil

- 4 large baking potatoes, peeled and thinly sliced

- 1 medium onion, chopped

- 1 (4 ounce) can sliced mushrooms, drained

- 1 red bell pepper, seeded and chopped

- 1 green bell pepper, seeded and chopped

- salt and pepper to taste

Directions

> Heat the oil in a large skillet over medium heat. Add the potatoes, and cook for about 10 minutes, stirringoccasionally, until you think they are about halfway done.

> Mix in the onion, mushrooms, redpepper, and green pepper.Continue to cook and stir until potatoes are golden brown and somewhat crisp, about 15 more minutes.Season with salt and pepper, and serve.

Roasted Potato Salad with Balsamic Dressing

Ingredients

- 10 red potatoes, scrubbed and dried with paper towels
- 3 tablespoons canola oil
- 1 tablespoon dried thyme
- 1 tablespoon chili powder
- 1 tablespoon kosher salt
- 1 tablespoon cracked black pepper
- 1 bunch green onions, sliced
- 3/4 cup roasted red peppers, drained and diced
- 1/2 cup kalamata olives, pitted and sliced
- 1 (10 ounce) can artichoke hearts, drained and chopped
- 1/4 cup chopped fresh parsley
- 1/2 cup crumbled Gorgonzola cheese
- 1/4 cup balsamic vinegar
- 1/4 cup extra-virgin olive oil
- 1 tablespoon Dijon mustard
- 1 teaspoon minced garlic
- 1 teaspoon dried oregano
- 1 teaspoon dried basil
- Salt and pepper to taste

Direction

> ➤ Preheat oven to 450 degrees F (230 degrees C).Cut the potatoes into 3/4-inch chunks, and place into a bowl. Drizzle with canola oil, and spread out onto a baking sheet. Turn potatoes so skin sides are down.

> ➤ Sprinkle the potatoes with thyme, chili powder, kosher salt, and pepper.Bake in the preheated oven until the potatoes are golden brown, about 45 minutes. Remove and allow to cool.

> ➤ In a large salad bowl, lightly toss the cooled potatoes, green onions, roasted red peppers, olives, artichoke hearts, parsley, andGorgonzola cheese until thoroughly combined.

> ➤ Place the balsamic vinegar, olive oil, Dijon mustard, garlic, oregano, and basil into a blender, and pulse a few times until the dressing is thickened and creamy.

> ➤ Season to taste with salt and pepper, pour over the potato salad, and toss lightly. Chill for 4 hours beforeserving.

Cucumber Potato Salad

Ingredients

- ❀ 5 pounds red potatoes
- ❀ 4 celery ribs, sliced
- ❀ 1 bunch green onions, sliced
- ❀ 2 tablespoons dill weed
- ❀ 2 teaspoons salt
- ❀ 2 cups mayonnaise
- ❀ 1 (16 ounce) bottle cucumber ranch salad dressing

Directions

> ➤ Place potatoes in a large kettle; cover with water. Bring to a boil. Reduce heat; cover and simmer for 20-25 minutes or until tender. Drain and cool. Cut potatoes into small cubes.

- ➢ In a large serving bowl, combine the potatoes, celery, onions, dill and salt. In a small bowl, whisk mayonnaise and salad dressing until blended.

- ➢ Pour over potato mixture and stir gently to coat. Cover and refrigerate for at least 6 hours before serving.

Cheesy Potatoes I

Ingredients

- ❀ 8 medium baking potatoes, peeled and sliced
- ❀ 1 onion, chopped
- ❀ 1 (1 pound) loaf processed cheesefood, sliced
- ❀ 1/2 cup butter, sliced
- ❀ Salt and pepper to taste
- ❀ 1 1/2 cups milk

Directions

- ➢ Preheat oven to 375 degrees F (190 degrees C).Place 1/2 the potatoes in a medium baking dish.

- ➢ Layer with 1/2 of the onion, 1/2 of the processed cheese, and 1/2 of the butter.Season with salt and pepper. Repeat layers, reserving 5 or 6 slices of the processed cheese. Pour in milk to approximately 1 inchdepth.

- ➢ Bake 40 minutes in the preheated oven, stirring twice. Top with remaining cheese food, and continue baking 30 minutes, or until potatoes are tender.

Pleasing Potato Pie

Ingredients

- ❀ 2 cups shredded peeled potatoes
- ❀ 1 1/2 cups shredded Cheddar cheese, divided
- ❀ 1 teaspoon salt, divided
- ❀ 4 eggs
- ❀ 1/2 cup milk
- ❀ 1 cup chopped fully cooked ham
- ❀ 1/2 cup chopped onion
- ❀ 1/2 teaspoon pepper

Directions

- ➢ Combine potatoes, 1/2 cup cheese and 1/2 teaspoon salt. Press into the bottom and up the sides of a greased 9-in. pie plate.

- ➢ In a bowl, beat eggs and milk. Add ham, onion, pepper and remaining cheese and salt; pour over potato crust (dish will be very full).

- ➢ Bakeat 350 degrees F for 45-50 minutes or until a knife inserted near thecenter comes out clean. Let stand 5 minutes before cutting.

Potato Leek Soup I

Ingredients

- ❀ 5 pounds white potatoes, peeled and quartered
- ❀ 6 cups chicken broth
- ❀ 2 leeks, bulb only
- ❀ 1/2 cup butter

* ❀ 1/4 cup white wine salt to taste
* ❀ 1/4 teaspoon freshly ground whitepepper

Directions

> Cook potatoes in chicken stock until soft. Set aside, do not drain.Put potatoes in the work bowl of a food processor in batches.

> Add5 cups of chicken stock from the potato cooking pot. Puree until smooth.Half the leeks lengthwise, and soak in water to clean.

> Finely slice. Saute in butter until transparent. Add white wine, and cook for 3 minutes.
> In a soup pot, combine remaining cup of chicken stock from thepotato cooking pot and sauteed leeks. Stir in pureed potatoes, and bring to a simmer.

> Season with salt and white pepper. Cook to desired consistency, add-ing more stock if necessary. Garnish with parsley.

Pork 'n' Potato Dinner

Ingredients

* ❀ 2 (1 inch thick) bone-in pork loin chops
* ❀ 1 tablespoon all-purpose flour
* ❀ 1 tablespoon vegetable oil
* ❀ 2 1/2 tablespoons grated Parmesan cheese, divided
* ❀ 1/8 teaspoon pepper
* ❀ 2 medium potatoes, thinly sliced
* ❀ 1 medium onion, thinly sliced
* ❀ 1 teaspoon beef bouillon granules
* ❀ 1/2 cup boiling water
* ❀ 1 1/2 teaspoons lemon juice

Directions

> ➤ Coat pork chops with flour. In a skillet over medium-high heat, brown chops in oil on both sides. Combine 1 tablespoon Parmesan cheese and pepper; sprinkle over chops.

> ➤ Arrange potato and onion slices over chops. Sprinkle with 1 tablespoon Parmesan cheese.Dissolve bouillon in boiling water; stir in lemon juice.

> ➤ Pour over chops. Sprinkle with the remaining Parmesan cheese. Cover and simmer for 18-22 minutes or until meat juices run clear.

Screaming Potatoes

Ingredients

> ❀ 2 pounds clean, scrubbed new red potatoes
> ❀ 1 tablespoon kosher salt
> ❀ 2 tablespoons water

Directions

> ➤ Place the potatoes in the bottom of a large cast iron skillet. Placeabout 2 tablespoons of water in the bottom of the pot and sprinklewith the salt.

> ➤ Cover tightly and place over low heat. Cook for 40-50 minutes. Do not lift the lid during this time.Occasionally give thepan a shake.

Curried Chicken and Potatoes

Ingredients

> ❀ 2 tablespoons olive oil

* 1 teaspoon cumin seed
* 1/2 teaspoon garam masala
* 1/4 teaspoon ground cardamom
* 1/4 teaspoon cayenne pepper
* 1/2 teaspoon black mustard seed
* 1/2 teaspoon salt
* 2 cloves garlic, minced
* 2 (4 ounce) chicken thighs, cut into bite size pieces
* 2 medium potatoes, diced
* 2 roma (plum) tomatoes, diced
* 1/2 bunch Swiss chard, chopped
* 1 (8 ounce) container plain yogurt

Directions

➢ In a large skillet, heat oil over medium heat. In hot oil, cook cumin seeds, garam masala, cardamom, cayenne pepper, mustard seeds, salt, and garlic.

➢ When seeds start to pop, stir in chicken andpotatoes. Cook for 15 minutes, or until chicken is nearly done.

➢ Stir in tomatoes, chard, and yogurt. Cover, and cook 15 minutes more, or until potatoes are tender and chicken is cooked through.

Carrot Soup with Potatoes and Cream

Ingredients

* 2 tablespoons butter
* 1 Spanish onion, chopped
* 6 cups reduced-fat chicken broth
* 5 carrots, peeled and sliced

- ❀ 3 small potatoes, peeled and sliced
- ❀ 1 teaspoon herbes de Provence
- ❀ 1 pinch dried thyme
- ❀ 1 bay leaf
- ❀ salt and pepper to taste
- ❀ 1/4 cup heavy cream
- ❀ 8 sprigs parsley

Directions

- ➤ Melt the butter in a large pot over low heat. When the butter begins to foam, add the onion; cook until the onion begins to turntranslucent, 3 to 4 minutes.

- ➤ Add the chicken broth, carrots, potatoes, herbes de Provence, thyme, and bay leaf; season with salt and pepper.

- ➤ Raise heat to medium-high and bring to a boil; reduce heat again to low and simmer until the potatoes are tender, about 30 minutes.

- ➤ Pour the soup into a blender, filling the pitcher no more than halfway. Securing the lid of the blender with a folded kitchen towel, start to blend using a few quick pulses before allowing to blend continually; puree in batches until smooth.

- ➤ Divide into eight soup bowls; garnish each portion with about 1/2 tablespoon heavy cream and a sprig of parsley.

Sweet Potato Puff

Ingredients

- ❀ 6 cups peeled, cubed sweet potatoes
- ❀ 4 eggs, separated
- ❀ 1/4 cup butter, softened
- ❀ 1/4 teaspoon salt
- ❀ 1/4 cup raisins

*   1/4 cup coarsely chopped walnuts
*   1/4 cup sugar

Directions

> Place the cubed sweet potatoes into a large pot and cover with water. Bring to a boil, then reduce heat to medium-low, and simmer until tender, about 30 minutes. Drain and let cool.

> Preheat oven to 350 degrees F (175 degrees C). Grease a 9x9 inch baking dish.Place the cooked sweet potatoes, egg yolks, butter, and salt into the work bowl of an electric mixer, and beat on high speed until thesweet potatoes are creamy and smooth, 3 to 5 minutes.

> Spoon thesweet potato mixture into the prepared baking dish, and level the top with a spoon. Sprinkle raisins and walnuts over the top of thecasserole, and lightly press them into the surface of the sweetpotatoes.

> In a mixing bowl, beat theegg whites until foamy, about 1 minute. Gradually pour in the sugar and continue beating until the meringueis glossy and holds soft peaks, 2 to 3 more minutes. Spread themeringue over the casserole.

> Bake in the preheated oven until the casserole is hot and the meringue is lightly browned, about 30 minutes

Cottage Cheese Potato Salad

Ingredients

*   3 eggs
*   4 large potatoes
*   1 cup diced celery
*   1/2 cup sliced radishes
*   1/2 cup diced green bell pepper
*   1/2 cup diced green onion
*   1 cup cottage cheese
*   3/4 cup mayonnaise
*   2 teaspoons salt, or to taste

- 1/4 teaspoon black pepper
- 1 tablespoon sliced black olives

Directions

> Place theeggs into a saucepan in a single layer and fill with water to cover theeggs by 1 inch. Cover the saucepan and bring the water to a boil over high heat.

> Once the water is boiling, remove from theheat and let theeggs stand in the hot water for 15 minutes. Pour out the hot water, then cool theeggs under cold running water in thesink. Peel once cold.

> Place the potatoes into a large pot and cover with salted water. Bring to a boil over high heat, then reduce heat to medium-low, cover, and simmer until tender, about 20 minutes.

> Drain and allow to steam dry for a minute or two. Rinse the potatoes in cold water,and allow to cool. Slice the cooled potatoes into a large salad bowl.

> Chop 2 hard-cooked eggs into the bowl with the potatoes, and mix in the celery, radishes, green pepper, and green onion.

> Stir together the cottage cheese and mayonnaise in a bowl, and pour over thepotato mixture.

> Toss lightly to combine, and season to taste with salt and pepper. Slice the remaining hard-cooked egg, arrange theslices on top of the salad for a garnish, and sprinkle with blackolives.

Party Size Potato Chip Chicken Bake

Ingredients

- 20 pounds cooked chicken breast-cut into bite size pieces
- 5 pounds celery, chopped
- 4 bunches green onion, diced
- 3 cups slivered, toasted almonds
- 1 gallon mayonnaise

- 2 cups fresh lemon juice
- salt and pepper to taste
- 6 cups crushed potato chip crumbs
- 4 cups shredded Cheddar cheese

Directions

➤ Preheat oven to 350 degrees F (175 degrees C) and lightly greasetwo 9x13 inch baking dishes.

➤ In a large bowl combine the chicken, celery, green onion and almonds; mix well. In a separate large bowl mix togethermayonnaise and lemon juice and season with salt and pepper to taste.

➤ Combine the two mixtures and blend all together.Spread potato chips in the bottom of the prepared baking dishes, then spread 1/2 of chicken mixture in each dish.

➤ Bake at 350 degrees F (175 degrees C) for 35 to 45 minutes, or until bubbly. Top with remaining potato chip crumbs and cheese andbake for another 5 to 10 minutes, or until cheese is melted and bubbly.

Garlic Potatoes

Ingredients

- 1 1/2 pounds red potatoes, cut into large chunks
- 1 clove garlic, halved lengthwise
- 1/2 cup milk
- 1 teaspoon salt
- 1 tablespoon chopped fresh parsley

Directions

➤ Place the potatoes and garlic into a large pot, and just cover with salted water. Bring to a boil; reduce heat to low, and cover. Simmer until very tender, about 20 minutes. Drain.

> Allow to steam dry for a minute or two. Return the potatoes to the pot. Pour in milk, and season with salt; mash until smooth. Stir in the parsley.

Sri Lankan Potato Curry

Ingredients

- ❋ 3/4 teaspoon coriander seed
- ❋ 1/4 teaspoon fennel seed
- ❋ 1/4 teaspoon cumin seed
- ❋ 4 leaves fresh curry
- ❋ 4 large potatoes - peeled and cubed
- ❋ 1 tablespoon ghee(clarified butter)
- ❋ 1/2 onion, finely chopped
- ❋ 1 clove garlic, minced
- ❋ 1 (1 inch) piece fresh ginger root, grated
- ❋ 1/2 teaspoon cumin seed
- ❋ 1/2 teaspoon coriander seed
- ❋ 1/2 cup coconut milk
- ❋ 1 tablespoon chopped fresh cilantro
- ❋ salt to taste

Directions

> In a small skillet, over a low heat, dry roast the 3/4 teaspoon coriander, 1/4 teaspoon fennel, and 1/4 teaspoon cumin seedsindividually until an aroma is starting to be given off.

> Combine all these with the curry leaves, and over a low heat, dry roast for about5 minutes more. Do not burn Grind the spices and leaves using a mortar and pestle or a clean coffee grinder. Set aside.

- ➢ Place potato cubes in a microwave-safe bowl, and microwave until about 1/2 cooked (time depends on individual microwave), about 3 to 5 minutes.

- ➢ n a large skillet, melt the ghee over medium heat. Cook the onion, garlic, and ginger in the ghee until golden and aromatic.

- ➢ Meanwhile, grind the remaining coriander and cumin seeds; add with one teaspoon fresh curry powder (prepared in the first step) to the onions and garlic.

- ➢ Cook, stirring, for 30 seconds. Stir in thepotatoes, and cook for 3 minutes. Stir in the coconut milk, bring to a simmer, and then reduce heat to low.

- ➢ Cover, and cook untilpotatoes are tender, about 7 minutes. Season with salt to taste. Top with chopped fresh cilantro, and serve.

Scrumptious Baked Chicken and Potatoes

Ingredients

- ❀ 5 pounds chicken parts
- ❀ 1 cup water
- ❀ 6 potatoes, quartered
- ❀ 2 tablespoons olive oil
- ❀ 2 teaspoons crushed dried rosemary
- ❀ 2 teaspoons crushed dried thyme
- ❀ salt and ground black pepper to taste

Directions

- ➢ Preheat an oven to 350 degrees F (175 degrees C).Place the chicken pieces in a large baking dish; pour the water into the bottom of the dish.

- ➢ Arrange the potatoes around and over thechicken pieces. Drizzle the olive oil over the mixture; season with the rosemary, thyme, salt, and pepper.

➤ Bake the chicken in the preheated oven until no longer pink at the bone and the juices run clear, about 1 hour.

➤ An instant-readthermometer inserted into the thickest part of the thigh, near thebone should read 180 degrees F (82 degrees C).

Zippy Potato Soup

Ingredients

❀ 3/4 pound sliced bacon, diced

❀ 1 medium onion, chopped

❀ 8 potatoes, peeled and cut into chunks

❀ 1 medium carrot, grated

❀ 5 cups water

❀ 1 (12 ounce) can evaporated milk

❀ 2 tablespoons butter or margarine

❀ 4 1/2 teaspoons minced fresh parsley

❀ 2 teaspoons Worcestershire sauce

❀ 1/2 teaspoon ground mustard

❀ 1/2 teaspoon ground nutmeg

❀ 1/4 teaspoon salt

Directions

➤ 1/8 teaspoon cayenne pepper In a large skillet, cook bacon and onion; drain and set aside.

➤ In a soup kettle or Dutch oven, cook the potatoes and carrot in water for20 minutes or until tender (do not drain).

➤ Stir in the remaining ingredients and the bacon mixture. Cook for 10 minutes or until heated through.

Cheesy Mushroom Potato Topper

Ingredients

- ❀ 1 dash ground black pepper
- ❀ 1 (10.75 ounce) can Campbell's® Condensed Cream of Mushroom
- ❀ Soup (Regular or 98% Fat Free)
- ❀ 4 hot baked potatoes, split
- ❀ 1/4 cup shredded Cheddar cheese

Directions

- ➢ Add the black pepper to the soup in the can and stir until the soup is smooth.

- ➢ Place the potatoes onto a microwavable plate. Spoon the soup on the potatoes. Sprinkle with the cheese.

- ➢ Microwave on HIGH for 4minutes or until the soup mixture is hot and the cheese is melted.

Sweet Potato Apple Scallop

Ingredients

- ❀ 2 pounds sweet potatoes
- ❀ 2 medium apples, peeled and cored
- ❀ 1 tablespoon lemon juice
- ❀ 1/2 cup packed brown
- ❀ 1/4 cup chopped pecans
- ❀ 1/2 teaspoon ground cinnamon
- ❀ 1/2 teaspoon pumpkin pie spice
- ❀ 1/2 teaspoon orangeextract
- ❀ 2 tablespoons butter or stick margarine

Directions

- ➤ Place sweet potatoes in a saucepan and cover with water. Bring to a boil; cook for 20-25 minutes or until tender.

- ➤ Drain and cool. Peel potatoes and cut into 1/4-in. slices. Place in a 13-in. x 9-in. x 2-in. baking dish coated with nonstick cooking spray.

- ➤ Cut apples into 1/4-in. rings; cut in half. Arrange over sweet potatoes. Sprinkle with lemon juice.

- ➤ Combine the brown sugar, pecans, cinnamon,pumpkin pie spice and orangeextract; sprinkleover apples. Dot with butter.

- ➤ Bake, uncovered, at 350 degrees F for 25-30 minutes or until apples are tender.

Mashed Potato Dream

Ingredients

- ✿ 4 large potatoes, peeled and quartered
- ✿ 1/4 cup butter
- ✿ 1 bunch green onions, sliced
- ✿ 1 tablespoon prepared horseradish
- ✿ 1 teaspoon garlic powder
- ✿ 2 tablespoons grated Parmesan cheese
- ✿ 1/2 cup milk
- ✿ freshly ground black pepper to taste
- ✿ salt to taste

Directions

- ➤ Bring a large pot of salted water to a boil. Add potatoes, and cook until tender, about 25 minutes; drain.

➤ Melt butter in a medium saucepan over medium heat. Stir in green onions, and cook until tender, 3 to 5 minutes.

➤ Mix green onions, horseradish, garlic powder, Parmesan chee-se, milk, pepper and salt with potatoes. Mash together with a potato masher.

Golden Potato Rounds

Ingredients

❀ 1 cup crushed cornflakes

❀ 1 1/2 teaspoons seasoned salt

❀ 4 medium potatoes, peeled and sliced 1/2-inch thick

❀ 1/4 cup butter or margarine, melted

Directions

➤ In a bowl, combine the cornflakes and seasoned salt. Dip potatoes in butter, then coat with cornflakemixture.

➤ Place on greased foil-lined baking sheets. Bake at 350 degrees F for 55-60 minutes or until tender.

Smushed Apples and Sweet Potatoes

Ingredients

❀ 2 large sweet potatoes, peeled and diced

❀ 2 tablespoons butter

❀ 1/4 cup white sugar

❀ 1 teaspoon ground cinnamon

❀ 1/2 teaspoon ground allspice

* 1 Granny Smith apple - peeled, cored and sliced
* 1/8 cup milk

Directions

> Place the sweet potato in a medium saucepan and fill with enough water to cover the potatoes. Bring to a boil, reduce heat to medium, and simmer for about 20 minutes or until tender. Remove from heat, drain and set aside.

> Melt butter over low heat in a small saucepan. Mix in the sugar, cinnamon and allspice. Add the apple slices, cover, and let simmer for 5 minutes, or until the apples are tender.

> Mix the apple mixtureinto the drained sweet potatoes along with the milk. Mix well using an electric mixer or just a fork until potatoes are mashed.

Potato Bean Skillet

Ingredients

* 1 pound fresh or frozen green beans, cut into 2 inch pieces
* 2 medium red potatoes, peeled and sliced
* 1 small onion, chopped
* 1 tablespoon olive or canola oil
* 3 tablespoons cider vinegar
* 2 tablespoons water
* 2 teaspoons sugar
* 1/2 teaspoon ground mustard
* 1/2 teaspoon salt
* 1/8 teaspoon pepper

Directions

> Place beans and potatoes in a saucepan; cover with water. Bring to a boil. Reduce heat; cover and simmer for 5 minutes; drain well.

> In a large skillet, sautebeans, potatoes and onion in oil until tender. In a small bowl, combine the remaining ingredients; pour overvegetables. Cook and stir over medium heat until the liquid is evaporated.

Carrot, Potato, and Cabbage Soup

Ingredients

- ❀ 4 large carrots, thinly sliced
- ❀ 2 large potatoes, thinly sliced
- ❀ 1 large onion, thinly sliced
- ❀ 1/4 medium head green cabbage, thinly sliced
- ❀ 2 cloves garlic, smashed
- ❀ 6 cups chicken stock
- ❀ 1 tablespoon olive oil
- ❀ 1/4 teaspoon dried thyme
- ❀ 1/4 teaspoon dried basil
- ❀ 1 teaspoon dried parsley
- ❀ 1 teaspoon salt
- ❀ ground black pepper to taste

> ## Directions

> Combine the carrots, potatoes, onion, cabbage, garlic, chicken stock, olive oil, thyme, basil, parsley, salt, and pepper in a stock pot over medium-high heat; bring to a simmer and cook until the carrots are tender, about 20 minutes. Transfer to a blender in small batches and blend until smooth.

Potato Rolls

Ingredients

* 7 cups all-purpose flour
* 1/2 cup sugar
* 1 (.25 ounce) package active dry yeast
* 1 teaspoon salt
* 2 cups milk
* 2/3 cup shortening
* 1/2 cup water
* 1 cup mashed potatoes (without added milk and butter)
* 2 eggs

Directions

➤ In a large mixing bowl, combine 2 cups flour, sugar, yeast and salt. In a saucepan, heat milk, shortening and water to 120 degrees F-130 degrees F.

➤ Add to dry ingredients; beat until moistened. Add mashed potatoes and eggs; beat until smooth. Stir in enoughremaining flour to form a stiff dough. Do not knead. Place in a greased bowl, turning once to grease top.

➤ Cover and refrigerate for several hours or overnight.Turn dough onto a lightly floured surface and punch down. Divide in half. With greased hands, shapeeach portion into 12 balls.

➤ Rolleach ball into an 8-in. rope; tie into a knot. Place 2 in. apart on greased baking sheets; tuck ends under.

➤ Cover and let rise untildoubled, about 2 hours. Bake at 375 degrees F for 25-30 minutes or until golden brown. Remove from pans to wire racks

Potato Soup with a Kick

Ingredients

- ❀ 1 pound ground beef
- ❀ 6 potatoes, peeled and cubed
- ❀ 1 onion, chopped
- ❀ 1 (16 ounce) can whole peeled tomatoes, with liquid
- ❀ 1 (8 ounce) can tomato sauce
- ❀ 3 cups water
- ❀ 2 teaspoons salt
- ❀ 1 teaspoon ground black pepper
- ❀ 1 teaspoon hot pepper sauce

Directions

➢ In a skillet, brown ground beef and onion. DrainIn a large saucepan, combine hamburger mixture,tomatoes (in juice), potatoes, and tomato sauce.

➢ Mix well. Stir in water, salt, pepper, and hot pepper sauce, and bring to a boil. Reduce heat,cover and simmer for 45 minutes or until potatoes are fork tender.

Roasted New Red Potatoes

Ingredients

- ❀ 3 pounds small red new potatoes, halved
- ❀ 1/4 cup olive oil
- ❀ 1 teaspoon
- ❀ Salt and freshly ground black pepper

Directions

➤ Adjust oven rack to lowest position and heat oven to 450 degrees. Toss potatoes with oil, salt and pepper. Arrange, cut side down, on a large lipped cookie sheet or jellyroll pan.

➤ Roast until tender and golden brown, about 30 minutes (check after20 minutes). Transfer to a serving dish.

Garden Potato Salad

Ingredients

❀ 6 large potatoes, cooked, peeled and cubed

❀ 4 hard-cooked eggs, sliced

❀ 2 celery ribs, sliced

❀ 6 green onions with tops, sliced

❀ 6 radishes, sliced

❀ 1 teaspoon salt

❀ 1/2 teaspoon pepper DRESSING

❀ 3 eggs, beaten

❀ 1/4 cup vinegar

❀ 1/4 cup sugar

❀ 1/2 teaspoon dry mustard

❀ 1/2 teaspoon salt

❀ 1 cup mayonnaise or salad dressing

Directions

➤ In a large bowl, combine potatoes, eggs, celery, green onions, radishes, salt and pepper; set aside. For dressing, combineeggs, vinegar, sugar, dry mustard and salt in a saucepan.

> Cook and stir over medium heat until thickened. Cool. Stir in mayonnaise; mix well. Pour over potato mixture; toss to coat. Refrigerate for several hours.

Delmonico Potatoes

Ingredients

- 1 (2 pound) package frozen hash brown potatoes, thawed
- 1 (8 ounce) package cubed processed cheese food
- 2 cups half-and-half
- 1/2 cup butter

Directions

> Preheat oven to 350 degrees F (175 degrees C). Place frozen potatoes in a 13 x 9 inch baking dish.

> In a saucepan on the stovetop or in microwave on low, melt together cheese and butter or margarine. When melted, blend in the cream. Pour mixture over frozen potatoes, and cover pan with foil. Bake for 1 hour. Remove foil, and bake 15 minutes more

Grilled Mustard Potato Salad

Ingredients

- 3 Yukon Gold potatoes, cubed
- 3 red potatoes, cubed
- 1/4 cup canola oil
- 3 tablespoons distilled whitevinegar
- 1 tablespoon Dijon mustard

- ❀ 1/2 teaspoon celery salt
- ❀ 1/4 teaspoon pepper

Directions

- ➢ Preheat an outdoor grill for high heat.Bring a large pot of salted water to a boil, and cook potatoes 10 to15 minutes, until tender but firm. Drain, and transfer to a medium bowl.

- ➢ In a small bowl, mix canola oil, vinegar, Dijon mustard, celery salt, and pepper. Toss 1/2 the mixture with the potatoes.

- ➢ Arrange potatoes in a single layer on a sheet of foil, and place on the prepared grill. Turning occasionally, cook 7 to 9 minutes, until lightly browned. Remove from heat, and cool. Toss with remaining oil mixture to serve

Man-Lovin' Potatoes

Ingredients

- ❀ 8 red potatoes
- ❀ 1 cup
- ❀ mayonnaise
- ❀ 1/2 cup sour cream
- ❀ 1 tablespoon onion powder
- ❀ 1 tablespoon garlic powder
- ❀ 1 teaspoon seasoned salt
- ❀ 1 teaspoon ground black pepper
- ❀ 3/4 cup crumbled cooked bacon
- ❀ 1/2 cup diced red onion
- ❀ 2 cups shredded American cheese
- ❀ 3 tablespoons grated Parmesan cheese

Directions

- ➢ Preheat an oven to 350 degrees F (175 degrees C). Grease a 9x13 inch baking dish. Slice potatoes with skins on into 1/4 inch thick slices. Place the potatoes into a large pot and cover with salted water.

- ➢ Bring to a boil over high heat, then reduce heat to medium-low, cover, and simmer until tender, 10 to 15 minutes. Drain and allow to steam dry for a minute or two.

- ➢ Mix together themayonnaise, sour cream, onion and garlic powders, seasoned salt, pepper, bacon, onion, and American cheese in a bowl.

- ➢ Stir in the potato slices. Pour mixture intoprepared baking dish. Sprinkle top with grated Parmesan cheese. Bake until bubbly and beginning to brown, 35 to 40 minutes.

Rosemary Mashed Potatoes and Yams with Garlic

Ingredients

- ❀ 8 cloves garlic
- ❀ 3 tablespoons olive oil
- ❀ 1 1/2 pounds potatoes, peeled and cubed
- ❀ 1 1/2 pounds sweet potatoes, peeled and cubed
- ❀ 1/2 cup milk
- ❀ 1/4 cup
- ❀ butter
- ❀ 1/2 teaspoon dried rosemary
- ❀ 1/2 cup grated Parmesan cheesesalt to taste
- ❀ ground black pepper to taste

Directions

- ➢ Preheat oven to 350 degrees F (175 degrees C). Put garlic in small ovenproof bowl, and drizzle with olive oil. Roast for 30 minutes, until very soft. Cool, peel, and reserve oil.

- Cook potatoes and yams in a large pot of salted water until tender, about 20 to 30 minutes. Drain, reserving 1 cup liquid.Place potatoes in a mixing bowl.

- Add milk, butter or margarine, rosemary, garlic, and reserved olive oil. Mash until smooth asdesired, adding reserved cooking liquid as needed. Mix in 1/4 cup cheese.

- Salt and pepper to taste. Transfer to a buttered or oiled 8 x 8 x 2 inch baking dish. Sprinkle with remaining cheese. Bake for 45 minutes, until heated through and golden on top.

Bologna Potato Soup

Ingredients

- 1 onion, peeled
- 2 (15 ounce) cans cut green beans, with liquid
- 1 1/2 pounds bologna, cut into pieces
- 8 potatoes, peeled and cubed
- 4 quarts water
- salt to taste
- ground black pepper to taste
- 1/2 cup cornstarch
- 1/2 cup cold water

Directions

- Place water in a 6-quart (or larger) pot. Bring to a boil. Place wholeonion and bologna into the water and boil for 30 minutes, adding more water as needed.

- Add potatoes and cook until tender.Remove onion and add the beans. Whisk the cornstarch and cold water together and also add. Cook until thickened.

Italian Mashed Potatoes

Ingredients

- 6 russet potatoes, peeled and cut into chunks
- 1 cup vegetable broth
- 1 teaspoon dried thyme
- 1 teaspoon dried rosemary
- 1 teaspoon dried oregano
- 1 teaspoon dried basil
- 1 teaspoon onion powder
- 1 teaspoon dried parsley
- 1 teaspoon dried sage
- 1 teaspoon minced garlic

Directions

- Place the potatoes into a large pot and cover with salted water. Bring to a boil over high heat, then reduce heat to medium-low, cover, and simmer until tender, about 20 minutes.

- Drain and allow to steam dry for a minute or two. Return the drained potatoes to thepot.Pour the vegetable broth, thyme, rosemary, oregano, basil, onion powder, parsley, sage, and garlic over the potatoes; mash with a potato masher.

Grated Potato Salad

Ingredients

- 6 cups grated peeled cooked potatoes
- 6 hard-cooked eggs, chopped
- 1 celery rib, chopped

- ❀ 1cup mayonnaise
- ❀ 3/4 cup sugar
- ❀ 1/4 cup milk
- ❀ 2 tablespoons cider vinegar
- ❀ 2 teaspoons prepared mustard

Directions

➢ In a large bowl, combine potatoes, eggs and celery. In a small bowl, whisk the mayonnaise, sugar, milk, vinegar, salt and mustard. Pour over potato mixture; stir until combined. Cover and refrigeratefor 4 hours.

Sweet Potatoes and Apples

Ingredients

- ❀ 1 (29 ounce) can sweet potatoes
- ❀ 1 (21 ounce) can apple pie filling
- ❀ 2 teaspoons brown sugar
- ❀ 1/2 teaspoon ground cinnamon

Directions

➢ In a large bowl, mix together sweet potatoes, apple pie filling, brown sugar and cinnamon. Transfer to a medium microwave-safe dish.

➢ Microwave on high 5 minutes, or until the mixtureis hot and bubbly.

Garlic Basil Mashed Potatoes

Ingredients

- 2 pounds potatoes, scrubbed and chopped
- 2 tablespoons butter
- 2 ounces cream cheese
- 1/3 cup sour cream
- 2 teaspoons dried basil
- 1/2 teaspoon garlic powder
- salt and ground black pepper to taste

Directions

- Place the potatoes into a large pot and cover with salted water. Bring to a boil over high heat, then reduce heat to medium-low, cover, and simmer until tender, about 20 minutes. Drain.

- Place drained potatoes, butter, cream cheese, sour cream, dried basil, and garlic powder in a large bowl.

- Mix well with an electric mixer on medium speed. Season to taste with salt and pepper.

Harvest Potato Casserole

Ingredients

- 8 large potatoes
- 2 bay leaves
- 1/4 cup butter or margarine, melted
- 1/2 teaspoon salt
- 1/4 teaspoon pepper

- 2 cups sour cream
- 1 (10.75 ounce) can condensed cream of chicken soup, undiluted
- 2 cups shredded Cheddar cheese, divided
- 1 (2 ounce) jar diced pimientos, drained
- 4 green onions, chopped
- 1/2 cup crushed cornflakes

Directions

> Place potatoes and bay leaves in a Dutch oven or large kettle; cover with water. Bring to a boil.

> Reduce heat; cover and simmer for 25-30 minutes or until tender. Remove from the heat; cool to room temperature. Place in the freezer (still covered by the cooking water) for 1 hour.

> Drain potatoes; peel and grate. Place in a greased 13-in. x 9-in. x 2-in. baking dish. Drizzle with butter. Sprinkle with salt and pepper; toss to coat. Combine the sour cream, soup, 1 cup cheese,pimientos and onion; spread over potatoes.

> Sprinkle with theremaining cheese; top with cornflakes (dish will be full). Bake, uncovered, at 350 degrees F for 45-50 minutes or until bubbly.

Potato Poofies

Ingredients

- 4 russet potatoes
- 1 tablespoon butter, softened
- 1/2 cup shredded Cheddar cheese
- 1/2 teaspoon garlic, minced
- 1/2 cup chopped fresh cilantro
- salt and pepper to taste

Directions

- ➢ Place potatoes into a largepot and cover with salted water. Bring to a boil, then reduce heat to medium-low, cover, and simmer untiltender, about 20 minutes. Drain and allow to steam dry until cool enough to handle.

- ➢ Peel the potatoes, and mash until smooth while they are still hot. Add the butter, Cheddar cheese, garlic, and cilantro, mash until the ingredients are incorporated, then season to taste with salt andpepper.

- ➢ Form the mashed potatoes into 10 balls, and slightly flatten between the palms of your hands.Preheat a large skillet over medium-high heat, and grease with cooking spray.

- ➢ Cook the poofies 5 at a time until golden brown on both sides, about 3 minutes per side. Repeat with remaining poofies. Poofies are best served warm.

Roasted Creole Potatoes

Ingredients

- ❁ 2 pounds cubed white potatoes
- ❁ 12 ounces andouille sausage, sliced
- ❁ 1/2 cup chopped green bell pepper
- ❁ 1/2 cup chopped onion
- ❁ 2 tablespoons olive oil
- ❁ 1 tablespoon paprika
- ❁ 1 tablespoon Creole seasoning
- ❁ 1 tablespoon garlic powder
- ❁ 1 teaspoon ground black pepper

Directions

- ➢ Preheat oven to 400 degrees F (200 degrees C).Place the potatoes,sausage, green pepper, and onion into a high-sided roasting pan. Drizzle with olive oil, and toss to coat. Sprinkle with paprika, Creoleseaso-ning, garlic powder, and black pepper; toss again to coat.

➤ Roast in preheated oven until the potatoes are tender and beginning to turn golden brown, 45 minutes to 1 hour. Stir occasionally during roasting.

Sally's Spinach Mashed Potatoes

Ingredients

* ❀ 1 (10 ounce) package frozen chopped spinach
* ❀ 6 potatoes, peeled and chopped
* ❀ 1/2 cup butter
* ❀ 1 cup sour cream
* ❀ 1 tablespoon chopped onion
* ❀ 1 teaspoon salt
* ❀ 1/4 teaspoon dried dill weed
* ❀ 1 cup shredded Cheddar cheese

Directions

➤ Preheat oven to 350 degrees F (175 degrees C). Lightly grease a medium casserole dish.Cook spinach according to package directions.

➤ Place potatoes in a pot with enough water to cover, and bring to a boil. Cook 15minutes, or until tender but firm. Drain, cool slightly, and mash.

➤ In a bowl, mix the spinach, mashed potatoes, butter, sour cream, onion, salt, and dill. Transfer to the prepared casserole dish. Top with Cheddar cheese. Bake 20 minutes in the preheated oven, until bubbly and lightly brown.

German Potato Pancakes

Ingredients

- 2 eggs
- 2 tablespoons all-purpose flour
- 1/4 teaspoon baking powder
- 1/2 teaspoon salt
- 1/4 teaspoon pepper
- 6 medium potatoes, peeled and shredded
- 1/2 cup finely chopped onion
- 1/4 cup vegetable oil

Directions

- In a large bowl, beat together eggs, flour, baking powder, salt, and pepper. Mix in potatoes and onion.

- Heat oil in a large skillet over medium heat. In batches, drop heaping tablespoonfuls of the potato mixture into the skillet.

- Press to flatten. Cook about 3 minutes on each side, until browned and crisp. Drain on paper towels.

Spiced Up Potatoes

Ingredients

- 2 (15 ounce) cans sliced potatoes, drained
- 2 tablespoons butter
- 1 teaspoon garlic salt
- 1 1/2 tablespoons Italian seasoning
- 1 1/2 tablespoons paprika

Directions

➤ Melt butter in a large skillet at a medium heat. Stir in the potatoes, garlic salt, Italian seasoning and paprika.

➤ Stir the potatoes around occasionally. Thepota-toes should cook for about 12 minutes or until potatoes are a red-brown color.

Cucumber Potato Salad

Ingredients

❀ 5 pounds red potatoes

❀ 4 celery ribs, sliced

❀ 1 bunch green onions, sliced

❀ 2 tablespoons dill weed

❀ 2 teaspoons salt

❀ 2 cups mayonnaise

❀ 1 (16 ounce) bottle cucumber ranch salad dressing

Directions

➤ Place potatoes in a large kettle; cover with water. Bring to a boil. Reduce heat; cover and simmer for 20-25 minutes or until tender. Drain and cool. Cut potatoes into small cubes.

➤ In a large serving bowl, combine the potatoes, celery, onions, dill and salt. In a small bowl, whisk mayonnaise and salad dressing until blended.

➤ Pour over potato mixture and stir gently to coat. Cover and refrigerate for at least 6 hours before serving.

Country Potato Dressing

Ingredients

- 1 large onion, chopped
- 3/4 cup chopped celery
- 1/4 cup butter or margarine
- 1/4 cup turkey or chicken broth
- 8 slices day-old whitebread, crusts removed and cubed
- 3 cups mashed potatoes
- 1 egg, beaten
- 1 1/2 teaspoons poultry seasoning
- 1 teaspoon salt
- 1/4 teaspoon pepper
- 1/4 teaspoon ground nutmeg

Directions

- In a small skillet, saute onion and celery in butter until tender. Remove from the heat; stir in broth. In a large bowl, combine bread cubes, potatoes, egg and seasonings

- Stir in onion mixture. Transfer to a greased 2-qt. baking dish. Cover and bake at 325 degrees F for 50-60 minutes or until a meat thermometer reads 160 degrees F.

Addictive Mashed Potatoes

Ingredients

- 6 medium potatoes, peeled and cubed

- ❀ 4 tablespoons butter, sliced
- ❀ 1 teaspoon extra virgin olive oil
- ❀ 1 large white onion, diced salt to taste
- ❀ 1/2 teaspoon brown sugar
- ❀ 3 tablespoons whipping cream
- ❀ 1/3 cup sour cream
- ❀ 1/2 cup cream cheese
- ❀ 1 tablespoon light soy sauce
- ❀ 1/4 cup freshly grated Parmesan cheese
- ❀ 1 tablespoon chicken bouillon granules
- ❀ 1 tablespoon dried parsley black pepper to taste

Directions

➢ In a large pot, cover potatoes with water and bring to a boil over high heat. Simmer on medium-high heat until the center of thepotatoes are tender when pricked with a fork, about 25 minutes. Drain, and return potatoes to pot.

➢ Meanwhile, heat butter and olive oil in a large skillet over medium heat. Stir in onions, sprinkle with salt, and cook 5 minutes. Reduceheat to medium low, and cook, stirring occasi-onally, until onions area deep golden brown, about 20 minutes. Stir in brown sugar.

➢ Pour whipping cream over the potatoes, and mash with a large fork or potato masher. Stir in sour cream, cream cheese, soy sauce,Parmesan cheese, bouillon granules, and dried parsley.

➢ Stir in caramelized onions, and season with black pepper. Mix with anelectric mixer until smooth. Reheat briefly over low heat, and serve.

Easy Potato Sausage Soup

Ingredients

- ❀ 2 onions, chopped

- ❀ 1/2 cup margarine
- ❀ 4 cups diced potatoes
- ❀ 1 (10 ounce) package frozen diced carrots
- ❀ 1 pound Polish sausage, sliced
- ❀ 1 green bell pepper, chopped
- ❀ 3 cups water
- ❀ 1 teaspoon salt
- ❀ 1/2 teaspoon ground black pepper
- ❀ 3 cups milk
- ❀ 3/4 cup dry potato flakes

Directions

➤ Using a large saucepan, brown onion in butter.Add potatoes, carrots, green peppers, sausage, water, salt and pepper. Cook on low, for about 45 minutes or until the potatoes arecreamy.

➤ Add milk and cook until heated through and then add instant potato flakes. If you want a creamy potato soup add a 1/2 cup potatoflakes, or if you want your soup thick like stew add 1 cup of potato flakes. Let soup sit for approximately 5 minutes in order to thicken and then serve.

Mediterranean Potato Salad

Ingredients

- ❀ 2 pounds potatoes
- ❀ 1 green bell pepper, minced
- ❀ 1 cucumber, sliced and quartered
- ❀ 1/2 cup sliced red onion
- ❀ 8 ounces crumbled feta cheese
- ❀ 1 lemon, juiced
- ❀ 1/2 cup Italian-style salad dressing
- ❀ salt and pepper to taste
- ❀ 3 pita breads, cut into wedges

Directions

➢ Bring a large pot of salted water to a boil. Add potatoes and cook until tender but still firm, about 15 minutes. Drain, cool and chop.

➢ In a large bowl, combine the potatoes, green peppers, cucumbers, red onion and cheese.Whisk together the lemon juice, salad dressing, salt and pepper. Pour over salad and toss to coat. Servewith pita bread wedges if desired.

Country Style Green Beans with Red Potatoes

Ingredients

❀ 1/2 pound smoked turkey tails

❀ 2 (14.5 ounce) cans green beans, drained and rinsed

❀ 1 large onion, chopped

❀ 10 small red potatoes, peeled and cubed

❀ 1 tablespoon seasoned salt

❀ 2 teaspoons ground black pepper

❀ 1 tablespoon garlic powder

Directions

➢ Place the turkey tails and onion into a 4 quart Dutch oven and fill half way full with water. Season with salt, pepper and garlic powder.

➢ Bring to a boil, then cover and simmer over low heat until meat falls off the bones, about 2 hours. Remove the bones and skin; return the meat to the pot. Discard bones and skin.

➢ Add the green beans to the Dutch oven and simmer for 20 minutes, then add the potatoes. Simmer for 10 to 15 minutes more, or until they can beeasily pierced with a fork.

Grilled Potatoes and Mushrooms

Ingredients

- 8 potatoes, sliced
- 1 (10.75 ounce) can condensed cream of mushroom soup
- 1 cup fresh sliced mushrooms
- 1 onion, sliced
- 1/2 cup butter seasoned
- salt to taste

Directions

- Preheat an outdoor grill for medium to low heat.Lay a piece of foil largeenough to hold all the ingredients flat on a table. Place the potatoes in the center of the foil, pour the soup over the potatoes, then top with the mushrooms and onion.

- Arrange thebutter all over and around the vegetables and then top off with your favorite seasonings. Now either fold foil over to seal or use another large piece to seal theentire package. Grill over medium to low heat on a top rack, if possible, for 1 hour.

Potatoes Supreme

Ingredients

- 8 potatoes, peeled and cubed
- 1 (10.75 ounce) can condensed cream of chicken soup, undiluted
- 3 cups shredded Cheddar cheese, divided
- 1 cup sour cream
- 3 green onions, chopped
- salt and pepper to taste

Directions

> ➢ Place potatoes in a saucepan and cover with water. Bring to a boil; cover and cook until almost tender. Drain and cool.

> ➢ In a large bowl, combine soup, 1-1/2 cups cheese, sour cream, onions, salt and pepper; stir in potatoes.

> ➢ Place in a greased 13-in. x 9-in.x 2-in. baking dish. Sprinkle with remaining cheese. Bake, uncovered, at 350 degrees F for 25-30 minutes or until heated through.

Celery Potato Chowder

Ingredients

- ❀ 1 medium onion, chopped
- ❀ 2 celery ribs, chopped
- ❀ 1/2 cup sliced fresh mushrooms
- ❀ 1 tablespoon butter or margarine
- ❀ 2 cups frozen corn, thawed
- ❀ 1 (10.75 ounce) can condensed cream of celery soup, undiluted
- ❀ 1 (10.75 ounce) can condensed cream of mushroom soup,
- ❀ undiluted
- ❀ 1 1/2 cups milk
- ❀ 1 cup mashed potatoes
- ❀ 5 bacon strips, cooked and crumbled

Directions

> ➢ In a large saucepan, saute the onion, celery and mushrooms in butter until tender. Add the corn, soups, milk and potatoes. Cook and stir over medium heat until heated through. Garnish with bacon.

Crunchy Praline Topped Sweet Potatoes

Ingredients

- 1 (24 ounce) package Simply Potatoes® Mashed Sweet Potatoes
- 1/2 teaspoon salt
- 1 cup corn flakes cereal, coarsely crushed
- 1/3 cup brown sugar
- 1/2 cup chopped pecans
- 2 tablespoons all-purpose flour
- 1/4 cup butter or margarine, melted

Directions

- Heat oven to 350 degrees F. Spray 1 1/2 quart casserole dish* with nonstick cooking spray. Stir Simply Potatoes® and salt incasserole dish until well blended.

- In medium bowl stir together all remaining ingredients. Spread top-ing evenly over Simply Potatoes®.

- Bake, uncovered, 25 to 30 minutes or until topping is light golden brown and potatoes are heated through.

Potato Delight

Ingredients

- 4 large baking potatoes
- 1 cup grated broccoli stems

- ❁ 1/2 cup chopped fresh
- ❁ mushrooms
- ❁ 1/4 cup sliced green onions
- ❁ 1/4 cup grated carrot
- ❁ 1/4 cup shredded red cabbage
- ❁ 1 1/2 cups diced fully cooked ham
- ❁ 1/4 cup butter or margarine
- ❁ Sour cream

Directions

> Bake potatoes in the oven or microwave until done. In a skillet, saute the next six ingredients in butter for 5 minutes or untilvegetables are tender. Serve over hot potatoes. Top with sour cream if desired.

Potato Soup Mix\

Ingredients

- ❁ 1 3/4 cups instant mashed potato flakes
- ❁ 1 1/2 cups dry milk powder
- ❁ 2 tablespoons chicken bouillon granules
- ❁ 2 teaspoons dried minced onion
- ❁ 1 teaspoon dried parsley
- ❁ 1/4 teaspoon ground whitepepper
- ❁ 1/4 teaspoon dried thyme
- ❁ 1/8 teaspoon ground turmeric
- ❁ 1 1/2 teaspoons seasoning salt

Directions

- Combine potato flakes, dry milk, bouillon granules, onion, parsley, pepper, thyme, turmeric and seasoning salt in a bowl and stir to mix. Pour into a 1 quart jar.

- Attach the following instructions: To serve, place 1/2 cup soup mix in bowl. Stir in 1 cup boiling water until smooth.

Garlic Rosemary Mashed Potatoes

Ingredients

- 2 pounds potatoes
- 4 cloves garlic
- 1/4 cup freshly grated Parmesan cheese
- 1 tablespoon butter or margarine
- 1 tablespoon chopped fresh rosemary
- 1/2 cup NESTLE® CARNATION® Evaporated Lowfat Milk
- salt and ground black pepper to taste

Directions

- PLACE potatoes and garlic in large saucepan. Cover with water; bring to a boil. Cook over medium-high heat for 15 to 20 minutes or until potatoes are tender; drain.

- RETURN potatoes and garlic to saucepan. Beat with hand-held mixer until combined. Add cheese, butter and rosemary; beat untilsmooth. Gradually beat in evaporated milk until fluffy. Season with salt and pepper.

Screaming Potatoes

Ingredients

- ✹ 2 pounds clean, scrubbed new red potatoes
- ✹ 1 tablespoon kosher salt

Directions

- ➤ Place the potatoes in the bottom of a large cast iron skillet. Placeabout 2 tablespoons of water in the bottom of the pot and sprinklewith the salt.

- ➤ Cover tightly and place over low heat. Cook for 40-50 minutes. Do not lift the lid during this time. Occasionally give thepan a shake.

Pineapple Sweet Potato Bake

Ingredients

- ✹ 6 large sweet potatoes
- ✹ 1 (20 ounce) can pineapplechunks
- ✹ 1 cup sugar
- ✹ 2 tablespoons cornstarch
- ✹ 1/2 cup butter or margarine, cubed
- ✹ 16 maraschino cherries Ground cinnamon

Directions

- ➤ Place sweet potatoes in a Dutch oven or large kettle and cover with water. Bring to a boil. Reduce heat; cover and simmer for 30-45minutes or until tender. Drain; cool slightly.

- Peel and cut each potato lengthwise into quarters; cut each quarter into two or threewedges. Place in a greased 13-in. x 9-in. x 2-in. baking dish.

- Drain pineapple, reserving juice. Sprinkle pineapple over potatoes. In a saucepan. combine sugar and cornstarch. Stir in the reserved pineapple juice until blended. Add butter. Bring to a boil; cook and stir for 2 minutes or until thickened.

- Pour over potatoes andpineapple. Top with cherries; sprinkle with cinnamon. Bake, un-covered, at 350 degrees F for 30-35 minutes or until heated through.

Streusel Sweet Potatoes

Ingredients

- 1 1/2 cups mashed sweet potatoes
- 1/4 cup milk
- 1 egg, lightly beaten
- 2 tablespoons sugar
- 2 tablespoons butter, melted
- 1/2 teaspoon ground cinnamon
- 1/2 teaspoon ground nutmeg
- 1/2 teaspoon vanilla extract
- TOPPING:
- 1/4 cup chopped pecans
- 1/4 cup packed brown sugar
- 1 tablespoon all-purpose flour
- 1 tablespoon butter, melted

Directions

- In a large bow, combine the first eight ingredients. Spoon into a greased 3-cup baking dish. Combine the topping ingredients;sprinkle over potato mixture.

> Bake, uncovered, at 350 degrees F for 30-35 minutes or until a therm-ometer inserted near the center reads 160 degrees F

Chili Potato Burritos

Ingredients

- ❀ 4 potatoes, peeled and chopped
- ❀ 1 cup shredded Colby-Monterey Jack cheese
- ❀ 2 teaspoons chili powder
- ❀ 1 teaspoon ground cumin
- ❀ 1 clove garlic, minced
- ❀ salt and pepper to taste
- ❀ 8 (6 inch) flour tortillas
- ❀ 1/2 cup red enchilada sauce

Directions

> Bring a large pot of salted water to a boil. Add potatoes, and cook until tender but still firm, about 15 minutes. Drain, cool and mash.

> Preheat oven to 350 degrees F (175 degrees C).In a medium mixing bowl, combine mashed potatoes, 3/4 cup cheese, chili powder, cumin, garlic, salt and pepper. Spoon evenly into tortillas, and roll up.

> Place rolled tortillas side by side in a 8x8 inch baking pan. Spread enchil-ada sauceevenly over the top, and sprinkle with remaining cheese.Bake in the preheated oven 15 minutes, or until cheese is bubbly.

Leslie's Salty Grilled Potatoes

Ingredients

- ❀ 4 medium potatoes
- ❀ 4 tablespoons butter, softened
- ❀ 4 tablespoons coarse salt
- ❀ 2 tablespoons garlic powder
- ❀ 1 tablespoon pepper
- ❀ 2 tablespoons Italian seasoning (optional)

Directions

- ➢ Preheat an outdoor grill for medium-low heat.Prepare four foil squares largeenough to fold over one potatoeach. Spread butter onto foil in a largeenough area that the potato will becompletely covered when rolled up.

- ➢ Sprinkle salt, garlic, pepper, and Italian seasoning evenly over foil. Roll each potato in the foil; puncture the package (including the potato) with a fork or knife afew times. Grill for 1 hour, or until soft, turning the potatoes often. Serve with your favorite toppings.

Pioneer Potato Candy

Ingredients

- ❀ 2 baking potatoes, peeled and cubed
- ❀ 1/2 teaspoon salt
- ❀ 2 teaspoons vanilla extract
- ❀ 2 pounds confectioners' sugar
- ❀ 1 pound chocolate confectioners' coating
- ❀ 1 cup flaked coconut

Directions

- ➤ Place potatoes in a medium saucepan with water to cover. Bring to a boil, then reduce heat and simmer 20 minutes, until potatoes aresoft. Drain and mash.

- ➤ In a large bowl, combine 1 cup mashed potatoes, salt and vanilla until smooth. Sift confectioners' sugar over potato mixture a cup at a time. Stir into potatoes. Mixture will liquefy at first when sugar is added, then gradually begin to thicken.

- ➤ When it becomes theconsistency of stiff dough, knead it, adding more sugar if necessary, or not using the whole amount if mixture is very stiff.

- ➤ Cover with a damp cloth and chill until mixture holds its shape when formed into a small (1/2 inch) ball.Form potato mixture into 1/2 inch balls.

- ➤ Melt confectioners' coating in a double boiler or in a small saucepan over low heat. Dip balls in melted chocolate, then roll in coconut. Let cool completely. Store in an airtight container.

Potato Coffee Cake

Ingredients

- ❀ 3/4 cup dry potato flakes
- ❀ 1 cup boiling water
- ❀ 1 cup warm milk
- ❀ 3 tablespoons butter, softened
- ❀ 2 eggs
- ❀ 1 cup white sugar
- ❀ 4 1/2 cups bread flour
- ❀ 1 (.25 ounce) package active dry yeast
- ❀ 3 tablespoons white sugar
- ❀ 1/2 teaspoon ground cinnamon

* ❀ 3 tablespoons butter, melted

Directions

- ➢ In a small bowl, dissolve potato flakes in boiling water. Let stand until lukewarm, about 15 minutes.

- ➢ Place ingredients in the pan of the bread machine in the order recommended by the manufacturer. Select Dough/Manual cycle;zpress Start. The mixing and first rise of the dough will be completed in the bread machine.

- ➢ When Dough/Manual cycle is finished, remove dough and briefly knead on a floured board. Divide dough into 3 round loaves and place in three lightly greased 8 inch pie pans.

- ➢ Cover and let raiseuntil doubled in size, about 60 minutes. Meanwhile, preheat oven to 350 degrees F (175 degrees C).

- ➢ In a small bowl, combine 3 tablespoons sugar with 1/2 teaspoon cinnamon. Brush risen loaves with melted butter and sprinkle with cinnamon sugar mixture. Bake in preheated oven for 20 minutes, or until golden brown.

Microwave Baked Potato

Ingredients

- ❀ 1 large russet potato
- ❀ 1 tablespoon butter or margarine
- ❀ 3 tablespoons shredded Cheddar cheese
- ❀ salt and pepper to taste
- ❀ 3 teaspoons sour cream

Directions

- Scrub the potato, and prick several time with the tines of a fork. Place on a plate.Cook on full power in the microwave for 5 minutes. Turn over, and continue to cook for 5 more minutes.

- When the potato is soft,remove from the microwave, and cut in half lengthwise. Season with salt and pepper, and mash up the inside a little using a fork.

- Top theopen sides with butter and 2 tablespoons of cheese. Return to themicrowave, and cook for about 1 minute to melt thecheese.Top with remaining cheese and sour cream, and serve.

Smoky Potato Cheese Soup

Ingredients

- ❁ 1 onion, chopped
- ❁ 1/4 cup margarine
- ❁ 2 (14.5 ounce) cans chicken broth
- ❁ 6 potatoes, peeled and cubed
- ❁ 1 pound smoked sausage
- ❁ 1 pound processed cheese, cubed
- ❁ 2 (12 fluid ounce) cans evaporated milk
- ❁ ground black pepper to taste
- ❁ 1 tablespoon cornstarch

Directions

- Saute the onions in butter or margarine in a large pan.Add the chicken broth and the cubed potatoes. Slice the smoked sausage into bite size pieces, and add to the soup.

- Simmer over medium heat until the potatoes are soft.Using a potato masher, lightly mash the potato mixture to break up the cubes a little bit, but not mashing as comple-tely as you would for mashed potatoes.

- Add the cubed cheese, and stir until melted. Stir in theevaporated milk. Season with black pepper. The soup should be pretty thick, but you can thicken it further with a paste of cornstarch and water.

- Use about 1 tablespoon of cornstarch at a time, and add it to thesoup until you have reached the desired thickness.

Fluffy Potato Casserole

Ingredients

- 2 cups mashed potatoes
- 1 (8 ounce) package cream cheese, softened
- 1 onion, chopped
- 2 eggs, beaten
- 1 tablespoon all-purpose flour
- 1/4 teaspoon salt
- 1/8 teaspoon ground black pepper
- 1/2 (6 ounce) can French fried onions

Directions

- Preheat oven to 300 degrees F (150 degrees C). Grease a 1 1/2 quart casserole dish.Combine mashed potatoes, cream cheese, onion, eggs, flour, salt and black pepper in an electric mixer.

- Beat 2 to 3 minutes atmedium speed. Pour into prepared casserole dish. Spread fried onions evenly over the top.Bake uncovered for 30 to 35 minutes.

Russian Potato Salad

Ingredients

- 5 large potatoes
- 1 (16 ounce) package turkey hot dogs
- 5 eggs
- 5 large dill pickles, chopped
- 1 bunch green onions, chopped
- 1 (15 ounce) can baby peas, drained
- salt to taste
- 1 cup mayonnaise

Directions

> Place the potatoes in a large pot, and fill with enough water to cover. Bring to a boil, and cook until a fork can beeasily insertedand removed, about 20 minutes. Drain and cool slightly.

> During thelast 10 minutes, boil the hot dogs and eggs. Drain everything, and set aside to cool. Peel the potatoes, and cut into cubes. Chop hot dogs. Placeeverything in a large bowl, and mix in the pickles, onions and peas.

> Peel theeggs, and grate them on top of the salad. Add mayonnaiseand salt to individual servings.

Irish Potato Soup

Ingredients

- 1 (1 pound) package bacon
- 1 onion, chopped
- 1 cup celery, chopped

- ❋ 6 potatoes, scrubbed and cubed
- ❋ salt and pepper to taste
- ❋ 2 (12 fluid ounce) cans evaporated milk

Directions

- ➢ Place the bacon in a large, deep skillet, and cook over medium-high heat, turning occasionally, until evenly browned, about 10 minutes.

- ➢ Drain the bacon slices on a paper towel-lined plate, crumble, and set aside.Cook and stir onion and celery in the remaining bacon grease over medium heat until the onion is translucent and tender.

- ➢ Drain excess grease, then stir in potatoes. Add water to cover all but 1 inch of thepotatoes. Bring to a boil over medium-high heat, then reduce tomedium-low, and simmer until potatoes are tender, about 15 minutes, stirring often.

- ➢ Stir in theevaporated milk, and continuecooking until warmed through. Season with salt and pepper. Stir in bacon just before serving.

Pineapple Sweet Potato Souffle

Ingredients

- ❋ 3 cups peeled, cubed sweet potatoes
- ❋ 1/2 cup brown sugar
- ❋ 1/4 cup margarine, softened
- ❋ 2 eggs
- ❋ 2 teaspoons vanilla extract
- ❋ 1/4 cup milk
- ❋ 1/4 cup all-purpose flour
- ❋ 1/4 cup margarine, melted
- ❋ 1 cup crushed pineapple, drained

- ❀ 1/2 cup white sugar
- ❀ 1 egg, lightly beaten

Directions

- ➢ Preheat an oven to 350 degrees F (175 degrees C). Grease a 2-quart baking dish.Place the sweet potatoes into a large pot and cover with water.

- ➢ Bring to a boil over high heat, then reduceheat to medium-low, cover, and simmer until tender, about 20 minutes. Drain and allow to steam dry for a minute or two. Mash sweet potatoes in a largebowl.

- ➢ Stir in the brown sugar, 1/4 cup softened margarine, 3 eggs,vanilla extract, and milk. Beat until fluffy. Pour into prepared baking dish. Mix flour, 1/4 cup melted margarine, pine-apple, white sugar, and 1 egg together in a bowl. Spoon over the sweet potato mixture.Bake in the preheated oven until golden brown, about 40 minutes.

Sweet Potato Crisp

Ingredients

- ❀ 3 cups mashed cooked sweet potatoes
- ❀ 1 cup white sugar
- ❀ 2 eggs
- ❀ 2 1/2 tablespoons butter, melted
- ❀ 1/2 cup milk
- ❀ 1/2 teaspoon salt
- ❀ 1 teaspoon vanilla extract
- ❀ 1 cup packed light brown sugar
- ❀ 1 cup coarsely chopped pecans
- ❀ 1/2 cup all-purpose flour
- ❀ 2 1/2 tablespoons melted butter

Directions

- ➤ Preheat the oven to 350 degrees F (175 degrees C). Butter a 9 inch square baking dish.

- ➤ In a medium bowl, mix together the sweet potatoes, white sugar, eggs, 2 1/2 tablespoons melted butter, milk, salt and vanilla until well blended. Spread evenly in the prepared baking dish.

- ➤ In a separate bowl, stir together the light brown sugar, pecans and flour. Stir in remaining 2 1/2 tablespoons of butter to make thecrumb topping.

- ➤ Spread topping over the sweet potatoes.Bake for 25 to 30 minutes in thepre-heated oven, until topping is browned and crispy.

Montreal Steak Seasoned Mashed Potatoes

Ingredients

- ❀ 3 pounds red potatoes, cut into chunks
- ❀ 1/4 cup butter
- ❀ 2 ounces cream cheese, cut into pieces
- ❀ 1/4 cup milk
- ❀ 2 tablespoons bacon bits
- ❀ 1/2 cup shredded Colby-Monterey Jack cheese
- ❀ 2 tablespoons Montreal steak seasoning
- ❀ 1/2 teaspoon kosher salt, or to taste

Directions

- ➤ Place the potatoes into a large pot and cover with salted water. Bring to a boil over high heat, then reduce heat to medium-low, cover, and simmer until tender, about 20 minutes.

- ➤ Drain.Mash the potatoes with a potato masher; mash in butter and cream cheese. Stir in milk, bacon bits, Colby-Jack cheese, and steakseasoning. Season to taste with salt.

Sweet Potatoes with Pecans and Sausage

Ingredients

- ❀ 3 pounds sweet potatoes
- ❀ 1 pound pork sausage
- ❀ 2 tablespoons butter
- ❀ 1/3 cup packed brown sugar
- ❀ 3/4 cup chopped pecans
- ❀ 1 teaspoon ground cinnamon

Directions

- ➤ Preheat oven to 350 degrees F (175 degrees C).Form sausage into round patties. Place patties in a large, deep skillet. Cook over medium high heat until brown.

- ➤ Drain and set aside.Wash yams, prick with fork and place on baking sheet. Bake for 1 hour or until yams are soft. Set aside to cool.

- ➤ Cut cooled yams into 1 to 2 inch cubes and place in 2 1/2 quart casserole dish. Add sausage, butter, brown sugar, pecans andcinnamon. Mix thoroughly, cover and bake for 30 to 40 minutes or until hot and bubbly.

Mashed Sweet Potatoes and Pears

Ingredients

- ❀ 2 pears, peeled and sliced
- ❀ 1/2 cup dry white wine
- ❀ 1/4 cup water
- ❀ 3 sweet potatoes, peeled and cubed

- ❋ 1 cup evaporated milk 1/4 teaspoon vanilla extract
- ❋ 1/4 cup brown sugar
- ❋ 2 tablespoons butter
- ❋ 1/2 teaspoon ground cinnamon
- ❋ 1/2 teaspoon ground nutmeg

Directions

- ➢ Place the pears, wine, and water in a small saucepan and bring to a boil over high heat. Turn heat to medium-low and simmer untilpears are soft, about 5-10 minutes. Remove pears from wine and reserve.

- ➢ Place the sweet potatoes into a large pot and cover with water. Bring to a boil over high heat, then reduce heat to medium-low, cover, and simmer until tender, about 20 minutes. Drain and allow to potatoes to steam dry for a minute or two.

- ➢ Stir the reserved pears, evaporated milk, vanilla, brown sugar, butter, cinnamon, and nutmeg into the sweet potatoes and mash until smooth. Transfer to a serving dish and serve hot.

Creamy Ham and Potatoes

Ingredients

- ❋ 4 medium red potatoes, thinly sliced
- ❋ 2 medium onions, finely chopped
- ❋ 1 1/2 cups cubed fully cooked ham
- ❋ 2 tablespoons butter or margarine
- ❋ 2 tablespoons all-purpose flour
- ❋ 1 teaspoon ground mustard
- ❋ 1/2 teaspoon salt
- ❋ 1/2 teaspoon pepper
- ❋ 1 (10.75 ounce) can condensed cream of celery soup, undiluted
- ❋ 1 1/3 cups water

* 1 cup shredded Cheddar cheese

Directions

> In a slow cooker, layer potatoes, onions and ham. In a saucepan, melt butter. Stir in flour, mustard, salt and pepper until smooth.

> Combine soup and water; gradually stir into flour mixture. Bring to a boil; cook and stir for 2 minutes or until thickened and bubbly. Pour over ham.

> Cover and cook on low for 8-9 hours or until potatoes aretender. If desired, sprinkle with cheese before serving.

Cheesy Baked Potatoes

Ingredients

* 2 large russet potatoes
* 1 egg, beaten
* 2 tablespoons milk
* 2 tablespoons mayonnaise
* 3/4 cup shredded Cheddar cheese, divided
* 1/4 teaspoon salt Dash pepper
* 2 tablespoons sliced green onion
* 2 bacon strips, cooked and crumbled

Directions

> Bake potatoes at 375 degrees F for 1 hour or until tender. When cool enough to handle, cut a thin slice off the top of each potato; scoop out pulp, leaving a thin shell.

> In a bowl, mash the pulp, egg, milk, mayonnaise, 1/2 cup of cheese, salt and pepper. Spoon into potato shells. Top with onion, bacon and remaining cheese.

> Place in a small ungreased baking pan. Bake, uncovered, at 375 degrees F for 25-30 minutes or until heated through.

Potato Cheese Calico Soup

Ingredients

* 1 pound potatoes, thinly sliced
* 1 cup sliced onion
* 2 1/2 cups chicken broth
* 1/2 cup milk
* 1 cup fresh sliced mushrooms
* 1/2 cup red bell pepper, diced
* 1/2 cup chopped green onions
* 1 cup freshly grated Asiago cheese
* salt and pepper to taste
* 2 tablespoons chopped fresh parsley
* 1 medium onion, chopped
* 1 medium onion, chopped

Directions

> In 3 quart saucepan, combine potatoes, onions and broth. Bring to a boil, reduce heat to low and cook for 10 minutes or until potatoes are tender.

> Transfer soup to a blender and puree. Return blended soup to saucepan and stir in milk, mushrooms, bell pepper and green onions.

> Simmer over medium-low heat and add cheese, a few tablespoons at a time, continually stirring to ensure it melts. Season with salt and pepper, sprinkle with parsley and serve.

Sweet Potato Pancakes

Ingredients

- ⚜ 1 pound sweet potatoes, peeled
- ⚜ 1/2 cup all-purpose flour
- ⚜ 1 teaspoon baking powder
- ⚜ 2 teaspoons white sugar
- ⚜ 1 teaspoon brown sugar
- ⚜ 2 teaspoons curry powder
- ⚜ 1 teaspoon ground cumin
- ⚜ 2 eggs, beaten
- ⚜ 1/2 cup vegetable oil for frying
- ⚜ 1/2 cup milk

Directions

- ➢ Shred the sweet potatoes, and place in a colander to drain for about 10 minutes. In a large bowl, stir together the flour, bakingpowder, white sugar, brown sugar, curry powder and cumin.

- ➢ Makea well in the center, and pour in eggs and milk. Stir until all of the dry ingredients have been absorbed. Stir in sweet potatoes.

- ➢ Heat oil in a large skillet over medium-high heat. Drop the potato mixture by spoonfuls into the oil, and flatten with the back of thespoon.

- ➢ Fry until golden on both sides, flipping only once. If they arebrowning too fast, reduce the heat to medium. Remove from the oil, and keep warm while the other pancakes are frying.

Sausage Potato Soup

Ingredients

- ⚜ 1 pound Bob Evans® Italian Sausage Roll

- ⚜ 2 tablespoons olive oil

- ⚜ 1 medium onion, chopped

- 1/4 teaspoon black pepper
- 1/4 teaspoon red pepper flakes
- 1 (48 ounce) can sodium-freechicken broth
- 1 (6 ounce) package precooked chicken strips, cut into pieces
- 1 (20 ounce) package Bob Evans® Home Fries Diced Potatoes
- 1 tablespoon parsley, chopped
- 1 bunch fresh kale, washed, chopped into pieces

Directions

> In soup pot, crumble and brown sausage with olive oil over medium heat. Add onions and saute for 3-4 minutes longer. Add salt,peppers, broth, chicken pieces, potatoes and parsley.

> Bring to boil and immediately turn down to simmer. Simmer for 10 minutes add kale. Cover and simmer for an additional 10 minutes. Refrigerateleftovers.

Pineapple Sweet Potatoes

Ingredients

- 6 sweet potatoes
- 1 (20 ounce) can crushed pineapple
- 1 cup packed brown sugar
- 1 pinch ground cinnamon
- 1 pinch ground ginger
- 1 pinch ground nutmeg
- 1 pinch ground cloves

Directions

> Preheat oven to 350 degrees F (175 degrees C). Butter one 9x13 inch baking dish. Bring a pot of salted water to a boil. Add potatoes; cook until tender but still firm. Drain, and transfer to a large bowl to cool. Peel andquarter.

> In a sauce pan, combine pineapple, sugar,cinnamon, ginger, nutmeg and cloves. Bring to boil and reduce heat. Arrange potatoes in a single layer in baking dish. Pour sauce over potatoes and bake for 45 minutes.

Brian's German Potato Salad

Ingredients

- 4 pounds red potatoes, halved
- 1 pound Bacon, cut into 1/2-inch pieces
- 1 cup chopped onion
- 1/4 cup all-purpose flour
- 1/4 cup white sugar
- 1 1/2 teaspoons salt
- 1 cup apple cider vinegar
- 2 teaspoons celery seed
- 2 tablespoons chopped fresh parsley

Directions

> Place the potatoes into a large pot and cover with salted water. Bring to a boil; reduce heat to medium-low, cover, and simmer until just tender, about 10 minutes.

> Drain and allow to steam dry for a minute or two; cut into 1/2-inch pieces and place into a large mixing bowl.

> Meanwhile, stir the bacon and onion together in a large skillet over medium heat until the fat has rendered from the bacon and theonion is very tender but not brown, about 15 minutes.

> Stir in theflour, sugar, and salt; cook for 1 minute. Pour in the vinegar; bring to a simmer and cook until slightly thickened, about 5 minutes.

> Pour the dressing over the potatoes and sprinkle with celery seed and parsley. Stir gently to combine. Serve hot.

Sweet Potato, Carrot, Apple, and Red Lentil Soup

Ingredients

- 1/4 cup butter
- 2 large sweet potatoes, peeled and chopped
- 3 large carrots, peeled and chopped
- 1 apple, peeled, cored and chopped
- 1 onion, chopped
- 1/2 cup red lentils
- 1/2 teaspoon minced fresh ginger
- 1/2 teaspoon ground black
- pepper
- 1 teaspoon salt
- 1/2 teaspoon ground cumin
- 1/2 teaspoon chili powder
- 1/2 teaspoon paprika
- 4 cups vegetable broth plain yogurt

Directions

- Melt the butter in a large, heavy bottomed pot over medium-high heat. Place the chopped sweet potatoes, carrots, apple, and onion in the pot.

- Stir and cook the apples and vegetables until the onions are translucent, about 10 minutes.

- Stir the lentils, ginger, ground black pepper, salt, cumin, chili powder, paprika, and vegetable broth into the pot with the appleand vegetable mixture.

- Bring the soup to a boil over high heat, then reduce the heat to medium-low, cover, and simmer until the lentils and vegetables are soft, about 30 minutes.

- Working in batches, pour the soup into a blender, filling the pitcher no more than halfway full.

- Hold down the lid of the blender with a folded kitchen towel, and carefully start theblen-der, using a few quick pulses to get the soup moving before leaving it on to puree.

- ➢ Puree in batches until smooth and pour into a clean pot. Alternately, you can use a stick blender and puree the soup right in the cooking pot.Return the pureed soup to the cooking pot.

- ➢ Bring back to a simmer over medium-high heat, about 10 minutes. Add water as needed to thin the soup to your preferred consistency. Serve with yogurt for garnish.

Confetti Scalloped Potatoes

Ingredients

- ❀ 1/2 cup butter
- ❀ 1/2 cup chopped green onion
- ❀ 1 (16 ounce) package frozen hash brown potatoes, thawed
- ❀ 1 (10.75 ounce) can condensed cream of mushroom soup
- ❀ 1 1/3 cups milk
- ❀ 1 cup shredded Cheddar cheese
- ❀ 1 small green bell pepper, cut into thin strips
- ❀ 1 dash pepper
- ❀ 1 cup crushed cheese flavored crackers, divided

Directions

- ➢ Preheat oven to 375 degrees F (190 degrees C).Melt butter in a large skillet over medium heat. Sauteonion until tender. Stir in potatoes, soup, milk, cheese, bell pepper, black pepper, and 1/2 cup cracker crumbs.

- ➢ Transfer to a 2 quartcasserole dish and top with remaining cracker crumbs.Bake in preheated oven for 35 to 40 minutes.

Campfire Baked Potatoes

Ingredients

- ❀ 4 medium baking potatoes
- ❀ 1/4 cup butter, softened

Directions

- ➤ Pokeeach potato several times all over with a fork. Smear each potato with 1 tablespoon of butter, then double wrap in aluminum foil. Bury the potatoes in the hot coals. Allow to cook for 30 to 60 minutes until soft.

French Potato Salad

Ingredients

- ❀ 9 potatoes
- ❀ 1/2 cup vegetable oil
- ❀ 1/4 cup tarragon vinegar
- ❀ 1/4 cup beef consomme
- ❀ 1/4 cup chopped green onions
- ❀ 2 tablespoons chopped fresh parsley
- ❀ 1 teaspoon salt
- ❀ 1 teaspoon ground black pepper

Directions

- ➤ Bring a large pot of salted water to a boil. Add potatoes; cook until tender but still firm, about 15 minutes. Drain, and transfer to a largebowl. Cool slightly. Peel and slice into a large bowl.

- ➤ In a small bowl, combine oil, vinegar, consomme, green onion, parsley, and salt and pepper.Gently toss warm potatoes with dressing. Cover, and refrigerateseveral hours or overnight.

Bacon-Wrapped Potatoes

Ingredients

- 1 small onion, thinly sliced
- 2 medium baking potatoes, halved lengthwise
- 4 bacon strips

Directions

- Layer onion slices on cut side of two potato halves; top with other potato half. Wrap each potato with two bacon strips. Secure with toothpicks.

- Place on a lightly greased baking pan. Bake, un-covered, at 325 degrees F for 1 hour and 20 minutes or until potato is tender and bacon is crispy. Discard toothpicks.

Savory Caribbean-Inspired Sweet Potato Cakes

Ingredients

- 2 sweet potatoes, peeled and cut into 1-inch cubes
- 1 tablespoon canola oil
- 1 fresh jalapeno chile, seeded and finely chopped
- 3 green onions with tops, thinly sliced
- 2 cloves garlic, minced
- 1 teaspoon brown sugar 1/4 teaspoon allspice
- salt and pepper to taste
- 1/4 cup canola oil

Directions

- Place the sweet potatoes in a pan, and fill with enough water to cover. Bring to a boil, and cook until potatoes areeasily pierced with fork, about 10 minutes.

➢ Drain, place the potatoes in a mixing bowl, and mash.Meanwhile, heat 1 tablespoon canola oil in a skillet over medium-high heat. Stir in the jalapeno pepper, green onions, and garlic.

➢ Cook and stir until the vegetables are soft, about 5 minutes. Stir thevege-tables, brown sugar, and allspice into the mashed sweetpotatoes. Season to taste with salt and pepper.

➢ Form the sweet potato mixture into 12 slightly flattened cakes about2 to 2 1/2 inches in diameter using your hands or large spoons. Place on a plate.

➢ Heat 1/4 cup canola oil in a skillet over medium-high heat. Place thesweet potato cakes in the skillet, four at a time, and cook, turning once, until golden brown on each side, 6 to 8 minutes. Add more oil if needed.

Cottage Cheese Potatoes

Ingredients

❀ 5 potatoes, peeled and cubed

❀ 1 small onion, chopped

❀ 1 1/2 cups chive-flavored cottagecheese

❀ 1 cup sour cream

❀ 1 cup shredded Cheddar cheese

Directions

➢ Place potatoes in a large pot of water and boil until tender when pierced with a fork.Preheat oven to 350 degrees F (175 degrees C). Butter a 9x3 inch casserole dish.

➢ In a large mixing bowl, combine potatoes, onion, cottage cheese, and sour cream. Transfer mixture to the prepared casseroledish. Top with Cheddar cheese.Bake at 350 degrees F (175 degrees C) for 30 to 40 minutes.

Ruth's Red Lentil and Potato Soup

Ingredients

- 2 tablespoons unsalted butter
- 1 large sweet onion, chopped
- 4 stalks celery, chopped
- 4 medium red potatoes, chopped
- 1 carrot, chopped
- 3 cloves garlic
- 1/4 teaspoon ground allspice
- 1/4 teaspoon cumin seeds
- 1/4 teaspoon cayennepepper
- 1/8 teaspoon ground cloves
- 1 dash pepper
- 1 quart vegetable broth
- 1 1/2 cups dry red lentils
- 2 cups water
- 1 cup roughly chopped kale
- 1/4 cup chopped fresh cilantro
- 1 teaspoon file powder

Directions

- Melt the butter in a large saucepan over medium heat. Stir in theonion and celery. Cook until tender. Mix in the potatoes, carrot, and garlic.

- Continue to cook and stir about 5 minutes, until the potatoes are well coated with butter. Season the mixture with allspice, cumin, cayenne pepper, cloves, and pepper.

- Pour in the vegetable broth, and mix in the lentils. Add water, increasing the amount as necessary to cover all ingredients. Bring to a boil, reduce heat, and stir in the kale.

➤ Cook, stirring occasionally, 35 to 45 minutes, until the lentils are tender. Mix in thecilantro and file powder. Continue cooking about 5 minutes, or to desired thickness.

Cream of Chicken and Potato Soup

Ingredients

- ❋ 1/2 cup butter
- ❋ 1/2 cup all-purpose flour
- ❋ 1 onion, chopped
- ❋ 1 bunch chopped fresh chives
- ❋ 2 quarts heavy cream
- ❋ 2 cups water
- ❋ 1 quart milk
- ❋ 3 teaspoons ground cumin
- ❋ 2 teaspoons salt
- ❋ 2 teaspoons ground black pepper
- ❋ 2 teaspoons garlic powder
- ❋ 2 teaspoons dried thyme
- ❋ 4 potatoes, peeled and cubed
- ❋ 1 pound skinless, boneless chicken breast halves - cut into cubes
- ❋ 3 tablespoons chopped fresh parsley

Directions

➤ Melt the butter in a large pot over medium heat. Stir in the flour until absorbed thoroughly by the butter. Add the onion and chives and saute for 5 minutes.

➤ Pour in the cream, water, milk, cumin, salt,ground black pepper, garlic powder, thyme, potatoes and chicken.

> Reduce heat to low and let simmer for 1 hour. Remove from heat, let cool slightly, pour into individual bowls and garnish each with parsley.

Garlic New Potatoes

Ingredients

* 1 (14 ounce) can Swanson® Seasoned Chicken Broth with Roasted Garlic
* 4 cups small new potatoes cut in half

Directions

> Place broth and potatoes in saucepan. Heat to a boil. Cover. Cook over low heat 15 minutes or until tender. Drain.

Spicy Sweet Potato Chips

Ingredients

* 2 tablespoons olive oil
* 2 tablespoons maple syrup
* 1/4 teaspoon cayenne pepper
* 3 large sweet potato, peeled and cut into 1/4-inch slices
* salt and pepper to taste

Directions

> Preheat oven to 450 degrees F (230 degrees C). Line a baking sheet with aluminum foil.

> Stir together olive oil, maple syrup, and cayenne pepper in a small bowl. Brush the sweet potato slices with the maple mixture and

> place onto the prepared baking sheet. Sprinkle with salt and pepper to taste.

> Bake in preheated oven for 8 minutes, then turn the potato slices over, brush with any remaining maple mixture, and continue baking until tender in the middle, and crispy on theedges, about 7 minutes more.

Twice Baked Cheesy Potatoes

Ingredients

* 5 potatoes
* 4 ounces American cheese, sliced into strips
* 1 tablespoon butter
* 3/4 cup sour cream

Directions

> Preheat oven to 350 degrees F (175 degrees C). Bake potatoes for 1 hour or until soft.

> In a microwave safe bowl, combine the cheese and butter. Cook in microwave for 1 1/2 minutes or until melted. Add sour cream and mix together.

> Cut potatoes in half, scoop out insides while being careful not to tear the skins. Add to cheese mixture and mix together untilsmooth.

> Stuff potato mixture back into potato shells and bake at 350 degrees F (175 degrees C) for 10 minutes.

Potato and Broccoli Casserole

Ingredients

* 1 head fresh broccoli, cut into florets
* 6 large potatoes, cubed

- 2 (10.75 ounce) cans condensed cream of broccoli soup
- 2 1/2 cups shredded Cheddar cheese
- 1 cup sour cream
- 1 teaspoon Dijon-style prepared mustard
- 1 cup crushed saltine crackers

Directions

- Preheat oven to 325 degrees F (165 degrees C). Lightly grease a 3 quart casserole dish.

- n a large bowl, mix together cream soups, cheddar cheese, sour cream, and mustard. Stir in potatoes and broccoli. Spoon into prepared casserole dish. Top with crushed crackers.

- Bake for 45 minutes to 1 hour, or until potatoes are tender.

Potato Soup with Fish and Cheese

Ingredients

- 4 tablespoons margarine
- 1 teaspoon paprika
- 2 small onion, chopped
- 4 cups water
- 10 potatoes, diced
- 2 cups half-and-half cream
- 1/2 pound cod fillets, cubed
- 2 eggs, lightly beaten
- 1 1/2 cups shredded Muenster cheese
- salt to taste

Directions

- ➤ Melt the butter or margarine in a large saucepan, and add thepaprika. Saute the onions in this mixture until they are soft. Add the water, bring it to the boil, and add the potatoes.

- ➤ Simmer gently until the potatoes are almost done. Depending on the size of thepotatoes it may be necessary to add more water during cooking.

- ➤ Add cream or milk and the fish; continue cooking, stirring occasionally, until potatoes begin to fall apart. If they remain very firm, mash them gently in the pan with a masher or wooden spoon.

- ➤ Add a little of the potato mixture to the beaten eggs, and then stir eggs into the soup. Remove from heat, and stir in the cheese. Correct the seasoning, and serve at once.

Bratwurst, Potato and Cabbage Soup

Ingredients

- ❀ 16 ounces bratwurst, casings removed
- ❀ 2 potatoes, peeled and cubed
- ❀ 1 onion, chopped
- ❀ 2 cups water
- ❀ 1 medium head cabbage, chopped
- ❀ 3 cups milk, divided
- ❀ 3 tablespoons all-purpose flour
- ❀ 4 ounces Swiss cheese, diced

Directions

- ➤ In a large skillet over medium high heat, saute the sausage for 10 minutes, or until browned and crumbled. Drain well and discard thefat.

- ➤ In a large pot over high heat, combine the browned sausage, potatoes, onion and water. Bring to a boil, reduce heat to low and simmer for 20 minutes.

- Add the cabbage, return to a boil, reduceheat and simmer for another 20 minutes. Add 2 1/2 cups of the milk and heat slowly to just under a boil. (Note: Don't try to do this too fast, or the milk will burn on the bottom of the pot.)

- In a separate small bowl, mix the flour with the remaining milk, and add to the pot slowly, stirring constantly, so that the flour does not clump. (Note: Make sure you get out all the lumps because they will not cook out on their own.)

- When the mixture in the pot thickens, add the cheese and stir off and on until the cheese has melted.

Spinach, Potato, and Nutmeg Soup

Ingredients

- 1 tablespoon vegetable oil
- 1 onion, chopped
- 1 1/2 quarts water
- 1 cube chicken bouillon
- 2 cups fresh spinach
- 4 small potatoes, peeled and halved
- ground nutmeg to taste
- 1/2 cup milk
- salt and pepper to taste

Directions

- Heat the oil in a skillet over medium heat. Cook and stir the onion until tender.

- In a saucepan, bring the water to a boil. Reduce heat to low, and dissolve the bouillon cube in the water.

- In a blender or food processor, blend the onion, spinach, potatoes, nutmeg, and about 2 cups of the bouillon until thick and smooth.

- Blend the potato mixture into the saucepan with the remaining bouillon. Bring to a boil, reduce heat, and simmer 20 minutes.

> Stir in the milk, and continue cooking 10 minutes. Season with salt, pepper, and more nutmeg to taste. Thus the soup is complete.

Deep Dish Potato and Pumpkin Pie

Ingredients

- ❀ 1 small sugar pumpkin
- ❀ 2 large russet potatoes
- ❀ 1 1/2 cups all-purpose flour
- ❀ 1/2 teaspoon salt
- ❀ 1/2 cup butter
- ❀ 4 tablespoons ice water
- ❀ 1 tablespoon olive oil
- ❀ 2 cups chopped onion
- ❀ 2 cloves garlic
- ❀ 1 1/3 cups fresh corn kernels
- ❀ 6 ounces shredded Monterey Jack cheese
- ❀ 2 teaspoons chopped fresh thyme
- ❀ 1/8 teaspoon ground allspice
- ❀ 1/2 teaspoon salt
- ❀ freshly ground black pepper

Directions

> Preheat the oven to 400 degrees F (200 degrees C).Split the pumpkin in half, spoon out the seeds and place thepumpkin halves face down on a baking sheet. Split the potatoes lengthwise and place on the pan with the pumpkin.

> Bake thepumpkin and potatoes for 1 hour. Remove them from the oven and let them cool. When the pumpkin has cooled, spoon out the flesh and put it into a large bowl. Cut the potato into 1/2 inch cubes.

➤ To make the dough in a food processor fitted with a steel blade, put the flour and salt into the processor. Add the butter. Run the machine in spurts until the butter is in bits no bigger than pea-size.

➤ Add 4 tablespoons ice water, and run the machine in spurts again just enough to bring the dough together. Turn the dough onto a work surface and knead it with your hands until the dough is soft and smooth, handling the dough as little as possible.

➤ Form it into a flattened ball. Chill the dough for at least 30 minutes. Preheat the oven to 375 degrees F (190 degrees C). On a floured surface, roll out the dough, and use it to line the bottom and sides of either a 9 inch square baking pan or a large deep dish pie pan.

➤ Pierce the dough with a fork in three places. Line the sides of the pan with aluminum foil, and crimp the foil gently to hold the dough in place.

➤ Bake the crust for 15 minutes. Remove the pan from the oven. Reduce the heat to 350 degrees F (175 degrees C). While the crust bakes, make the filling.

➤ Heat the oil in a large skillet over medium heat. Add the onions, and cook them, stirring frequently, until they soften, about 5 minutes.

➤ Add the garlic, and cook for 3 to 4 minutes more, stirring frequently. Add the corn and cook for 2 more minutes. Remove the skillet from the heat.

➤ Stir in the pumpkin, potato, cheese, thyme, allspice, salt, and pepper. Mix well, then spoon into pre-baked pie shell.

➤ Bake the pie at 350 degrees F (175 degrees C) for 30 minutes or until veggies and cheese are piping hot. Serve immediately.

Shredded Potato Quiche

Ingredients

❋ 1 (16 ounce) package frozen shredded hash brown potatoes, thawed

❋ 1/4 cup butter, melted

❋ 5 eggs, lightly beaten

❋ 1 1/2 cups shredded Swiss cheese

- ❀ 1 cup cooked ham
- ❀ 1/4 cup milk
- ❀ salt and pepper to taste

Directions

- ➢ Preheat oven to 375 degrees F (190 degrees C). Lightly grease a 9 inch pie pan.

- ➢ Press potatoes into greased pie plate. Brush with melted butter. Bake in preheated oven until lightly browned, about 10 to 15minutes.

- ➢ In a large bowl, stir together beaten eggs, milk, cheese, ham, salt and pepper. Pour egg mixture into baked crust.Bake in preheated oven until center is set, about 20 minutes.

- ➢ Thequiche will be browned on top and a knife inserted into the center will come out clean.

Dilled Creamed Potatoes

Ingredients

- ❀ 2 pounds new potatoes
- ❀ 2 tablespoons olive oil
- ❀ 1 small onion, diced
- ❀ 3 cloves garlic, minced
- ❀ 1 quart heavy cream
- ❀ 1 cup chopped freshdill
- ❀ salt and pepper to taste

Directions

- ➢ Place the potatoes in a large pot with enough water to cover. Bring to a boil, and cook 15 minutes, or until tender.

> Heat the olive oil in a skillet over medium heat, and cook the onion and garlic until tender.

> Drain potatoes, and return to the pot. Pour in the cream, and mix in the onion, garlic, and dill. Bring to a boil, reduce heat to low, and simmer 20 minutes, stirring occasion-nally, until thickened. Season with salt and pepper.

Country-Italian Chicken and Potatoes

Ingredients

- 2 tablespoons olive oil
- 1 pound boneless, skinless chicken breasts, cut into 1-inch cubes
- 2 cloves garlic, finely chopped
- 2 medium potatoes, cut into 1-inch cubes
- 1 medium green or red bell
- pepper, cut into large pieces
- 1 (26 ounce) jar Ragu® Old World Style® Pasta Sauce
- 1 teaspoon dried basil leaves, crushed

Directions

> Heat olive oil in 12-inch skillet over medium-high heat and cook chicken with garlic until chicken is thoroughly cooked.

> Removechicken and set aside.Add potatoes and bell pepper in same skillet. Cook over medium heat, stirring occasionally, 5 minutes.

> Stir in remainingingredients. Bring to a boil over high heat. Reduce heat to low and simmercovered, stirring occasionally, 35 minutes or until potatoes are tender. Return chicken to skillet and heat through.

Potato Chip Cookie Mix in a Jar

Ingredients

- 1 cup white sugar
- 1 1/2 cups crushed potato chips
- 2/3 cup chopped pecans
- 2 1/2 cups all-purpose flour
- 1 teaspoon baking powder

Directions

- In a small bowl, stir together theflour and baking powder. Layer ingredients in order given in a 1 quart "wide mouth" canning jar. Itwill be a tight fit.

- Press each layer firmly in place before adding next ingredient. Decorate the jar and attatch a tag with the followingdirections:

- Empty jar of cookie mix into large mixing bowl. Mix thoroughly. Add: 2 sticks butter, softened and 1 teaspoon vanilla. Mix until blended completely.

- Shape into balls the size of walnuts. Flatten. Bake at 350 degrees F (175 degrees C) for 14 to 18 minutes until edges are very lightly browned. Cool 5 minutes on the cookiesheets. Remove cookies to wire racks to cool completely.

Chipotle Sweet Potatoes

Ingredients

- 2 sweet potatoes, peeled and cubed
- 1/4 cup softened butter
- 2 chipotle peppers in adobo sauce, chopped
- 2 tablespoons adobo sauce from chipotle peppers

* 2 tablespoons half-and-half cream salt to taste

Directions

- ➤ Place the sweet potatoes into a large pot and cover with salted water. Bring to a boil over high heat, then reduce heat to medium-low, cover, and simmer until tender, about 20 minutes. Drain and allow to steam dry for a minute or two.

- ➤ Place the potatoes into a bowl and add the butter, chipotle chiles, adobo sauce, and half-and-half. Mash well with a potato masher, and season to taste with salt to serve.

Bacon Potato Bundles

Ingredients
* 4 large baking potatoes, peeled and quartered
* 8 slices onion
* 8 green peppers, sliced
* 4 bacon strips
* salt and pepper to taste

Directions

- ➤ Place the potatoes on four pieces of greased heavy-duty aluminum foil. Place onion and green pepper between potato quarters; top with bacon. Sprinkle with salt and pepper.

- ➤ Wrap in foil. Grill,covered, over medium-high heat for 40-50 minutes or until the potatoes are tender, turning once.

Savory Grilled Potatoes

Ingredients

- 1/4 cup mayonnaise
- 1 tablespoon grated Parmesan cheese
- 1 garlic clove, minced
- 1/2 teaspoon minced fresh parsley
- 1/4 teaspoon salt
- 1/4 teaspoon paprika
- 1/4 teaspoon pepper
- 2 medium baking potatoes, cut into 1/4 inch slices
- 1 small onion, sliced and separated into rings

Directions

- 2 tablespoons butter   In a large bowl, combine the first seven ingredients. Add potatoes and onion; toss gently to coat. Spoon onto a double thickness of greased heavy-duty foil (about 18 in. square).

- Dot with butter. Fold foil around potato mixture and seal tightly. Grill, covered, overmedium heat for 30-35 minutes or until potatoes are tender, turning once.

Potato Cake

Ingredients

- 1 potato, cubed
- 1 cup butter
- 2 cups packed brown sugar
- 4 eggs
- 2 cups all-purpose flour
- 2 teaspoons baking powder

- ❀ 1 teaspoon ground cinnamon
- ❀ 1 teaspoon ground nutmeg
- ❀ 1/2 teaspoon ground cloves
- ❀ 1 cup milk
- ❀ 1 (1 ounce) square semisweet chocolate, melted
- ❀ 1 cup chopped pecans

Directions

- ➢ Preheat oven to 350 degrees F (175 degrees C). Bring a saucepan of water to a boil. Add potato and cook until tender but still firm, about 15 minutes.

- ➢ Drain, cool and mash. Grease and flour a 10 inch Bundt pan.Cream butter, gradually add brown sugar until light and fluffy. Add eggs, one at a time, beating well after each addition. Beat inmashed potatoes.

- ➢ Combine flour, baking powder, cinnamon, nutmeg, and cloves; add to creamed mixture alternately with milk, beginning and ending with flour mixture. Stir in melted chocolate and pecans. Pour batter into a prepared 10 inch Bundt pan.

- ➢ Bake at 350 degrees F (175 degrees C) for 1 hour or until cake tests done. Cool in pan 20 minutes; remove cake from pan, and coolcompletely before serving.

Corny Ham and Potato Scallop

Ingredients

- ❀ 5 potatoes, peeled and cubed
- ❀ 1 1/2 cups cubed cooked ham
- ❀ 1 (15 ounce) can whole kernel corn, drained
- ❀ 1/4 cup chopped green bell pepper
- ❀ 2 teaspoons instant minced onion
- ❀ 1 (10.75 ounce) can condensed Cheddar cheese soup
- ❀ 1/2 cup milk
- ❀ 3 tablespoons all-purpose flour

Directions

➢ In a slow cooker, combine potatoes, ham, corn, green pepper, and onion. In a small bowl, stir together soup, milk, and flour untilsmooth.

➢ Pour soup mixture over ham and vegetables, and stir gently to coat.Cover, and cook on Low for about 8 hours, or until potatoes are tender.

Eureka Potato Salad

Ingredients

* 8 potatoes, peeled and cubed
* 1 cup sour cream
* 1/2 cup creamy salad dressing, e.
* g. Miracle Whip в„ў
* 1/2 cup shredded Monterey Jack cheese
* 2 hard-cooked eggs, peeled and chopped
* salt and pepper to taste

Directions

➢ Place the potatoes into a large pot, and fill with enough water to cover. Bring to a boil, and cook for about 10 minutes, or until easily pierced with a fork.

➢ Drain, and set aside to cool.In a serving bowl, mix together the sour cream, salad dressing, shredded cheese and hard-cooked eggs. When the potatoes arecool, stir into the dressing.

➢ If you like it creamier, mix longer. Season with salt and pepper to taste.

Sweet Potato Soup

Ingredients

- ❀ 2 sweet potatoes
- ❀ 2 white potatoes
- ❀ 1 turnip
- ❀ 1/2 cup heavy whipping cream
- ❀ 6 cups chicken broth
- ❀ 1 tablespoon brown sugar
- ❀ 1 1/2 teaspoons ground nutmeg
- ❀ 2 tablespoons margarine
- ❀ salt to taste
- ❀ ground black pepper to taste

Directions

- ➢ Peel and cut vegetables into small, uniform pieces. Place in a pot, and cover with the chicken stock; use only the amount of stockneeded to cover.

- ➢ Bring to a boil, and cook until vegetables aretender.Place vegetables and liquid into a food processor. Puree.

- ➢ Return pureed vegetables to the saucepan.Slowly stir in thecream, brown sugar, nutmeg, and butter. Add salt and pepper to taste.

Onion Potato Pie

Ingredients

- ❀ 8 cups frozen shredded hash brown potatoes, thawed
- ❀ 6 tablespoons butter, divided
- ❀ 3/4 teaspoon salt, divided

- 1 cup diced sweet onion
- 1/4 cup chopped sweet red pepper
- 1 cup shredded Cheddar cheese
- 3 eggs, lightly beaten
- 1/3 cup milk

Directions

> Gently squeeze potatoes to removeexcess water. Melt 5 tablespoons butter; add to potatoes along with 1/2 teaspoon salt. Press in bottom and up sides of a greased 9-in.

> pie plate to form a crust. Bake at 425 degrees F for 25-30 minutes or until edges arebrowned. Cool to room temperature.In a saucepan over medium heat, saute the onion and red pepper in remaining butter until tender, about 6-8 minutes.

> Spoon into crust; sprinkle with cheese. Combine theeggs, milk and remaining salt; pour over onion mixture.

> Bake at 350 degrees F for 20-25 minutes or until a knife inserted near the center comes out clean. Let stand 5 minutes beforeserving.

Potato Chowder Soup I

Ingredients

- 2 cups peeled and diced potatoes
- 1/2 cup diced carrots
- 1/2 cup diced celery
- 1/4 cup chopped onion
- 1 teaspoon salt
- 1/4 cup butter
- 2 cups milk
- 1/4 cup all-purpose flour

* 2 (15 ounce) cans whole kernel corn, drained
* 2 1/2 cups shredded Cheddar cheese

Directions

➢ Place potatoes, carrots, celery, onion and salt in a large pot with water to cover. Bring to a boil, reduce heat and simmer 20 minutes.

➢ Meanwhile, combine butter, milk and flour in a small saucepan over medium-low heat. Stir constantly until smooth and thick.

➢ Pour milk mixture into cooked vegetables. Stir in corn and cheeseuntil cheese is melted. Serve.

Roasted Garlic Mashed Potatoes

Ingredients

* 1 medium head garlic
* 1 tablespoon olive oil
* 2 pounds russet potatoes, peeled and quartered
* 4 tablespoons butter, softened
* 1/2 cup milk
* salt and pepper to taste

Directions

➢ Preheat oven to 350 degrees F (175 degrees C).Drizzle garlic with olive oil, then wrap in aluminum foil. Bake in preheated oven for 1 hour.

➢ Bring a large pot of salted water to a boil. Add potatoes, and cook until tender, about 15 minutes. Drain, cool and chop. Stir in butter, milk, salt and pepper.

➢ Remove the garlic from the oven, and cut in half. Squeeze thesoftened cloves into the potatoes. Blend potatoes with an electric mixer until desired consistency is achieved.

Cheesy Potato Salad

Ingredients

- ❀ 2 1/2 pounds red potatoes, cubed
- ❀ 1 cup sour cream
- ❀ 1/2 cup mayonnaise
- ❀ 1/4 cup white sugar
- ❀ 1/2 bunch green onions, chopped
- ❀ 1 cup shredded Cheddar cheese
- ❀ 1 tablespoon real bacon bits

Directions

- ➢ Place the potatoes into a pot, and fill with enough water to cover. Bring to a boil, and cook for about 10 minutes, or until easilypierced with a fork. Drain, and set aside to cool.

- ➢ In a large bowl, mix together the sour cream, mayonnaise, sugar, half of the onions, and half of the cheese. Gently stir in the cooled potatoes. Top with remaining cheese and onions, and sprinklebacon bits over the top.

Oven-Fried Potatoes

Ingredients

- ❀ 12 medium potatoes, peeled and cubed
- ❀ 1/4 cup grated Parmesan cheese
- ❀ 2 teaspoons salt
- ❀ 1 teaspoon garlic powder
- ❀ 1 teaspoon paprika
- ❀ 1/2 teaspoon pepper
- ❀ 1/3cup   vegetable oil

Directions

- ➤ Place potatoes in two large resealable plastic bags. Combine theParmesan cheese and seasonings; add to potatoes and shake to coat. Pour oil into two 15-in. x 10-in. x 1-in. baking pans;

- ➤ Pour potatoes into pans. Bake, uncovered, at 375 degrees F for 40-50 minutes or until tender.

Spinach and Sweet Corn Mashed Potatoes

Ingredients

- ❀ 1 1/2 pounds new potatoes, scrubbed and quartered
- ❀ 1/4 teaspoon salt
- ❀ 1/2 cup butter, softened
- ❀ 1/2 cup heavy cream
- ❀ salt and pepper to taste
- ❀ 1 tablespoon olive oil
- ❀ 1 1/2 cups whole kernel corn
- ❀ 1 (10 ounce) package fresh spinach, stems removed
- ❀ 1 1/2 teaspoons minced garlic

Directions

- ➤ Place potatoes in a pot and cover with water.Bring to a boil and add 1/4 teaspoon salt. Boil until potatoes are tender, about 15minutes.

- ➤ Drain water and mash potatoes together with butter and heavy cream until light and fluffy. Season with salt and pepper to taste.

- ➤ Heat a large skillet over medium heat. Pour in olive oil and sautecorn 2 to 3 minutes. Stir spinach and garlic into skillet and saute an additional 1 minute, until spinach is wilted. Fold mixture into mashed potatoes. Adjust season-ings and serveimmedia-tely.

Bratwurst Potato Skillet

Ingredients

- 2 tablespoons vegetable oil
- 2 medium red potatoes, cut into 1/4 inch slices
- 2 fully cooked bratwurst, cut into
- 1 inch pieces
- 1 small onion, chopped
- 1/3 cup chopped green pepper
- 2 tablespoons soy sauce
- 1 tablespoon orange juice
- 1/2 teaspoon dried basil
- 1/4 teaspoon salt

Directions

- Dash pepper In a heavy skillet, heat oil over medium-high heat. Add the potatoes; cover and cook for 6 minutes or until browned and crisp-tender,stirring occasionally. Add bratwurst, onion and green pepper.

- Cook and stir for 5 minutes or until meat is heated through and vegetables are crisp-tenderCombine the soy sauce, orange juice, basil, salt and pepper; add to the skillet.Cook and stir 1-2 minutes longer or until meat andvegetables areevenly coated.

Sage Mashed Potatoes

Ingredients

- 4 medium potatoes, peeled and cut into 1/8-inch slices
- 1 medium onion, chopped
- 1/4 cup water
- 2 tablespoons olive or canola oil
- 1 tablespoon minced fresh sage

- ❀ 1/2 teaspoon salt
- ❀ 1/8 teaspoon pepper
- ❀ 1/2 cup reduced-fat plain yogurt

Directions

- ➢ In a greased 11-in. x 7-in. x 2-in. baking dish, layer the potatoes and onion. Combine the water, oil, sage, salt and pepper; pour overpotato mixture.

- ➢ Cover and bake at 450 degrees F for 45-50 minutes or until potatoes are tender, stirring twice. Transfer to a mixingbowl; add yogurt and mash

Pesto Pasta with Green Beans and Potatoes

Ingredients

- ❀ 1/2 pound dry penne pasta
- ❀ 4 red potatoes, cut into
- ❀ 1/4 inch slices
- ❀ 1/4 pound fresh green beans, cut into 2 inch pieces
- ❀ 1 tablespoon olive oil
- ❀ 1 clove garlic, minced salt and pepper to taste
- ❀ 1/2 cup plain yogurt
- ❀ 1/3 cup pesto
- ❀ 1/4 cup grated Parmesan cheese

Directions

- ➢ Bring a large pot of lightly salted water to a boil, and cook thepenne pasta for 8 to 10 minutes, until al dente. Remove from heat, drain, and return to the pot.

- ➢ Bring a medium saucepan of water to a boil, and cook the potatoes about 7 minutes. Place the green beans in the saucepan with the potatoes. Continue cooking about 3 minutes. Drain the partiallycooked potatoes and green beans, and set aside.

- ➢ Heat the olive oil in a large skillet over medium heat, and saute thegarlic about 1 minute. Stir in the potatoes and green beans. Season with salt and pepper. Cook and stir until potatoes and beans aretender and lightly browned.

- ➢ Toss the potato mixture into the pot with the drained pasta. Mix in the yogurt, pesto, and Parmesan cheese. Reserve a little Parmesan to sprinkle on top when serving.

Pittsburgh Potatoes

Ingredients

- ❀ 7 potatoes, scrubbed
- ❀ 2 cups processed cheese food (such as Velveeta®), cubed
- ❀ 1/4 cup butter or margarine
- ❀ 1 1/2 cups sour cream
- ❀ 1/3 cup finely chopped yellow onions
- ❀ 1 teaspoon salt
- ❀ 1/4 teaspoon pepper
- ❀ 2 tablespoons butter or margarinepaprika

Directions

- ➢ Preheat an oven to 350 degrees F (175 degrees C).Place the potatoes into a large pot and fill with enough water to cover.

- ➢ Bring to a boil, and cook until tender enough to pierce with a fork; drain, and and cut into cubes.

- ➢ Melt cheese and 1/4 cup butter in a large saucepan over medium low heat, stirring frequently. Remove the pan from the heat; stir in the sour cream, onion, salt, and pepper.

- ➢ Stir the potatoes into the cheese mixture, and transfer to a 2 quart casserole dish. Dot thetop of the potatoes with the remaining 2 table-spoons of butter, and sprinkle with paprika.

- ➢ Bake in preheated oven until hot, about 30 minutes. Cool beforeserving.

Roasted Garlic Potato Soup

Ingredients

* 6 potatoes, peeled and cut into 1 inch pieces
* 2 tablespoons olive oil, divided
* 1/2 teaspoon ground black
* pepper
* 1 onion, chopped
* 6 cloves garlic, peeled
* 3 cups chicken broth
* 1 cup water
* 1 cup whole milk
* salt to taste

Directions

➤ Preheat oven to 425 degrees F (220 degrees C).Place potatoes in a shallow roasting pan and drizzle with 1 tablespoon olive oil. Sprinkle with pepper; stir to coat.

➤ Bake for 25 minutes, or until potatoes are browned. Reserve 1 cup of roasted potatoes.In a 3 quart saucepan heat remaining oil; saute onions for 5 minutes. Add potatoes and garlic and stir in broth and water.

➤ Bring to a boil, reduce heat and simmer, uncovered, for 20 minutes.Spoon half of broth mixture into a blender; blend until nearly smooth.

➤ Repeat with remaining mixture; return all to pot. Stir in milk and season with salt to taste. Ladle into bowls and top with reserved roasted potatoes.

Blueberry Potato Cake

Ingredients

- ❀ 1 large potato, peeled and cubed
- ❀ 1 cup shortening
- ❀ 2 cups white sugar
- ❀ 4 eggs
- ❀ 2 teaspoons vanilla extract
- ❀ 2 cups all-purpose flour
- ❀ 2 teaspoons baking powder
- ❀ 1/4 teaspoon salt
- ❀ 2 cups blueberries

Directions

- ➢ Preheat oven to 350 degrees F (175 degrees C). Grease and flour a 9x13 inch pan. Bring a small pot of water to boil, add potato and let it boil until tender (approximately 10 minutes). Drain well, thenmash. Set aside 1 cup.

- ➢ Sift together the flour, baking powder and salt. Stir in theblueberries to coat them in the flour mixture. Set aside.

- ➢ In a large bowl, cream together the shortening and sugar until light and fluffy. Mix in the warm mashed potato. Beat in theeggs one at a time, then stir in the vanilla. Stir in the flour mixture with theblueberries, mixing just until incorporated.

- ➢ Pour batter into prepared pan. Bake in the preheated oven for 45 minutes, or until a toothpick inserted into the center of the cake comes out clean. Allow to cool.

Potato Crunchy Tenders

Ingredients

- ❋ 1/2 cup vegetable oil for frying
- ❋ 1 1/2 cups milk
- ❋ 1 egg
- ❋ 1 (7.6 ounce) package garlic flavored instant mashed potatoes
- ❋ 2 teaspoons salt
- ❋ 2 teaspoons ground black pepper
- ❋ 1 1/2 pounds chicken tenders

Directions

➤ Heat the oil in a large skillet over medium heat. While the oil is heating, beat the milk and egg together in a bowl. In another bowl, stir together the instant mashed potatoes, salt, and pepper.

➤ Stir the chicken tenders with the milk mixture to coat thoroughly, then shake off excess milk and dip each tender into the potato flakes.

➤ Place the breaded tenders into the hot oil, and fry untilgolden brown, 7 to 10 minutes. Remove from oil and drain on paper towels.

Green Beans and Potatoes

Ingredients

- ❋ 3 cups thinly sliced potatoes
- ❋ 2 cups frozen green beans
- ❋ 1/2 teaspoon dried thyme
- ❋ 1/4 teaspoon ground black pepper
- ❋ 1 teaspoon vegetarian Worcestershire sauce
- ❋ 1 cup vegetable broth, divided
- ❋ 1 teaspoon cornstarch
- ❋ 1/4 cup chopped fresh parsley

Directions

> - In a large skillet over medium-high heat combine potatoes, green beans, thyme, pepper, Worcestershire sauce and 3/4 cup of broth.

> - Bring to a boil; reduce heat to medium-low, cover and simmer 15 to20 minutes or until vegetables are tender.

> - In a small bowl blend remaining broth and cornstarch.Stir inparsley; add to potato mixture. Cook, stirring, until bubbly and thickened.

Coconut Sweet Potatoes

Ingredients

- ❁ 1 1/2 pounds sweet potatoes
- ❁ 1/3 cup crushed pineapple
- ❁ 2 tablespoons butter, melted
- ❁ 1 tablespoon orange juice
- ❁ 1 egg, beaten
- ❁ 1 teaspoon salt
- ❁ 1/4 teaspoon ground mace
- ❁ 1/8 teaspoon ground ginger
- ❁ 1/3 cup flaked coconut
- ❁ 1/3 cup finely chopped pecans
- ❁ 2 tablespoons brown sugar

Directions

> - Place sweet potatoes in a Dutch oven; cover with water. Bring to a boil. Reduce heat; cover and cook for 30-35 minutes or until tender. Drain; cool slightly.

> - Peel the potatoes and place in a large mixing bowl; mash. Add thepineapple, butter, orange juice, egg, salt, mace and ginger; mix well. Transfer to a greased 11-in. x 7-in. x 2-in. baking dish.

- Bake, uncovered, at 400 degrees F for 20-30 minutes or until heated through. Combine the coconut, pecans and brown sugar; sprinkle over the top. Bake 8-10 minutes longer or until topping is lightly browned.

Ham N Cheese Potato Bake

Ingredients

- 1 (24 ounce) packagefrozen O'Brien hash brown potatoes
- 2 cups cubed fully cooked ham
- 3/4 cup shredded Cheddar
- cheese, divided
- 1 small onion, chopped
- 2 cups sour cream
- 1 (10.75 ounce) can condensed cheddar cheese soup, undiluted
- 1 (10.75 ounce) can condensed cream of potato soup, undiluted
- 1/4 teaspoon pepper

Directions

- In a large bowl, combine potatoes, ham, 1/2 cup cheese and onion. In another bowl, combine sour cream, soups and pepper; add to potato mixture and mix well.

- Transfer to a greased 3-qt. baking dish. Sprinkle with remaining cheese. Bake, uncovered, at 350 degrees F for 60-65 minutes or until bubbly and potatoes are tender. Let stand for 10 minutes before serving.

Lemon Horseradish New Potatoes

Ingredients

- 1/4 cup butter
- 1/2 teaspoon salt

- 1/4 teaspoon pepper
- 2 tablespoons prepared horseradish
- 2 tablespoons fresh lemon juice
- 1 1/2 pounds small new potatoes, unpeeled

Directions

> Preheat oven to 350 degrees F (175 degrees C).Melt butter in a 2 quart casserole dish in the oven. Stir in salt, pepper, horseradish and lemon juice.

> Place potatoes in dish and toss to coat with butter mixture.Cover and bake in preheated oven for 1 hour, or until potatoes are tender.

Rum and Sweet Potato Casserole

Ingredients

- 3 cups mashed sweet potatoes
- 1 cup white sugar
- 2 eggs, beaten
- 1/2 cup milk
- 1 teaspoon vanilla extract
- 1/2 cup butter, melted
- 1/3 cup dark rum
- 1 cup brown sugar
- 1 cup chopped pecans
- 1/3 cup self-rising flour
- 1/3 cup butter, melted

Directions

> Preheat oven to 350 degrees F (175 degrees C). Grease a 9x13 inch baking dish.In a large bowl, mix the sweet potatoes and sugar.

- Stir in theeggs. Mix in milk, vanilla extract, and 1/2 cup melted butter. Gradually stir in the rum until well blended. Transfer the mixture to the prepared baking dish.

- In a medium bowl, mix the brown sugar, pecans, flour, and 1/3 cup melted butter. Sprinkle this mixture over the mashed sweet potato mixture.

- Bake 30 minutes in the preheated oven. Allow to sit at least 10 minutes before serving.

Teriyaki Potatoes

Ingredients

- ❋ 1 1/2 pounds small red potatoes, quartered
- ❋ 1 tablespoon butter or margarine
- ❋ 1 tablespoon teriyaki or soy sauce
- ❋ 1/4 teaspoon garlic salt (optional)
- ❋ 1/4 teaspoon Italian seasoning
- ❋ 1 dash black pepper
- ❋ 1 dash cayenne pepper

Directions

- Place potatoes in an ungreased 1-1/2-qt. micro-wave-safe dish. Dot with butter.

- Add remaining ingredients; toss to coat. Cover and microwave on high for 12-15 minutes or until potatoes are tender, stirring twice.

Sri Lankan Potato Curry II

Ingredients

- 1/2 pound potatoes, peeled and cut into 1 1/2-inch cubes
- 1 teaspoon salt
- 1 cup coconut cream
- 3 green chile peppers, chopped
- 4 fresh curry leaves
- 1/2 teaspoon cayenne pepper
- 3/4 teaspoon saffron powder
- 1 clove garlic, minced
- 1/2 cup water

Directions

- ➢ Combine the potatoes, salt, coconut cream, green chiles, curry leaves, cayenne pepper, saffron powder, garlic, and water in a saucepan.

- ➢ Cook over medium heat, stirring frequently, until thecoconut cream thickens, about 15 to 20 minutes.Test the potatoes for doneness by piercing them with the tip of a paring knife.

- ➢ When the potatoes are tender, remove the pan from the heat. Let stand for 5 minutes before serving. Serve with plain rice.

Two-Tone Baked Potatoes

Ingredients

- 6 medium russet potatoes
- 6 medium sweet potatoes
- 2/3 cup sour cream, divided
- 1/3 cup milk
- 3/4 cup shredded Cheddar cheese
- 4 tablespoons minced chives, divided
- 1 1/2 teaspoons salt, divided

Directions

- Pierce russet and sweet potatoes with a fork. Bake at 400 degrees for 60-70 minutes or until tender. Set sweet potatoes aside.
- Cut a third off the top of each russet potato; scoop out pulp, leaving skins intact. Place pulp in a bowl; mash with 1/3 cup sour cream, milk, cheese, 2 tablespoons chives and 3/4 teaspoon salt. Setaside.
- Cut off the tip of each sweet potato; scoop out pulp, leaving skins intact. Mash pulp with remaining sour cream, chives and salt.
- Stuff mixture into half of each potato skin; spoon russet potato filling into other half. Place on a baking sheet. Bake at 350 degrees for 15-20 minutes or until heated through.

Mediterranean Potato Salad

Ingredients

- 2 pounds small red potatoes, unpeeled, cooked, cooled, and cut in bite-size pieces
- 1 pint grape tomatoes, halved
- 1 cup sliced celery
- 1 cup sliced green onions, with green
- 1/2 cup basil leaves, shredded
- 2 garlic cloves, crushed
- 2 tablespoons white balsamic vinegar, or other white vinegar
- 6 tablespoons extra-virgin olive oil
- 2 teaspoons Dijon mustard
- Salt and freshly ground black pepper, to taste

Directions

- In a large bowl, combine potatoes, tomatoes, onions, basil, and celery.In a small bowl, whisk together garlic, vinegar, oil, mustard, salt and pepper.

> ➤ Add dressing to potatoes and toss. Refrigerate until ready to serve.

BBQ Potato Roast

Ingredients

- ❀ 10 potatoes, peeled and halved
- ❀ 1/2 cup vegetable oil
- ❀ 2 tablespoons seasoned salt

Directions

> ➤ Preheat grill for high heat.Place potatoes in a large saucepan with enough lightly salted water to cover. Bring to a boil. Cook 15 minutes, or until tender but firm.

> ➤ Drain potatoes, and pat dry. Coat thoroughly with vegetable oil and seasoned salt.

> ➤ Place potatoes on the preheated grill. Cook approximately 20 minutes, turning periodically.

Sweet Potato Corn Bread

Ingredients

- ❀ 2 cups all-purpose flour
- ❀ 2 cups cornmeal
- ❀ 1/2 cup sugar
- ❀ 7 teaspoons baking powder
- ❀ 2 teaspoons salt
- ❀ 4 egg, beaten
- ❀ 3/4 cup milk

- 1/3 cup vegetable oil
- 2 2/3 cups mashed cooked sweet potatoes

Directions

- In a large bowl, combine the first five ingredients. In a small bowl, combine theeggs, milk, oil and sweet potatoes.

- Stir into dryingredients just until moistened. Pour into a greased 13-in. x 9-in. x 2-in. baking pan.

- Bake at 425 degrees F for 30-35 minutes or until a toothpick inserted near the center comes out clean. Cut into squares. Serve warm.

Potato Wedges with Dip

Ingredients

- 1 large baking potato
- olive oil-flavored cooking spray
- 1/4 teaspoon salt
- 1 dash garlic salt dash cayenne pepper
- BACON HORSERADISH DIP:
- 1/3 cup sour cream
- 1/2 teaspoon prepared horseradish
- 1 bacon strip, cooked and crumbled

Directions

- Pierce potato and place on a microwave-safe plate. Microwave on high for 3 minutes or until still firm but almost tender.

- Cut into eight wedges; place on a baking sheet coated with nonstick cookingspray. Spritz wedges with olive oil-flavored spray; sprinkle with salt, garlic salt and cayenne.

> Bake at 425 degrees F for 20-25 minutes or until golden brown. In a small bowl, combine the dip ingredients. Serve with potato wedges.

Potato Cheese Casserole

Ingredients

- ❀ 4 pounds potatoes, peeled
- ❀ 1 (8 ounce) package cream cheese, softened
- ❀ 1/2 cup butter or margarine, softened
- ❀ 1/4 cup milk
- ❀ 1 teaspoon salt
- ❀ 1/4 teaspoon pepper
- ❀ 1 cup chopped green pepper
- ❀ 1/2 cup shredded Cheddar cheese
- ❀ 1/2 cup grated Parmesan cheese
- ❀ 1/2 cup snipped chives
- ❀ 1 (2 ounce) jar diced pimientos, drained

Directions

> Cook potatoes in boiling water until tender; drain and mash. Add cream cheese, butter, milk, salt and pepper; mix well. Stir in green pepper, cheeses, chives and pimientos.

> Spread in a greased 13-in. x 9-in. x 2-in. baking dish. Bake, uncovered, at 350 degrees F for 50-60 minutes or until browned and heated through.

My Grandmother's Potato Chip Cookies

Ingredients

- ❀ 2 cups butter, softened
- ❀ 1 cup white sugar
- ❀ 1 teaspoon vanilla extract
- ❀ 3 1/2 cups all-purpose flour
- ❀ 1 1/2 cups crushed salted potato chips

Directions

- ➢ Preheat an oven to 350 degrees F (175 degrees C). Grease baking sheets.Mash the butter, sugar, and vanilla extract together in a bowl until creamy and well combined; mix in the flour a little at a time.

- ➢ Gently fold in the potato chips. Drop dough onto the prepared bakingsheets by teaspoonful.

- ➢ Bake in the preheated oven until theedges are golden brown, about15 minutes. Remove cookies from sheets immediately and cool on wire racks.

Sweet Potato Pudding

Ingredients

- ❀ 6 large sweet potatoes, peeled and quartered
- ❀ 1/2 cup butter, melted
- ❀ 2/3 cup dark brown sugar
- ❀ 2/3 cup white sugar
- ❀ 4 eggs, beaten
- ❀ 2/3 cup orange juice
- ❀ 2 teaspoons vanilla extract

Directions

- ➤ Preheat oven to 350 degrees F (175 degrees C). Butter a 2 1/2 quart baking dish.

- ➤ Bring a large pot of water to a boil. Add potatoes and cook until tender, about 20 minutes. Drain and mash.

- ➤ In a large bowl, combine the mashed sweet potatoes, butter, brown sugar, white sugar, eggs, orange juice and vanilla; stir until smooth.

- ➤ Pour into buttered dish. Bake in preheated oven 40 minutes.

Authentic Potato Pancakes

Ingredients

- ❀ 10 russet potatoes, peeled and shredded
- ❀ 1 carrot, peeled and shredded
- ❀ 1 onion, finely diced
- ❀ 5 cloves garlic, crushed
- ❀ 1 tablespoon chopped flat leaf parsley
- ❀ 1 tablespoon chopped fresh dill
- ❀ 2 tablespoons fresh lemon juice
- ❀ 1/4 cup olive oil
- ❀ 2 tablespoons all-purpose flour
- ❀ 2 cups dry bread crumbs salt and pepper to taste

Directions

- ➤ olive oil for frying, as needed   Mix potatoes, carrot, onion, garlic, parsley, and dill in a large bowl. Stir in lemon juice, 1/4 cup of olive oil, flour, bread crumbs, salt, and pepper. Knead just until mixture holds together.

> Heat the remaining 1/4 cup olive oil in a skillet over medium heat. Working in batches, drop spoonfuls of potato mixture in hot oil. Cook approximately 4 minutes per side, or until golden brown. Serve hot.

Slow Cooker Creamy Potato Soup

Ingredients

- 6 slices bacon, cut into 1/2 inch pieces
- 1 onion, finely chopped
- 2 (10.5 ounce) cans condensed chicken broth
- 2 cups water
- 5 large potatoes, diced
- 1/2 teaspoon salt
- 1/2 teaspoon dried dill weed
- 1/2 teaspoon ground whitepepper
- 1/2 cup all-purpose flour
- 2 cups half-and-half cream
- 1 (12 fluid ounce) can evaporated milk

Directions

> Place bacon and onion in a large, deep skillet. Cook over medium-high heat until bacon is evenly brown and onions are soft. Drain off excess grease.

> Transfer the bacon and onion to a slow cooker, and stir in chicken broth, water, potatoes, salt, dill weed, and white pepper. Cover, and cook on Low 6 to 7 hours, stirring occasionally.

> In a small bowl, whisk together the flour and half-and-half. Stir into the soup along with theevaporated milk. Cover, and cook another30 minutes before serving.

Slow Cooker Potato Soup

Ingredients

- 8 pounds potatoes, peeled and cubed
- 1 small onion, chopped
- 2 tablespoons butter
- 2 cubes chicken bouillon
- 2 tablespoons dried parsley
- 6 cups water
- 2 cups milk
- 1/2 cup all-purpose flour

Directions

- Place the potatoes, onion, butter, chicken bouillon cubes, parsley and water into a slow cooker. Set on low and let cook for 6 to 8 hours.

- At least half an hour before serving, stir together the milk and flour until no lumps remain, and mix into the soup. Cook for 30 minutes or until the soup is thickened.

Potato Chip Cookies IV

Ingredients

- 1 cup vegetable oil
- 1 cup confectioners' sugar
- 1 1/2 cups all-purpose flour
- 1 teaspoon vanilla extract
- 1 1/2 cups crushed light potato chips
- 1/3 cup confectioners' sugar for decoration

Directions

➢ Preheat oven to 350 degrees F (175 degrees C).Cream the shortening and the sugar together until light. Stir in the vanilla and the flour then carefully fold in the potato chips.

➢ Drop by spoonfuls onto an ungreased baking sheet. Bake at 350 degrees F (175 degrees C) for 15 to 18 minutes or until just goldenbrown, do not over bake.

➢ Sprinkle warm cookies with confectioners' sugar and remove to wire racks to cool.

Tex-Mex Potatoes

Ingredients

❋ 4 baking potatoes

❋ 1 tablespoon vegetable oil

❋ 1 onion, chopped

❋ 1 large green bell pepper, chopped

❋ 1 teaspoon minced garlic

❋ 1 (16 ounce) can chili beans in spicy sauce, undrained

❋ 1 tablespoon vegetarian Worcestershire sauce

❋ 1/2 teaspoon minced jalapeno peppers

❋ 1 cup shredded Monterey Jack cheese

Directions

➢ Scrub potatoes and prick in several places with toothpick or sharp knife. Place on paper towel in microwave and cook at high power for 8 minutes

➢ Turn and rotate potatoes and cook for another 8 to 10 minutes or until tender. Alternately you can bake potatoes in a 400 degrees F (200 degrees C) oven for about 1 hour or until tender

- Over medium high, heat oil in a medium skillet. Saute onions and bell peppersuntil softened. Stir in beans, Worcestershire sauce, and jalapeno peppers.

- Reduce heat to low, cover and simmer for 5 to 6 minutes.Split potatoes and top with bean mixture. Sprinkle with cheese.

Potato Cutlets

Ingredients

- 5 medium-size potatoes, washed thoroughly
- 2 teaspoons salt
- 2 tablespoons garam masala
- 2 tablespoons coriander powder
- 2 tablespoons black pepper
- 10 cilantro leaves, chopped
- 6 tablespoons bread crumbs oil for frying

Directions

- Place unpeeled potatoes in a large saucepan, fill with water, and place over high heat. Bring to a boil; cook until potatoes are soft and tender. Drain, cool, and peel potatoes.

- Place potatoes in a large bowl. Add salt, garam masala, coriander powder, pepper, and cilantro. Mash with a large fork or potatomasher until there are no lumps.

- Shape potatoes into flat cutlets, about 2 or 3 inches in diameter and 1 inch thick. Coat each cutlet lightly in bread crumbs, and set aside.

- Heat about 2 tablespoons oil in a large skillet over medium heat. Fry potato cutlets in batches until golden brown on both sides. Between batches, add oil as needed.

Potato Clam Chowder

Ingredients

- 2 bacon strips, diced
- 1 cup chopped onion
- 2 tablespoons all-purpose flour
- 2 (6 ounce) cans minced clams
- 1 cup water
- 1/2 teaspoon salt
- 1/4 teaspoon dried thyme
- 1/4 teaspoon dried savory
- 1/8 teaspoon pepper
- 4 medium potatoes, peeled and cubed
- 2 cups milk
- 2 tablespoons minced fresh parsley

Directions

- In a 3-qt. saucepan or Dutch oven, cook bacon until crisp. Removebacon; set aside. Saute onion in drippings until tender. Add flour; stir until smooth. Drain clams, reserving juice; set clams aside.

- Gradually add water and clam juice to pan; cook and stir over medium heat until smooth and bubbly. Add salt, thyme, savory, pepper and potatoes; bring to a boil.

- Reduce heat; cover andsimmer for 25 minutes or until potatoes are tender, stirring often. Add bacon, clams, milk and parsley; heat through.

Kerry's Sweet Potato Latkes

Ingredients

- 1 large sweet potato, peeled and grated

- 1/2 onion, grated
- 2 eggs
- 1/4 teaspoon black pepper
- 2 teaspoons olive oil, or more if needed
- 1/2 teaspoon salt
- 1 cup applesauce
- 1 cup plain nonfat yogurt

Directions

- Preheat oven to 200 degrees F (95 degrees C). Line a baking sheet with paper towels.

- Fill a bowl with lightly-salted water. Rinse the grated sweet potato in the water, and drain into a sieve. Pat the grated sweet potato drywith a cloth or paper towels, then place into a bowl.

- Squeezeexcess moisture from the grated onion, and place into the bowl with the sweet potato. Stir theeggs and pepper into the mixture until well combined.

- Heat the olive oil in a nonstick skillet over medium heat until it shimmers, and spoon about 1 heaping tablespoon of the potatomixture per patty into the hot oil. Flatten the patties with a fork, and fry until golden brown and crisp on the bottom, 5 to 8 minutes.

- Flip and cook on the other side, sprinkle with salt, then set the cooked patties aside on the prepared baking sheet in the preheated oven while you finish cooking the latkes.

- Stir the potato mixture beforecooking each batch of patties. Serve hot with applesauce andyogurt.

Mashed Potato Salad

Ingredients

- 5 red potatoes

- ❀ 5 Yukon Gold potatoes
- ❀ 2 tablespoons butter salt and pepper to taste
- ❀ 1/2 cup mayonnaise
- ❀ 1/2 cup prepared mustard
- ❀ 1/2 cup sour cream
- ❀ 1 stalk celery, finely chopped
- ❀ 1 red onion, finely diced
- ❀ 2 small sweet pickles, finely chopped
- ❀ 1 green bell pepper, chopped

Directions

> Cube potatoes, if desired you may peel them. Place potatoes in a large saucepan and cover with water. Cook over medium heat until potatoes are tender. Drain and place cooked potatoes in a largebowl.

> Mash potatoes with butter and salt and pepper to taste. Oncemashed stir in the mayonnaise, mustard and sour cream, mixingwell. Stir in the celery, onion, pickles and green pepper. Serve warm or at room temperature.

Oven-Roasted Potatoes

Ingredients

- ❀ 4 baking potatoes
- ❀ 2 tablespoons butter or margarine, melted
- ❀ 2 teaspoons paprika
- ❀ 1 teaspoon salt
- ❀ 1/2 teaspoon
- ❀ pepper

Directions

> Peel potatoes and cut into large chunks; place in a shallow 2-qt baking pan. Pour butter over and toss until well coated.

> Sprinkle with paprika, salt and pepper. Bake, uncovered, at 350 degrees F for 45-60 minutes or until potatoes are tender.

Roasted Sweet Potatoes & Onions

Ingredients

* 2 large sweet potatoes, peeled and cut in 1-inch chunks
* 2 medium Vidalia or other sweet onions, cut in 1-inch chunks
* 3 tablespoons olive oil
* 1/4 cup amaretto liqueur
* 1 teaspoon dried thyme
* Salt and freshly ground black pepper, to taste
* 1/4 cup sliced almonds, toasted

Directions

> Heat oven to 425 degrees F.Toss first 6 ingredients in a shallow medium-sized baking dish.Cover; bake 30 minutes. Uncover; bake 20 minutes more. Sprinklewith almonds

---

Southwestern Style Twice Baked Potatoes

Ingredients

* 4baking potatoes
* 1/2 onion, diced
* 1/2 cup milk
* salt and pepper to taste
* 3 tablespoons butter

- 1 green bell pepper, seeded and diced
- 1 red bell pepper, seeded and diced
- 2 jalapeno peppers, seeded and chopped
- 1 tablespoon minced garlic
- 2 cups shredded Cheddar cheese
- 4 tablespoons bacon bits
- 1/4 cup sour cream

Directions

- Cook each potato in the microwave until tender enough to pierce with a fork, about 8 minutes. Allow potatoes to cool, then slice in half lengthwise.

- Preheat the oven to 350 degrees F (175 degrees C).Scoop out the centers of the potato halves, leaving about 1/2 inch of potato in the skin to keep its shape.

- Place skins on a greasedbaking sheet and place the scoopings into a bowl. Mash the potato in the bowl with milk, salt, pepper and butter until smooth, or assmooth as you prefer.

- Stir in the green and red peppers, jalapeno and garlic until evenly distributed. Mound the mixture into thepotato skins.

- Sprinkle cheese and bacon bits over the top.Bake for 15 minutes in the preheated oven, or until the cheese is starting to toast.

Suzy's Potato Skins

Ingredients

- 10 potatoes
- salt and pepper to taste
- 1/2 cup chopped green onions
- 1 cup chopped tomatoes
- 1 (4 ounce) can diced green chiles
- 1 cup shredded Cheddar cheese

❋ 1 cup sour cream

Directions

➤ Preheat oven to 350 degrees F (175 degrees C).Pierce potatoes deeply with a fork and bake for 45 minutes or until tender.Increase the heat of the oven to 375 degrees F (190 degrees C).

➤ When the potatoes are cool enough to handle cut them in half lengthwise and scoop out nearly all of the potato (reserve rest of potato for a later use of your choice).

➤ Salt and pepper the potatoskins to taste. Sprinkle green onions, tomatoes, chilis and cheese into the potato skin. Arrange potato skins on a baking sheet.

➤ Bake 10 minutes, or until cheese has melted. You may want to cut the baked skins in half crosswise before serving for tidy eating.Serve with sour cream on the side, for people to scoop onto their potato skins if they'd like.

Sweet Potatoes with Poblano Butter Topping

Ingredients

❋ 1 sweet potato
❋ 1 fresh poblano pepper, seeded and finely chopped
❋ 1 cup light soy butter, softened
❋ 1 teaspoon lime juice
❋ 1/4 cup chopped fresh cilantro
❋ 1 teaspoon freshly ground black pepper, or to taste

Directions

➤ Preheat oven to 400 degrees F (200 degrees C). Pierce the sweet potato in several places with a fork.

➤ Roast the sweet potato in preheated oven until easily pierced with a fork, 1 to 1 1/2 hours.

➤ Meanwhile, place the poblano pepper, soy butter, lime juice, and pepper in the bowl of a food processor.

> Process until well blended, about 1 minute. If not using immediately, place poblano-soy butter in a covered container and refrigerate up to 1 month.

> To serve, slice the sweet potato in half and spread with 1 tablespoon poblano butter.

Cilantro Potatoes

Ingredients

* 1 bunch fresh cilantro, chopped
* 1 garlic clove, minced
* 1/4 cup olive oil
* 3 pounds potatoes, peeled and cubed
* 1/2 teaspoon salt

Directions

> In a large skillet, cook cilantro and garlic in oil over medium heat for1 minute. Add the potatoes; cook and stir for 20-25 minutes or until tender and lightly browned. Drain. Sprinkle with salt.

Shearers' Mince and Potato Hot Pot

Ingredients

* 5 medium potatoes, peeled and thinly sliced
* 1 tablespoon olive oil
* 1 pound ground beef
* 1 onion, chopped
* 1 tablespoon tomato sauce

- ❀ 1tablespoon Worcestershiresauce
- ❀ salt and pepper to taste
- ❀ 1/4 cup butter
- ❀ 1/4 cup all-purpose flour
- ❀ 2 cups milk
- ❀ 1 cup shredded sharp Cheddar cheese
- ❀ 1 (6 ounce) can mushrooms, drained
- ❀ 2 tablespoons butter, diced

Directions

- ➢ Preheat oven to 350 degrees F (175 degrees C). Place potato slices in a medium bowl with enough water to cover.

- ➢ Heat oil in a medium saucepan over medium heat. Stir in ground beef, onion, tomato sauce, and Worcestershire sauce. Season with salt and pepper. Cook until beef isevenly browned and onions aretender.

- ➢ In a separate medium saucepan over medium heat, melt 1/4 cup butter, and thoroughly blend in flour. Gradually stir in milk. Cook and stir 5 minutes, or until thickened.

- ➢ Reduce heat, and blendCheddar cheese into the mixture. Season with salt and pepper to taste.Line a medium baking dish with 1/2 the potato slices.

- ➢ Pour in theground beef mixture, and top with mushrooms. Cover with thecheese saucemixture. Top with remaining potatoes.

- ➢ Dot with 2 tablespoons butter.Bake 30 to 40 minutes in the preheated oven, until lightly browned.

Beefy Potato Volcano

Ingredients

- ❀ 3 large baking potatoes, 10 to 12 ounces each, preferably Idaho, washed and dried

- ❀ 1 teaspoon vegetable oil
- ❀ 1 pound ground turkey or lean ground beef
- ❀ 1 teaspoon dried Italian seasoning
- ❀ 1 (8 ounce) can peas, drained
- ❀ 1 (8 ounce) can sliced carrots, drained
- ❀ 1 (8 ounce) can cut green beans, drained
- ❀ 1 cup canned diced tomatoes, drained
- ❀ 1 (15 ounce) can beef or turkey gravy

Directions

> Preheat the conventional oven to 450 degrees F. Place the potatoes in a microwave-safe, oven-proof glass baking dish, such as a pieplate, that fits in the microwave oven.

> Microwave the potatoes at full power for 10 minutes (the amount of time it takes to preheat theoven). Transfer the potatoes to the conventional oven and bake until tender, about 20 minutes.

> Ten to 15 minutes before the potatoes are done baking, heat the oil in a large skillet over medium-high heat. Add the ground turkey and cook until lightly browned, chopping and turning as needed with a spatula so the turkey browns evenly, about 5 minutes.

> Add theseasoning to the skillet, followed by the peas, carrots, green beans, tomatoes and gravy to make the stew. Stir gently to combine and simmer for 5 minutes. Keep warm.

> To serve: Cut each potato in half across its equator and seteach half, cut-side down on a plate so that it looks like a small mountain.

> Cut a slit in the top of each potato half and squeeze the sides gently forcing some of the potato to 'erupt' from the top. Ladle 1 cup ofthe stew over each potato to resem-ble flowing lava; serve immediately.

Potato Flake Cookies

Ingredients

- ❀ 1/2 cup butter
- ❀ 1 cup white sugar
- ❀ 1 egg
- ❀ 1 1/2 cups buttermilk baking mix
- ❀ 1 1/2 tablespoons coconut extract
- ❀ 1 1/4 cups dry potato flakes

Directions

> ➤ Cream together butter or margarine, sugar, egg, and coconut flavoring. Add baking mix to mixture. Fold in potato flakes.

> ➤ Drop by teaspoon on lightly greased cookie sheet and bake at 350 degrees F (175 degrees C) for 12 minutes or until lightly browned.

Green Bean and Potato Salad

Ingredients

- ❀ 1 1/2 pounds red potatoes
- ❀ 3/4 pound fresh green beans, trimmed and snapped
- ❀ 1/4 cup chopped fresh basil
- ❀ 1 small red onion, chopped
- ❀ salt and pepper to taste
- ❀ 1/4 cup balsamic vinegar
- ❀ 2 tablespoons Dijon mustard
- ❀ 2 tablespoons fresh lemon juice
- ❀ 1 clove garlic, minced
- ❀ 1 dash Worcestershire sauce
- ❀ 1/2 cup extra virgin olive oil

Directions

- ➢ Place the potatoes in a large pot, and fill with about 1 inch of water. Bring to a boil, and cook for about 15 minutes, or until potatoes aretender.

- ➢ Throw in the green beans to steam after the first 10 minutes. Drain, cool, and cut potatoes into quarters. Transfer to a large bowl, and toss with fresh basil, red onion, salt and pepper. Set aside.

- ➢ In a medium bowl, whisk together the balsamic vinegar, mustard, lemon juice, garlic, Worcestershire sauce and olive oil. Pour over thesalad, and stir to coat. Taste and season with additional salt andpepper if needed.

Potato Spinach Casserole

Ingredients

- ❀ 7 large potatoes, peeled and cubed
- ❀ 1 (10 ounce) package frozen chopped spinach, thawed and drained
- ❀ 1 cup sour cream
- ❀ 1/4 cup butter
- ❀ 2 tablespoons chopped green onions
- ❀ 2 teaspoons salt
- ❀ 1/4 teaspoon black pepper
- ❀ 1 cup shredded Cheddar cheese

Directions

- ➢ Preheat oven to 400 degrees F (200 degrees C). Grease a 2 quart casserole dish.

- ➢ Bring a large pot of salted water to a boil. Add potatoes and cook until tender, about 15 minutes. Drain and mash.

- ➢ In a large bowl combine mashed potatoes, spinach, sour cream, butter, green onions, salt and pepper. Spoon into prepared dish.

- ➢ Bake for 15 minutes. Top with cheese and bake 5 minutes longer.

Feta and Bacon Stuffed Chicken with Onion

Ingredients

- 3/4 pound bacon, cut into 1 inch pieces
- 1 cup crumbled feta cheese
- 3 tablespoons sour cream
- 1/8 tablespoon dried oregano
- 1/8 teaspoon ground black pepper
- 3 (4 ounce) skinless, boneless chicken breast halves
- 1 cup all-purpose flour
- 2 eggs, beaten
- 1 cup dry bread crumbs
- 4 potatoes, peeled and cubed
- 1 sweet onion (such as Vidalia®), chopped
- 2 tablespoons butter
- 3 tablespoons sour cream

Directions

- ➢ Preheat an oven to 350 degrees F (175 degrees C). Place the bacon in a large, deep skillet, and cook over medium-high heat, turningoccasionally, until evenly browned but still soft.

- ➢ Reserve the bacon grease in the skillet, and cool the bacon slices on a paper towel-lined plate. Once cool, mix the bacon together with the feta cheese,3 tablespoons of sour cream, oregano, and black pepper in a small bowl; set aside.Lay a chicken breast flat onto your work surface.

- ➢ Use the tip of a sharp boning or paring knife to cut a 2-inch pocket in the chicken breast. Repeat with the remaining chicken breasts. Spoon thebacon mixture into the pockets. Pour the flour, egg, and bread crumbs into separate, shallow dishes. Gently press the chicken breasts into the flour to coat. Dip each into the beaten egg, then press into bread crumbs.

- ➢ Reheat the bacon grease over medium heat. Brown the chicken breasts on both sides in the hot fat, about 2 minutes per side.Reservethe bacon grease in the pan.

- ➤ Place the breasts on a baking dish, and bake in the preheated oven until the chicken is no longer pink and the filling is hot, 20 to 25 minutes. An instant-readthermometer inserted into the center should read at least 165 degrees F (74 degrees C).

- ➤ Meanwhile, place the potatoes into a large pot and cover with salted water. Bring to a boil over high heat, then reduce heat to medium-low, cover, and simmer until tender, about 20 minutes. Drain.

- ➤ While the potatoes are boiling, cook the onion in the remaining bacon grease over medium heat until very tender and golden brown, about 10 minutes.

- ➤ Once the potatoes are done, mashtogether with the onion, butter, and remaining 3 tablespoons of sour cream. Serve the chicken breasts accomp-anied by the mashedpotatoes.

Creamy Potato Lasagna

Ingredients

- ❋ 1 (12 ounce) jar Alfredo sauce
- ❋ 1 cup milk
- ❋ 3 pounds potatoes, peeled and sliced lengthwise about 1/8 inch thick
- ❋ 5 tablespoons grated Parmesan cheese
- ❋ 1/2 teaspoon salt
- ❋ 1/2 teaspoon ground black pepper
- ❋ 1 1/2 cups diced ham
- ❋ 1 (10 ounce) package chopped frozen broccoli, thawed
- ❋ 2 cups shredded Swiss cheese

Directions

- ➤ Preheat oven to 400 degrees F (200 degrees C).Lightly grease a 9x13 inch baking dish. In a medium bowl, whisk together the Alfredo sauce and milk.

- ➤ Spread 1/4 cup of the sauce in the bottom of the baking dish. Then layer 1/3 of the potatoes over the sauce in the dish. Sprinkle with 1 tablespoon of Parmesan cheese and salt and pepper to taste.In a separate medium bowl, combine the ham, broccoli and 1 1/2 cups of the Swiss cheese.

> Mix well and spread 1/3 of this mixtureover the potatoes in the baking dish. Then top with another layer of potatoes, followed by the ham mixture, finally topping all with theremaining Swiss cheese and Parmesan cheese. Pour the remaining Alfredo sauce over all.

> Cover and bake at 400 degrees F (200 degrees C) for 45 minutes, then uncover and bake at 350 degrees F (175 degree C) foradditional 25 minutes or until potatoes are tender. Let stand 10 to15 minutes before serving.

Chicken, Spinach, and Potato Soup

Ingredients

- 1 pound skinless, boneless chicken thighs
- 2 cups chicken stock
- 4 cups water
- 3 tablespoons olive oil
- 1 large onion, thinly sliced
- 6 cloves garlic, chopped
- 2 large potatoes, cubed
- 1 (16 ounce) can garbanzo beans, drained
- 1 (10 ounce) bag fresh spinach
- 1/2 cup diced roasted red peppers (optional)
- salt and pepper to taste
- 1/4 cup grated Parmesan cheese

Directions

> Bring chicken thighs, chicken stock, and water to a simmer in a largesaucepan over medium-high heat. Reduce heat to medium-low, and continue simmer in until the chicken is no longer pink in the center, about 20 minutes.

- Remove the chicken thighs, and set aside to cool. Reserve the broth.While the thighs are cooling, heat olive oil in a large pot over medium heat. Stir in onion and garlic. Cook and stir until the onion has softened and turned translucent, about 5 minutes.

- Add thepotatoes, then strain the reserved cooking liquid into the pot. Bring to a boil over high heat, then reduce heat to medium-low, and simmer until the potatoes are tender, about 25 minutes.

- Cut the cooked chicken into cubes and add to the simmering potatoes. Cook for 5 minutes, then stir in the garbanzo beans,spinach, and roasted pepper; simmer 10 more minutes. Season to taste with salt and pepper, and sprinkle with grated Parmesancheese before serving.

Lena's Potato Salad

Ingredients

- 8 extra largeeggs
- 8 large potatoes, peeled and chopped
- 1 (3 ounce) jar pitted and sliced green olives
- 1/2 cup mayonnaise
- 2 tablespoons Dijon mustard salt and pepper to taste

Directions

- Placeeggs in a saucepan with enough cold water to cover. Bring water to a boil, and immediately remove from heat. Cover pan, and let eggs stand in hot water for 10 to 12 minutes. Removeeggs from hot water, cool, and peel. Do not chop.

- In a pot with enough water to cover, boil the potatoes 15 minutes, or until tender. Remove from heat, and allow to remain in the hot water about 10 minutes. Drain, and cool.

- Place theeggs and potatoes in a large bowl. By hand, mix in theolives, mayonnaise, and mustard, and mash theeggs and potatoes. Season with salt and pepper. Cover, and refrigerate until serving.

Anna's Linguica and Potato Stew

Ingredients

* 6 slices bacon
* 1 large onion, sliced
* 2 cloves garlic, chopped
* 1 pound linguica sausage, sliced
* 3 pounds potatoes, cubed
* 4 small zucchini, sliced
* 2 (8 ounce) cans tomato sauce
* 1/2 cup red wine
* 1/4 cup chopped fresh parsley
* 1 tablespoon dried basil
* salt and pepper to taste

Directions

➢ In a skillet over medium-high heat, cook the bacon until crisp and evenly brown. Drain, reserving juices, and break into bite-sizepieces. Place the pieces in a slow cooker. Cook the onion and garlic in the reserved bacon juices over medium heat until tender.

➢ Drain, and place in the slow cooker. Quickly brown thelinguica sausage in the skillet over medium-high heat, and place in the slow cooker.Add the potatoes, zucchini, tomato sauce, and red wine to the slow cooker, and season with parsley, basil, salt, and pepper.

➢ Stir toevenly distribute ingredients. Cover, and cook 2 1/2 hours on High, stirring occasionally, until the potatoes are tender.

Slashed Sea Bass with Red Onions, Mushrooms,

Ingredients

- 1 tablespoon butter
- 2 portobello mushroom caps, sliced
- 1 red onion, sliced
- 1 teaspoon fresh lemon juice sea salt to taste
- cracked black pepper to taste
- 2 (4 ounce) fillets sea bass
- 2 tablespoons chopped fresh chervil
- 1 teaspoon chili oil
- 1/2 cup pesto sauce

Directions

- Preheat the oven broiler. Place new potatoes in a pot with enough water to cover, and bring to a boil. Cook 10 minutes or until tender. Melt the butter in a skillet over medium heat, and saute the mushrooms and onion until tender.

- Sprinkle with lemon juice, and season with sea salt and cracked black pepper.Slash the sea bass fillets on both sides, and insert the chervil. Rub with chili oil, sea salt, and cracked black pepper.

- Place fillets on a baking sheet, and broil 5 minutes on each side, or until easily flaked with a fork. Drizzle with pesto sauce, and serve over new potatoes,mushrooms, and onion.

Mustard Mashed Potatoes

Ingredients

- 5 red potatoes, scrubbed and halved
- 2 tablespoons butter
- 1/4 cup milk

- salt and pepper to taste
- 1/4 cup whole grain mustard

Directions

> Place the potatoes into a large pot and cover with salted water. Bring to a boil over high heat, then reduce heat to medium-low, cover, and simmer until tender, about 20 minutes.

> Drain and allowto steam dry for a minute or two. Mash potatoes in a large bowl with the butter and milk, and season with salt and pepper.

> Whip the potatoes using an electric mixer set on medium until smooth, 3 to 4 minutes, adding more milk if the potatoes are too dry. Beat in the whole grain mustard, and serve immediately.

Sweet Potato Cookies

Ingredients

- 1/4 cup milk
- 2 cups sifted all-purpose flour
- 1 teaspoon baking powder
- 1/2 teaspoon salt
- 1/2 cup butter
- 1/4 cup white sugar
- 1 egg
- 1 teaspoon ground cinnamon
- 1/2 cup honey
- 1 cup peeled, shredded sweet potato
- 1/2 teaspoon baking soda

Directions

- Preheat oven to 350 degrees F (175 degrees C).Combine sugar and butter or margarine. Blend in egg, honey, and sweet potato.Sift together flour, baking soda, baking powder, salt, and cinnamon.

- Blend in butter mixture and milk.Drop from a teaspoon 2 inches apart onto greased cookie sheets. Bake for 15 to 20 minutes until brown

Delicious Stuffed Potato Pancakes

Ingredients

- 8 potatoes, peeled and shredded
- 1/4 cup all-purpose flour
- 1/2 teaspoon baking powder
- 3 eggs
- salt and black pepper to taste Filling:
- 1/2 pound ground beef
- 1/2 onion, grated
- 1 pinch garlic salt
- 1 egg
- 1/4 cup bread crumbs
- 2 teaspoons vegetable oil

Directions

- Mix together the potatoes, flour, baking powder, 3 eggs, and salt and pepper in a bowl. In another bowl, mix the ground beef, onion, garlic salt, 1 egg, and bread crumbs until well-combined.

- Heat the oil in a skillet over medium-low heat, and drop a rounded tablespoon of potato mixture into the hot skillet. Spread and flatten the pancake out a little, and place about 2 teaspoons of beefmixture on the pancake, spreading the filling out almost to theedges of the pancake.

- Drop another rounded tablespoon of potato mixture on top of the beef, and spread it out to completely cover the beef. Fry until the bottom of the pancake is golden brown, about5 minutes, then flip and fry the other side until golden, 1 to 2 more minutes.

Kentucky Bourbon Sweet Potatoes

Ingredients

- 6 large sweet potatoes, peeled and sliced
- 1 cup white sugar
- 1/2 cupbutter
- 1/2 cup bourbon
- 1/2 teaspoon vanilla extract

Directions

- Preheat oven to 350 degreesF (175 degrees C).Arrangesweet potatoes in a 9x13 inch baking dish.Combine sugar, butter, bourbon and vanilla extract in a large saucepan and heat to a boil.

- As soon as the sauce comes to a boil pour it over the sweet potatoes.Bake 30 to 40 minutes or until the sweet potatoes are soft.

Red Pepper Potato Soup

Ingredients

- 1 red bell pepper
- 1/2 cup butter
- 1 1/2 cups chopped onion
- 1 1/2 cups chopped celery

- 6 cloves garlic, minced
- 8 cups chicken stock, divided
- 1 teaspoon salt
- 1 teaspoon ground black pepper
- 1 1/2 cups chopped carrot
- 1/4 teaspoon ground nutmeg
- 1/4 teaspoon cinnamon
- 3 large potatoes, peeled and cut into 1/2-inch cubes
- 1/2 teaspoon dried sage
- 1/4 teaspoon ground ginger

Directions

> Preheat an oven to 425 degrees F (220 degrees C). Grease a baking sheet. Place the red bell pepper on the prepared baking sheet and roast in the preheated oven until the skin blisters, 15 to 20 minutes.

> Handling carefully, cut small slits with a knife into each of the 4 sides of the hot pepper. Immediately plunge the pepper a smallbowl full of ice water for 2 minutes. Slice the pepper in half. Removeand discard the skin. Chop the flesh into small pieces. Set aside.

> While the pepper roasts, melt the butter in a large pot over medium heat. Cook the onion, celery, and garlic in the melted butter until tender, about 5 minutes. Pour 3 cups of the chicken stock into thepot; season with salt and pepper. Add 3 more cups of the chickenstock, the carrots, nutmeg, and cinnamon.

> Stir the potatoes into the soup along with the remaining 2 cups of stock; bring to a boil for 10 minutes. Add the roasted pepper, sage, and ginger. Continueboiling until the potatoes and carrots are tender, another 10 to 15 minutes. Serve hot.

Easy Cheesy Bacon Potato Soup

Ingredients

- 3 potatoes, diced

- 1 onion, chopped
- 1 1/2 cups water
- 2 cubes chicken bouillon
- 8 ounces cheese spread with bacon

Directions

> In a covered medium saucepan over high heat, combine thepotatoes, onions, water and bouillon. Bring all to a boil and cook for about 15 to 20 minutes, or until potatoes are tender.

> Add the cheese spread and mash with a potato masher. Add more water if a thinner soup is desired.

New England Potato Soup

Ingredients

- 1 medium onion, chopped
- 1 celery rib, thinly sliced
- 2 tablespoons butter or margarine
- 1 (14.5 ounce) can chicken broth
- 3 medium potatoes, peeled and cubed
- 1 1/2 teaspoons sugar
- 1/2 teaspoon salt
- 1/2 teaspoon dried rosemary, crushed
- 1/2 teaspoon dried thyme
- 1/8 teaspoon pepper
- 1/3 cup all-purpose flour
- 2 1/2 cups milk, divided
- 1 1/2 cups cubed fully cooked ham
- 1 cup frozen peas

Directions

> ➤ In a saucepan, saute onion and celery in butter until tender. Add broth, potatoes, sugar, salt, rosemary, thyme and pepper; bring to a boil. Reduce heat; cover and simmer for 15-20 minutes or until potatoes are tender.

> ➤ Combine flour and 1/2 cup milk until smooth; gradually stir into soup. Bring to a boil; cook and stir for 2 minutes. Stir in ham, peas and remaining milk; heat through.

Herbed Potato Soup

Ingredients

- ❀ 2 medium potatoes, peeled and diced
- ❀ 2 cups water
- ❀ 1 large onion, chopped
- ❀ 1/4 cup butter,cubed
- ❀ 1/4 cup all-purpose flour
- ❀ 1 teaspoon salt
- ❀ 1/2 teaspoon dried thyme
- ❀ 1/4 teaspoon dried rosemary, crushed
- ❀ 1/4 teaspoon pepper
- ❀ 1 1/2 cups milk

Directions

> ➤ Place potatoes and water in a large saucepan; cook over medium heat until tender. Meanwhile, in another saucepan, saute onion butter until tender. Stir in the flour, salt, thyme, rosemary, andpepper.

> ➤ Gradually add milk. Bring to a boil; cook and stir for 2 minutes. Add potatoes with cooking liquid; heat through.

Rosy Potato Soup

Ingredients

- ❀ 1 large onion, chopped
- ❀ 3/4 cup chopped celery
- ❀ 3 tablespoons butter or margarine
- ❀ 1 tablespoon all-purpose flour
- ❀ 1/2 teaspoon salt
- ❀ 3 cups milk
- ❀ 3 medium potatoes - peeled, cooked and sliced
- ❀ 1 tablespoon minced fresh parsley
- ❀ 1 tablespoon paprika

Directions

> In a large saucepan, saute onion and celery in butter until tender. Stir in flour and salt until blended. Gradually add milk. Bring to a boil; cook and stir for 2 minutes or until thickened and bubbly. Reduceheat. Add potatoes, parsley and paprika; heat through.

Seasoned Potato Fries

Ingredients

- ❀ 2 russet potatoes, sliced into 1/4 inch strips
- ❀ 1 tablespoon vegetable oil
- ❀ 1 tablespoon Italian seasoning
- ❀ 1 tablespoon garlic powder
- ❀ 1/4 teaspoon salt
- ❀ 1/4 teaspoon pepper

Directions

- Place potato strips in a large resealable plastic bag; add oil. Seal bag and shake gently to coat. Add seasonings; shake again.

- Placeseasoned strips on a baking sheet coated with nonstick cooking spray. Bake potato strips at 425 degrees F for 25 minutes or until crispy. Serve immediately.

Potato Pancakes

Ingredients

- 5 pounds potatoes, peeled
- 1 onion
- 3 eggs, beaten
- 2 1/2 cups dry pancake mix
- 2 teaspoons salt
- 1 teaspoon ground black pepper
- 1 tablespoon vegetable oil

Directions

- In a food processor grate potatoes and onion. In a large bowl combinepotatoes, onions, eggs, pancake mix, salt and pepper.

- Heat oil in a large skillet over medium heat. Spoon potatoes into skillet and cook as you would pancakes, for 3 to 4 minutes on each side.

English Baked Potatoes

Ingredients

- 4 large potatoes, cut into wedges
- salt and pepper to taste
- 2 tablespoons olive oil

Directions

➢ Preheat the oven to 350 degrees F (175 degrees C).In a large bowl, toss potato wedges and olive oil until the potatoes are coated. Spread the wedges out on a large baking sheet. Season with salt and pepper to taste.

➢ Bake for 20 minutes in the preheated oven, turn over, and bake for an additional 10 to 15 minutes, or until tender. Serve plain, withvinegar, or dip in ketchup.

Mountain Mama's Potato Pancakes

Ingredients

❋ 2/3 cup instant mashed potato flakes

❋ 1/3 cup complete dry pancakemix

❋ 1/2 cup chopped onion

❋ 1 cup shredded Cheddar cheese

❋ 1 cup skim milk

❋ 1 egg, beaten

❋ 1 tablespoon extra-virgin olive oil

❋ 1/2 teaspoon garlic powder

❋ salt and pepper to taste

❋ 1 pinch cayenne pepper (optional)

Directions

➢ Stir together the potato flakes, pancake mix, onion, Cheddar cheese, milk, egg, olive oil, garlic powder, salt, pepper, and cayenne pepper in a bowl until well combined.Grease a griddle or large skillet, and placeover medium heat.

➢ Drop pancakes, 1/4 cup at a time, onto the hot griddle, and cook until theedges look dry and 1 bubble appears in the center, about 3 minutes. Flip the pancakes, and cook until browned on the other side, about 3 more minutes.

Serbian Ground Beef, Veggie, and Potato Bake

Ingredients

- ❀ 1 pound ground beef
- ❀ 1 tablespoon olive oil
- ❀ 1 green bell pepper, chopped
- ❀ 1 onion, chopped
- ❀ 1 carrot, shredded
- ❀ 2 celery stalks, chopped
- ❀ 1/2 tablespoon paprika
- ❀ 1/2 teaspoon salt
- ❀ 3/4 teaspoon black pepper
- ❀ 1/4 teaspoon crushed red pepper
- ❀ 1 pinch ground cinnamon
- ❀ 1 pinc
- ❀ h ground cloves
- ❀ 1/4 cup water
- ❀ 1/8 cup red wine
- ❀ 1 cube beef bouillon
- ❀ 2 tablespoons half-and-half
- ❀ 2 potatoes, peeled and sliced

Directions

- ➢ Preheat oven to 400 degrees F (200 degrees C). Lightly grease a casserole dish.In a skillet over medium heat, cook the beef until evenly brown. Remove beef from skillet, reserving juices, and set aside. Mix in theolive oil, and saute the green pepper, onion, carrot, and celery until tender.

- ➢ Return beef to the skillet, and season with paprika, salt, black pepper, red pepper, cinnamon, and cloves. Stir in the water and red wine until heated through. Dissolve the beef bouillon cube into the mixture. Remove skillet from heat, and mix in the half-and-half.

- Layer the bottom of the prepared casserole dish with enough potato slices to cover. Place the beef and vegetable mixture over thepotatoes, and top with remaining potatoes.

- Cook, covered, 45 minutes in the preheated oven, or until the potatoes are tender.

Blue Cheese Potatoes Delmonico

Ingredients

- 8 medium potatoes, peeled and cubed
- 1/2 cup butter
- 1/2 cup all-purpose flour
- 1 cup milk
- 1 cup cream
- 1/2 cup crumbled blue cheese
- 1/3 cup bread crumbs

Directions

- Preheat the oven to 375 degrees F (190 degrees C). Place thepotatoes in a large saucepan with water to cover. Bring to a boil over medium-high heat, and cook until tender, about 8 to 10minutes. Drain, and transfer to a casserole dish.

- Melt the butter in a medium saucepan over medium-high heat. Whisk in the flour, and cook for 5 minutes, stirring constantly. Gradually whisk in the milk and cream so there are no lumps.

- Reduce heat and simmer for 20 minutes. Remove from heat and whisk in the blue cheese until smooth. Pour over the potatoes in thedish. Sprinkle breadcrumbs over the top.Bake for 25 minutes in the preheated oven, or until top is nicely browned.

Roasted Potato and Garlic Salad

Ingredients

- 8 red potatoes - unpeeled, scrubbed and cubed
- 2 red bell peppers
- 2 medium heads garlic
- 1/2 cup olive oil
- salt and pepper to taste
- 1/3 cup balsamic vinegar
- 1/3 cup olive oil
- 1 teaspoon dried oregano

Directions

- Preheat oven to 400 degrees F (200 degrees C).Place 1/2 cup of olive oil in a large bowl. Toss the cubed potatoes in the oil until coated, and then spread them evenly on a bakingsheet.Pass the red peppers through the bowl of oil, making sure they areevenly coated.

- Place on a separate baking sheet. Cut about 1/2 inch off the tops of the garlic and drizzle with theremaining oil from the bowl. Place on the baking sheet with the red peppers. Sprinkle the potatoes,peppers and garlic with salt and pepper, and then place both sheets in the oven for about 20 minutes.

- Check the potatoes: they should be soft, brown and crispy. If not, return them to the oven for an additional 10 minutes or until they aredone. The peppers and garlic will take longer, and are done when the skins on the peppers are black and garlic is dark brown (nomore than 40 minutes total).

- Onceeverything has been roasted, place the potatoes in a largebowl and seal the peppers in a plastic bag to let them steam for 10 minutes. (This will loosen their skins.)
- Take the peppers out of the bag, remove their skins and seeds and chop them up. Add to the bowl with the potatoes and stir to mix.

- Turn the garlic heads upside down and squeeze the softened garlic past into a separate, small bowl. Mix in the balsamic vinegar, 1/3 cup olive oil and oregano until smooth. Pour the dressing onto thepotatoes and peppers and toss to coat.

➤ Season to taste withadditional salt and pepper. Best when served warm or at room temperature. To prepare in advance for an occasion, refrigerateand then reheat in the microwave just until warmed through.

Oven Baked Potato Wedges

Ingredients

- ❀ 2 teaspoons olive oil
- ❀ 5 large russet potatoes, peeled and cut into wedges
- ❀ 1/2 cup melted butter
- ❀ 1 cup seasoned bread crumbs

Directions

➤ Preheat oven to 350 degrees F (175 degrees C). Grease a baking sheet with the olive oil.Brush potato wedges with butter, and roll in bread crumbs. Placewedges on prepared baking sheet.

➤ Bake in preheated oven for 20 minutes. Remove from oven and turn wedges; cook for 10 to 15 minutes, or until tender.

Sweet Potato Gnocchi

Ingredients

- ❀ 2 (8 ounce) sweet potatoes
- ❀ 1 clove garlic, pressed
- ❀ 1/2 teaspoon salt
- ❀ 1/2 teaspoon ground nutmeg
- ❀ 1 egg
- ❀ 2 cups all-purpose flour

Directions

- Preheat the oven to 350 degrees F (175 degrees C). Bake sweet potatoes for 30 minutes, or until soft to the touch. Remove from theoven, and set aside to cool.

- Once the potatoes are cool enough to work with, remove the peels, and mash them, or press them through a ricer into a large bowl.Blend in the garlic, salt, nutmeg, and egg. Mix in the flour a little at a time until you have soft dough. Use more or less flour as needed.

- Bring a large pot of lightly salted water to a boil. While you wait for the water, make the gnocchi. On a floured surface, roll the dough out in several long snakes, and cut into 1-inch sections.

- Drop thepieces into the boiling water, and allow them to cook until they floatto the surface.Remove the floating pieces with a slotted spoon, and keep warm in a serving dish. Serve with butter or cream sauce.

Easy Creamy Potato Ecstasy

Ingredients

- 2 cups water
- 2 potatoes - peeled and cubed
- 2 stalks celery, chopped
- 1/2 cucumbers, sliced
- 6 baby carrots, sliced
- 2 cloves garlic, minced
- 2 onions, sliced
- 2 button mushrooms, chopped
- 2 cubes chicken bouillon

Directions

- Bring water to a boil in a large saucepan over high heat. Place thepotatoes and celery in the water and boil for 10 minutes. Then add the cucumber, carrots, garlic, onion, mushrooms and bouillon.

- Reduce heat to medium and let simmer for 10 more minutes. Transfer mixture to a blender or food processor and puree for 40 seconds, or until smooth.

Healthy Potato Salad

Ingredients

- 2 pounds small red potatoes, quartered
- 5 hard-cooked eggs
- 3/4 cup fat-free mayonnaise
- 2 teaspoons cider vinegar
- 1 teaspoon sugar
- 1 teaspoon ground mustard
- 1/2 teaspoon salt
- 1/4 teaspoon pepper
- 1 large sweet onion, chopped
- 2 celery ribs, chopped
- 1/2 cup chopped green onions
- 1/2 cup julienned sweet red pepper
- 1/4 cup minced fresh parsley

Directions

- Place the potatoes in a saucepan and cover with water. Bring to a boil. Reduce heat; cover and simmer for 12-14 minutes or untiltender. Drain; cool for 30 minutes.

- Sliceeggs in half (discard yolks or save for another use). Cut thewhites into 1/2-in. pieces.In a large bowl, combine the mayonnaise, vinegar, sugar, mustard, salt and pepper.

- Add the potatoes, egg whites, onion, celery, green onions, red pepper and parsley; toss to coat. Cover and refrigeratefor 2 hours or until chilled.

Cheesy Potato Kugel

Ingredients

- 3 pounds peeled and shredded potatoes
- 4 eggs
- salt and pepper to taste
- 5 tablespoons olive oil
- 1 onion, chopped
- 2 1/2 cups Cheddar cheese, shredded

Directions

- Preheat oven to 350 degrees F (175 degrees C). Grease a 9x5 inch loaf pan.Place potatoes in a colander and squeeze out moisture.In a large bowl combineeggs, salt, pepper, oil and onion.

- Placepotatoes and cheese in the bowl and mix well. Pour mixture into theprepared loaf pan.Bake at 350 degrees F (175 degrees C) for 1 hour. Raise heat to 450 degrees F (230 degrees C) and bake for 5 to 10 minutes untilbrowned, serve hot.

Potato Soup a la Inge

Ingredients

- 5 potatoes, peeled and cubed
- 5 cubes chicken bouillon
- 2 1/2 quarts water
- salt and pepper to taste
- 1 dash garlic powder
- 1 pinch ground nutmeg
- 1 pint heavy whipping cream
- 3 green onions, chopped

Directions

> In a large pot over high heat, combine the potatoes, bouillon, water, salt and pepper, garlic powder and nutmeg. Cook for about 15 minutes or until potatoes are tender. Add the heavy cream and the green onions.

> Stir well and allow soup to bubble up, about 5minutes. Remove from heat and pour into individual bowls. Garnish with bacon bits and enjoy!

Vegetarian Purple Potatoes with Onions and

Ingredients

* 6 purple potatoes, scrubbed
* 1 tablespoon olive oil
* 1 large red onion, chopped
* 8 ounces sliced fresh mushrooms salt and black pepper to taste
* 2 tablespoons olive oil
* 1/4 teaspoon crushed red pepper flakes
* 1 tablespoon chopped capers
* 1 teaspoon chopped fresh tarragon

Directions

> Cut each potato into wedges by quartering the potatoes, then cutting each quarter in half. Heat 1 tablespoon of olive oil over medium heat in a large skillet, and cook and stir the onion andmushrooms until the mushrooms start to release their liquid and theonion becomes translucent, about 5 minutes.

> Transfer the onionand mushrooms into a bowl, and set aside.Heat 2 more tablespoons of olive oil over high heat in the same skillet, and place the potato wedges into the hot oil. Sprinkle with salt and pepper, and allow to cook, stirring occasionally, until thewedges are browned on both sides, about 10 minutes.

> Reduce heat to medium, sprinkle the potato wedges with red pepper flakes, and allow to cook until the potatoes are tender, about 10 more minutes. Stir in the onion and mushroom mixture, toss the vegetables
> together, and mix in the capers and fresh tarragon.

Potato Chip Chicken

Ingredients

- 1 cup crushed potato chips
- 1 tablespoon minced fresh parsley
- 1/2 teaspoon salt
- 1/2 teaspoon paprika
- 1/4 teaspoon onion powder
- 4 skinless, boneless chicken breast halves
- 2 tablespoons mayonnaise

Directions

- In a large resealable plastic bag, combine the potato chips, parsley, salt, paprika and onion powder. Brush chicken with mayonnaise; ad chicken to the crumb mixture and shake to coat.

- Place in anungreased microwave-safe 11-in. x 7-in. x 2-in. baking dish. Cover with microwave-safe paper towels; cook on high for 8-10 minutes or until chicken juices run clear.

Potato Dumplings I

Ingredients

- 6 cups baked potatoes -- peeled, cooled and riced
- 6 eggs
- 1 teaspoon salt
- 2 cups all-purpose flour
- 3 slices bread
- 2 tablespoons butter

Directions

➤ The day before, boil potatoes with the skins on until tender. Cook enough to make at least 6 cups cold riced potatoes. Peel thepotatoes, and rice them. Refrigerate them until needed.

➤ Brown 2 to 3 pieces of bread in butter or margarine for croutons. Cut into small pieces ,and let cool.Combine riced potatoes, 5 or 6 beaten eggs, salt, and flour. Add croutons, and mix together. The mixture should stick together.

➤ Too much flour will make them heavy.Form into balls about the size of tennis balls. Drop into boiling water in a large pot. Cover and cook for 10 minutes. Serve immediately.

SwansonB® Ultimate Mashed Potatoes

Ingredients

❀ 3 1/2 cups SwansonB® Chicken Broth

❀ 5 large potatoes, cut into 1-inch pieces

❀ 1/2 cup light cream

❀ 1/2 cup sour cream

❀ 1/4 cup chopped fresh chives

❀ 2 tablespoons butter

❀ 3 slices bacon, cooked and crumbled (reserve some for garnish)

❀ Generous dash ground black pepper

Directions

➤ Heat the broth and potatoes in a 3-quart saucepan over medium-high heat to a boil.Reduce the heat to medium. Cover and cook for 10 minutes or until the potatoes are tender. Drain, reserving the broth.

➤ Mash the potatoes with 1/4 cup broth, light cream, sour cream, chives, butter, bacon and black pepper. Add the additional broth, if needed, until desired consistency.B Garnish with the remaining bacon.

Italian Potato Salad

Ingredients

- 6 medium red potatoes, cooked and cubed
- 2 garlic cloves, minced
- 1/2 cup chopped red onion
- 3 plum tomatoes, quartered
- 1/3 cup olive or vegetable oil
- 3 leaves fresh basil, chopped
- 1 (5 ounce) jar stuffed green olives, drained and halved
- 1 teaspoon dried oregano
- 1 1/2 teaspoons salt
- 1/4 teaspoon pepper Lettuce Leaves

Directions

> In a large bowl, combine the first 10 ingredients; toss to coat. Cover and refrigerate until serving. Serve salad in a lettuce-lined bowl ifdesired.

Norwegian Potato Klub

Ingredients

- 6 slices bacon
- 2 cups all-purpose flour
- 1/2 teaspoon baking powder
- 10 medium potatoes, peeled and shredded
- 2 teaspoons salt

Directions

- ➤ Place bacon in a large skillet over medium-high heat. Remove bacon from the pan, and reserve the grease.

- ➤ In a medium bowl, stir together the flour and baking powder. Stir in potatoes to make a sticky dough.

- ➤ Bring a large pot of water to a boil, and add 2 teaspoons of salt. Squeeze the potato mixture into 6 or 7 dumplings, or your desired size.

- ➤ Drop carefully into the boiling water. Simmer for 45 to 60minutes. Remove to a platter with a slotted spoon.

- ➤ Serve with bacon grease brushed over the top, and crumbled bacon. These may also be sliced and fried the next day for another great meal.

Parmesan Red Potatoes

Ingredients

- ❉ 4 medium unpeeled red potatoes, quartered
- ❉ 1/3 cup grated Parmesan cheese
- ❉ 3 teaspoons garlic powder
- ❉ 1 (14.5 ounce) can chicken broth
- ❉ 2 tablespoons minced fresh parsley

Directions

- ➤ Place potatoes in a 6-qt. pressure cooker. Sprinkle with Parmesan cheese and garlic powder; add broth. Close cover securely; place pressure regulator on vent pipe. Bring cooker to full pressure over high heat. Reduce heat to medium-high; cook for 6 minutes.

- ➤ (Pressure regulator should maintain a slow steady rocking motion; adjust heat if needed.)Remove from the heat; immediately cool according to manufacturer's directions until pressure is completely reduced.Sprinkle with parsley.

Buttermilk Parmesan Potatoes

Ingredients

- ❀ 14 small potatoes, peeled and cubed
- ❀ 1 tablespoon butter
- ❀ 2 cloves garlic, minced
- ❀ 1/4 cup minced red onion
- ❀ 3 tablespoons butter
- ❀ 1/3 cup all-purpose flour
- ❀ 1/2 teaspoon salt
- ❀ 1/4 teaspoon pepper
- ❀ 1 cup 2% milk
- ❀ 1 cup buttermilk
- ❀ 1 cup freshly grated Parmesan cheese, divided

Directions

- ➤ Preheat oven to 350 degrees F (175 degrees C).Lightly grease 9x13 inch baking dish. Arrange potatoes over thebottom of the dish, and set aside.Melt 1 tablespoon butter in a saucepan over medium heat.

- ➤ Addthegarlic and onion; cook and stir until the onion is transparent, about 5 minutes. Stir in 3 tablespoons butter until melted. Sprinkle the flour, salt, and pepper over the onion mixture. Cook and stir until mixturebubbles and thickens, about 2 minutes.

- ➤ Continue to stir the flour mixture while gradually pouring in the milk and buttermilk, and return the mixture to boiling. Stir in 3/4 cup Parmesan cheese; cook for 2 minutes until melted, and mixture is smooth. Pour the mixture over the potatoes in the baking dish, stirring to coat evenly.

- ➤ Bake in preheated oven for 1/2 hour, and stir. Bake 1/2 hour longer, stir the potato mixture again, and sprinkle with remaining 1/4 cup Parmesan cheese. Bake for 20 minutes more.

Garlic Potato Biscuits

Ingredients

- ❀ 1/2 pound diced peeled potatoes
- ❀ 3 cloves garlic, peeled
- ❀ 1/3 cup butter or margarine, softened
- ❀ 1 teaspoon salt
- ❀ 1/4 teaspoon pepper
- ❀ 2 cups all-purpose flour
- ❀ 1 tablespoon baking powder
- ❀ 1/3 cup milk

Directions

- ➤ Place potatoes and garlic cloves in a saucepan. Add enough water to cover. Bring to a boil. Reduce heat; cover and simmer until tender.

- ➤ Drain well. Mash potatoes and garlic with butter, salt and pepper. In a bowl, combine flour and baking powder; stir in potato mixture until mixture resembles coarse crumbs. Add milk and stirwell.

- ➤ Turn onto a lightly floured surface. Roll to 1/2-in. thickness; cut with a floured 2-in. biscuit cutter. Place 1 in. apart on an ungreased baking sheet. Bake at 450 degrees F for 10-12 minutes or untilgolden brown. Serve warm.

Sausage-Potato Casserole

Ingredients

- ❀ 3 large baking potatoes, peeled and thinly sliced
- ❀ ground black pepper to taste
- ❀ 1 cup shredded Cheddar cheese
- ❀ 1 pound Polish kielbasa
- ❀ 1/2 teaspoon dried dill weed

* 1/4 teaspoon caraway seed
* 2/3 cup milk

Directions

> Preheat oven to 375 degrees F (190 degrees C). Using two long sheets of aluminum foil on top of each other, fold one long edgetogether and open out to make a large sheet of foil.

> Line a 13x9 pan with the foil, allowing edges to hang outside panArrange the slicedpotatoes, overlapping slightly, in bottom of pan. Pepper to taste. Top with half of the cheese.

> Cut sausage in half crosswise and lengthwise and place, cut side down on top. Top with remaining cheese, the dill weed, caraway seed and milk. Seal edges of foil tightly.Bake at 375 degrees F (190 degrees) for 1 hour.

Octoberfest German Potato Salad

Ingredients

* 3 pounds potatoes, peeled and sliced
* 1/2 cup chopped onion
* 2 teaspoons salt
* 1/2cup mayonnaise
* 1/4 cup vegetable oil
* 1/2 cup cider vinegar
* 2 tablespoons white sugar
* 2 tablespoons dried parsley ground black pepper to taste

Directions

> Bring a large pot of salted water to a boil. Add peeled and cut potatoes; cook until tender but still firm, about 15 minutes. Drain, and transfer to a large bowl. Add onions.

> In a large bowl, whisk together the mayonnaise, oil, vinegar, sugar, parsley, salt and pepper. Gently stir in the potatoes and onion. Let stand for 1 hour before serving to enhance flavors.

Southern Candied Sweet Potatoes

Ingredients

- 6 large sweet potatoes
- 1/2 cup butter
- 2 cups white sugar
- 1 teaspoon ground cinnamon
- 1 teaspoon ground nutmeg
- 1 tablespoon vanilla extract salt to taste

Directions

> Peel the sweet potatoes and cut them into slices.Melt the butter or margarinein a heavy skillet and add the sliced sweet potatoes.

> Mix the sugar, cinnamon, nutmeg and salt. Cover the sweet potatoes with sugar mixture and stir.

> Cover skillet, reduce heat to low and cook for about 1 hour or until potatoes are "candied". They should be tender but a little hard around theedges.

> Also the saucewill turn dark. You will need to stir occasionally during the cooking. Stir in the vanilla just before serving. Serve hot.

Sweet Potato Casserole I

Ingredients

- 1 (40 ounce) can sweet potatoes, drained
- 1 cup white sugar
- 2 eggs

- 1/3 cup milk
- 1 teaspoon vanilla extract
- 1 cup packed brown sugar
- 1 cup chopped pecans
- 1/3 cup all-purpose flour
- 2/3 cup melted butter

Directions

- Preheat oven to 350 degrees F (175 degrees C). Butter one 2 quart baking dish.Heat, drain and mash sweet potatoes. Combine with them with the white sugar, eggs, 1/3 cup of the melted butter, milk and vanilla. Place in the prepared baking dish.

- In a separate bowl combinethe brown sugar, chopped pecans, flour and 1/3 cup of the melted butter. Sprinkle over the top of thesweet potato mixture. Bake at 350 degrees F (175 degrees C) for 35 minutes or until a knife inserted near the center comes out clean.

Sarah Contona's Sweet Potato Pie

Ingredients

- 1 1/2 cups crushed graham crackers
- 1/2 teaspoon ground cinnamon
- 2 tablespoons brown sugar
- 1/2 cup butter, melted
- 1 (8 ounce) package cream cheese, softened
- 1 (29 ounce) can sweet potatoes, drained and mashed
- 1/4 cup packed brown sugar
- 1/4 cup light cream
- 2 eggs, lightly beaten
- 2 tablespoons vanilla
- 1 (10.5 ounce) package miniaturemarshmallows

Directions

- ➤ Preheat oven to 350 degrees F (175 degrees C). Lightly grease a 9 inch springform pan.In a medium bowl, mix graham crackers, cinnamon, 2 tablespoons brown sugar, and butter. Press mixture into the preparedspringform pan to form a crust.

- ➤ Bake 10 minutes in the preheated oven, until lightly browned.In a large bowl, blend cream cheese, sweet potatoes, 1/4 cup brown sugar, light cream, eggs, and vanilla. Pour into the baked crust.

- ➤ Bake pie 1 hour in the preheated oven, placing marshmallows on top to melt during the last 10 minutes.

Honeyed Sweet Potatoes

Ingredients

- ❁ 2/3 cup honey
- ❁ 1/2 cup butter, melted
- ❁ 1 teaspoon salt
- ❁ 8 sweet potatoes, sliced

Directions

- ➤ Preheat the oven to 350 degrees F (175 degrees C). Grease a 9x13 inch baking dish.In a large bowl, stir together the honey, butter and salt. Add the sweet potatoes, and stir to coat. Transfer to the prepared baking dish.

- ➤ Pour any liquid from the bowl over the potatoes.Cover, and bake for 30 minutes in the preheated oven, basting frequently.

Thanksgiving Sweet Potatoes

Ingredients

- 2 (15 ounce) cans sweet potatoes
- 1/4 cup orange juice
- 3/4 cup all-purpose flour
- 1/2 cup white sugar
- 1 teaspoon ground cinnamon
- 1 pinch salt
- 1/2 cup margarine
- 1 1/2 cups miniaturemarshmallows

Directions

- Preheat oven to 350 degrees F (175 degrees C).Place sweet potatoes in a 10x6 inch shallow baking dish and pour orange juice over.In a small bowl, combine flour, sugar, cinnamon and salt; mix together and cut in margarine.

- Sprinkle over sweet potatoes.Bake for 30 minutes. Remove from oven, sprinkle withmarshmallows and broil until browned.

Cream of Sweet Potato Soup

Ingredient
- 3 large sweet potatoes
- 3 (14 ounce) cans low-sodium chicken broth
- 1/4 cup brown sugar, or more to taste
- 1/2 teaspoon salt (to taste)
- 1/4 teaspoon ground nutmeg Black pepper to taste
- Cayenne pepper to taste
- 1/3 cup heavy cream

Directions

- Preheat oven to 350 degrees F (175 degrees C).Bake sweet potatoes in preheated oven until soft, about 1 1/2 hours (you can also use a microwave). Remove and let cool slightly.

- Peel sweet potatoes, and puree with chicken broth in batches, using enough chicken broth so that it purees smoothly. Bring pureeto a simmer in a large saucepan over medium-high heat, then reduce heat to medium-low.

- Stir in the sugar, salt, nutmeg, black pepper, and cayenne pepper; cover, and let simmer for 10 minutes. Remove from heat, and stir in cream.

Potato Casserole I

Ingredients

- 8 potatoes, peeled and diced
- 1/4 cup butter
- 1 onion, chopped
- 1 (10.75 ounce) can condensed cream of chicken soup
- 1/4 cup sour cream
- 3/4 cup shredded Cheddar cheese
- salt to taste
- ground black pepper to taste
- 1/4 cup shredded Cheddar cheese

Directions

- Bring a large pot of salted water to a boil and add potatoes. Cook until tender, then drain water. While potatoes are cooking, heat a small skillet over medium heat. Melt butter and saute onion until golden brown. Set aside.

- Preheat oven to 350 degrees F (175 degrees C).Mash potatoes with cream of chicken soup and sour cream until smooth and creamy. Mix in onions, 3/4 cup cheese, salt, and
- pepper.

> Spoon into a 2 quart casserole dish and bake in preheated oven for 30 minutes. Sprinkle remaining 1/4 cup cheese over top and bake an additional 10 minutes. Serve hot.

Danish Potato Soup

Ingredients

* 1 ham bone water
* 2 potatoes, peeled and diced
* 6 green onions, sliced
* 3 stalks celery, chopped
* 1/4 cup minced fresh parsley
* 2 cups chopped cabbage
* 2 carrots, diced
* 3 tablespoons all-purpose flour
* 1 cup light cream ground nutmeg

Directions

> In a soup kettle, bring ham bone and 2 quarts water to a boil. Reduce heat and simmer 1 hour or until meat pulls away from the bone. Remove ham bone. When cool enough to handle, trim any meat and dice.

> Discard bone. Return ham to kettle along with potatoes, onions, celery, parsley, cabbage and carrots; cook 40 minutes. Stir together flour and 1/4 cup cold water. Slowly pour into the soup, stirring constantly.

> Bring soup to a boil; cook 2 minutes. Reduce heat; stir in cream. Remove from theheat. Sprinkle a dash of nutmeg on each bowlful just before serving.

Brandied Candied Sweet Potatoes

Ingredients

- 2 pounds sweet potatoes, peeled and diced
- 1/2 cup butter
- 1/2 cup packed brown sugar
- 1/2 cup brandy
- 1/2 teaspoon salt

Directions

> Place sweet potatoes in a large saucepan with enough water to cover. Bring to a boil. Cook 15 minutes, or until tender but firm. Drain, and set aside.

> In a large skillet over low heat, melt the butter. Stir in the brown sugar, brandy, and salt. Add the sweet potatoes, and stir to coat. Cook, stirring gently, until sweet potatoes are heated through and well glazed.

Potato Leek Soup II

Ingredients

- 2 tablespoons unsalted butter
- 1 cup sliced leeks
- 1 cup chopped onion
- 1 2/3 cups chicken broth
- 4 cups milk
- 1 1/3 cups potato flakes
- 1 teaspoon salt
- 1/2 teaspoon celery salt
- 2 tablespoons chopped fresh parsley

Directions

> Melt the butter in a large pot over medium heat. Saute the leeks and onion in the butter for 5 minutes, or until tender. Pour in the broth and the milk and mix well.

- Bring to a boil, reduce heat to low and simmer for 5 minutes. Stir in the potato flakes, salt, celery salt and parsley. Allow to thicken and heat through.

Loaded Potatoes

Ingredients

- 4 large baking potatoes
- 2 tablespoons butter, melted
- 3 tablespoons grated Parmesan cheese
- 1/2 teaspoon dried rosemary, crushed
- 1/4 teaspoon salt
- 1/8 teaspoon pepper
- 1/2 cup shredded Cheddar cheese
- 1/4 cup real bacon bits
- 1 green onion, chopped

Directions

- Scrub potatoes. With a sharp knife, slice potatoes thinly but not all the way through, leaving slices attached at the bottom. Place on a microwave-safe plate; drizzle with butter.

- Combine the Parmesan cheese, rosemary, salt and pepper; sprinkleover potatoes and between slices

- .Microwave, uncovered, on high for 12-18 minutes or until potatoes are tender. Top with cheddar cheese, bacon and onion. Microwave for 1-2 minutes longer or until cheese is melted.

Asparagus Potato Soup

Ingredients

- 2 cups diced peeled potatoes
- 1/2 pound fresh asparagus, chopped
- 1/2 cup chopped onion
- 2 celery ribs, chopped
- 1 tablespoon chicken bouillon granules
- 4 cups water
- 1/4 cup butter or margarine
- 1/2 cup all-purpose flour
- 1 cup whipping cream
- 1/2 cup milk
- 1/2 teaspoon salt Dash pepper
- 12 bacon strips, cooked and crumbled
- 3/4 cup shredded Cheddar cheese

Directions

➢ In a large saucepan or soup kettle, combine the potatoes, asparagus, onion, celery, bouillon and water. Bring to a boil.Reduce heat; cover and simmer for 15 minutes or until vegetables are tender.

➢ Stir in the butter.In a bowl, combine flour, cream, milk, salt and pepper until smooth; add to the vegetable mixture. Bring to a boil; cook and stir for 2minutes or until thickened. Garnish with bacon and cheese.

Sweet Potato Cake

Ingredients

- 2 1/4 cups sifted cake flour
- 3 teaspoons baking powder
- 1/2 teaspoon baking soda
- 1/2 teaspoon salt
- 1 1/2 teaspoons ground cinnamon

- 1/2 teaspoon ground allspice
- 1/2 teaspoon ground ginger
- 1/2 cup butter
- 1 cup dark brown sugar
- 1 cup white sugar
- 2 eggs
- 3/4 cup buttermilk
- 3/4 cup mashed sweet
- potatoes
- 1/2 cup chopped golden raisins

Directions

- Preheat oven to 350 degrees F (175 degrees C). Grease two 9 inch round cake pans.Sift together flour, baking powder, soda, salt, cinnamon, allspice, and ginger.

- Mix together buttermilk, potatoes, and raisins in a medium bowl. In a large bowl, cream butter or margarine. Gradually add white and brown sugars, creaming until fluffy. Add eggs one at a time,beating thoroughly after each addition.

- Beating only until smooth after each addition, alternately add dry ingredients in fourths and potato mixture in thirds to creamed mixture. Turn batter intoprepared pans, and spread evenly.

- Bake for about 30 minutes, or until cake tests done. Cool, and remove from pans. Frost as desired.

Slimmed-Down Potato Salad

Ingredients

- 1 (12 ounce) package silken tofu
- 3 tablespoons fresh lemon juice
- 1 tablespoon prepared yellow mustard

- ❀ 1 clove garlic, minced
- ❀ 1 teaspoon salt
- ❀ 2 tablespoons olive oil
- ❀ 1 cup chopped celery
- ❀ 1 red bell pepper, seeded and cubed
- ❀ 3 eggs, hard-boiled, shelled, and chopped
- ❀ 1/2 cup chopped green onions
- ❀ 1/2 cup chopped dill pickles
- ❀ salt and ground black pepper to taste
- ❀ 2 tablespoons whole milk

Directions

- ➢ Place the potatoes in a Dutch oven and fill with enough water to cover. Bring to a boil; reduce heat to medium-low. Cover and
- ➢ simmer until potatoes are tender, and a fork can beeasily inserted and removed, about 20 minutes.

- ➢ Drain and cool slightly. Peel, cut into cubes, and place in a large bowl.To make the dressing, combine the tofu, lemon juice, mustard, garlic, and 1 teaspoon of salt in the bowl of a food processor. Blend until smooth.

- ➢ With the processor running, add the olive oil in a thin, steady stream, blending just until mixture thickens. Set aside.Combine the celery, red bell pepper, eggs, green onions, and pickles in the bowl with the potatoes.

- ➢ Pour the dressing over the potato mixture, and toss lightly to evenly coat all ingredients.Season to taste with salt and pepper. Cover and chill at least 4 hours.

- ➢ Just before serving, toss the salad with milk, 1 tablespoon at a time, to reach the desired consistency.

Balsamic Vinegar Potato Salad

Ingredients

- 10 medium red potatoes, diced
- 1 small onion, chopped
- 1/2 cup diced roasted red peppers
- 1 (4 ounce) can sliced black olives, drained
- 1 (10 ounce) can quartered artichoke hearts, drained
- 1/2 cup balsamic vinegar
- 3 teaspoons olive oil
- 1 teaspoon dried oregano
- 1 teaspoon dried basil
- 1/2 teaspoon mustard powder
- 2 tablespoons chopped fresh parsley

Directions

> Place potatoes in a saucepan with enough water to cover. Bring to a boil, then cook for 5 to 10 minutes, until tender. Drain, andtransfer to a large bowl.Add the onion, red peppers, olives, and artichokes to the bowl with the potatoes.

> In a separate bowl, whisk together the balsamicvinegar, olive oil, oregano, basil, mustard powder and parsley. Pour over the vegetables, and stir to coat. Chill for at least 4 hours or overnight before serving.

Sweet Potatoes 'n' Pears

Ingredients

- 9 cups cubed peeled sweet potatoes
- 4 cups water
- 1 (15 ounce) can pear halves, drained
- 1/3 cup packed brown sugar
- 1/4 cup butter, softened
- 1/4 teaspoon ground cinnamon

Directions

> Place the sweet potatoes in a shallow 3-qt. microwave-safe dish; add water. Cover and microwave on high for 18-20 minutes or until tender.

> Drain and place in a large mixing bowl. Add the remaining ingredients; beat until combined.

Barbequed Potato and Garlic Scape Packets

Ingredients

* 8 red potatoes, cut into 1-inch cubes
* 20 garlic scapes, cut into 11/2-inch pieces
* 1/4 cup extra-virgin olive oil kosher
* salt and pepper to taste

Directions

> Preheat an outdoor grill for medium-high heat and lightly oil the grate. Cut 6 18-inch pieces of aluminum foil and set aside.

> Combine the potatoes and scapes in a mixing bowl. Drizzle with olive oil; season to taste with salt and pepper. Divide the mixture among the pieces of aluminum foil and fold theedges of the foil over the potato mixture to seal the packets.

> Place the packets onto the preheated grill and close the lid. Cook until the potatoes are tender and easily pierced with a fork, 20 to 25 minutes. Rotate the packets halfway through cooking.

Loaded Baked Potato Casserole

Ingredients

* 1 (32 ounce) bag Simply
* Potatoes® Southwest Style Hash Browns
* 1 (6 ounce) can French's® French Fried Onions

- 🏵 1 cup frozen peas

- 🏵 1 cup shredded Cheddar cheese

- 🏵 4 slices bacon, cooked and crumbled

- 🏵 2 (10.75 ounce) cans

- 🏵 Campbell's® Condensed Cream of Celery Soup (Regular or 98% Fat Free)

- 🏵 1 cup milk

Directions

- ➤ Stir the potatoes, 1 1/3 cups of theonions, peas, cheese and bacon in a 13 x 9-inch (3-quart) shallow baking dish. Stir the soup and milk in a medium bowl. Pour the soup mixture over the potato mixture. Cover.

- ➤ Bake at 350 degrees F for 30 minutes or until hot. Stir.Sprinkle with the remaining onions. Bake for 5 minutes more or until the onions are golden brown.

Classic American-Style Potato Salad

Ingredients

- 🏵 2 pounds red boiling potatoes, scrubbed

- 🏵 2 tablespoons red wine vinegar

- 🏵 1/2 teaspoon salt

- 🏵 1/2 teaspoon freshly ground black pepper

- 🏵 3 hard-cooked eggs

- 🏵 1 small celery stalk

- 🏵 1/4 cup chopped sweet pickle (not relish)

- 🏵 3 scallions

- 🏵 2 tablespoons chopped fresh parsley

- 🏵 1/2 cup mayonnaise

- 🏵 2 tablespoons Dijon-style mustard

Directions

- Place potatoes in a pot with water to cover. Bring to a boil, cover and simmer, stirring to ensureeven cooking, until a thin-bladed paring knife or a metal skewer inserted into a potato can beremoved with no resistance, 25 to 30 minutes. Drain, rinse under cold water and drain again.

- Cool slightly.Cut warm potatoes into 3/4-inch dice with a serrated knife. Layer them in a bowl, seasoning with vinegar, salt and pepper as you go.

- Cut eggs, celery and pickle in 1/4-inch dice and thinly slice scallions. Add to potatoes, along with parsley. Stir in mayonnaise and mustard until everything is combined. Chill, covered, beforeserving.

Horseradish Potatoes

Ingredients

- 1/4 cup butter or margarine
- 1 tablespoon prepared horseradish
- 2 teaspoons lemon juice
- 1/2 teaspoon salt
- 1/8 teaspoon pepper
- 12 small new potatoes

Directions

- Place butter in an ungreased microwave-safe 1-qt. dish. Microwave, uncovered, on high for 40 seconds or until melted.

- Stir inhorseradish, lemon juice, salt, pepper and potatoes. Cover and microwave on high for 10 minutes, stirring once. Let stand for 2 minutes. Stir before serving.

Baking Potato Soup

Ingredients

- 4 large potatoes, peeled and diced

- 1/4 cup butter
- 1 teaspoon salt
- 1/2 teaspoon ground black pepper
- 4 1/2 cups water, divided
- 3 (1 ounce) packages white gravy mix

Directions

> Place potatoes in a pot with water to cover. Bring to a boil, introduce butter, salt and pepper. Reduce heat to medium low and simmer until potatoes are tender, 10 to 20 minutes more.

> Meanwhile, prepare gravy mix. Bring 3 1/2 cups of water to a boil in a large saucepan. Combine the remaining cup of water with thegravy mix and stir to dissolve. Stir into boiling water.

> Drain potatoes and add to boiling gravy mix. Continue to boil 5 minutes more, adding water to thin if desired. Serve at once.

Potato Penne Soup

Ingredients

- 1/2 cup margarine
- 1 onion, chopped
- 10 cups water
- 2 large carrots, chopped
- 5 potatoes, peeled and cubed
- 1/2 cup pearl barley
- 2 (14.5 ounce) cans fat-freechicken broth
- 1 cup penne pasta
- 3 stalks celery, chopped, with leaves
- 4 tablespoons chicken bouillon powder
- 1 red bell pepper, diced

- ❋ 1 green bell pepper, chopped
- ❋ 1/2 teaspoon ground whitepepper
- ❋ 1 1/2 cups cauliflower florets, broken into bite size pieces
- ❋ 3/8 cup chopped fresh parsley
- ❋ 3/4 teaspoon dried thyme
- ❋ 3 tablespoons all-purpose flour
- ❋ 2 cups whole milk
- ❋ 2 tablespoons soy sauce

Directions

- ➢ In a large saute pan, melt margarine, add onions and cook over medium heat until translucent. Reduce heat to low.In a large stock pot, add water and bring to a boil. Add carrots, potatoes, pearl barley, and cook for 10 minutes.

- ➢ Add chicken broth, penne, celery (including leaves), chicken soup base, red bell pepper and green bell pepper and bring back to a boil. Reduce heat and cook for 15 minutes.Add white pepper, cauliflower florets, parsley, thyme and cook for an additional 5 minutes.

- ➢ In a food processor or blender, puree 3 cups of all-ready cooked soup and return to stock pot.In a small mixing bowl, mix together flour and 3/4 cup whole milk; blend well. Add flour mixture to the cooked onions and mix well.

- ➢ Gradually add remainder of milk, stirring constantly until soup is heated through.Add onion mixture to soup and stir. Add soy sauce and bring to a boil. Adjust seasonings to taste and serve soup hot.

Golden Potato Rounds

Ingredients

- ❋ 1 cup crushed cornflakes
- ❋ 1 1/2 teaspoons seasoned salt
- ❋ 4 medium potatoes, peeled and sliced 1/2-inch thick
- ❋ 1/4 cup butter or margarine, melted

Directions

> ➢ In a bowl, combine the cornflakes and seasoned salt.Dip potatoes in butter, then coat with cornflakemixture.

> ➢ Place on greased foil-lined baking sheets.Bake at 350 degrees for 55-60 minutes or until tender.

Beef-Stuffed Potatoes

Ingredients

* ❀ 6 medium baking potatoes
* ❀ 1 pound ground beef
* ❀ 2 tablespoons chopped onion
* ❀ 1/3 cup sour cream
* ❀ 1 (4 ounce) can chopped green chilies
* ❀ 3 tablespoons butter or margarine
* ❀ 1tablespoon Worcestershiresauce
* ❀ 1 teaspoon salt
* ❀ 1/2 teaspoon garlic powder
* ❀ 1/2 teaspoon chili powder
* ❀ 3/4 cup shredded Cheddar cheese

Directions

> ➢ Bake potatoes at 375 degrees F for 1 hour or until tender. Cool. Meanwhile, in a large skillet, cook the beef and onion over medium heat until the meat is no longer pink; drain. Cut a thin slice off thetop of each potato.

> ➢ Carefully scoop out pulp, leaving a thin shell; place pulp in a bowl. Add sour cream, chilies, butter, Worcestershire sauce, salt, garlic powder and chili powder; mash or beat. Stir in meat mixture until combined. Stuff into potato shells.

> ➢ Place on an ungreased baking sheet. Sprinkle with cheese. Bake at 350 degrees F for 10-15 minutes or until heated through.

Bengaladumpa Vepudu (Potato Stir-Fry)

Ingredients

- ❋ 1/4 cup cooking oil
- ❋ 4 dried red chile peppers
- ❋ 1 tablespoon cumin seeds
- ❋ 2 teaspoons skinned split black lentils (urad dal)
- ❋ 1/2 teaspoon mustard seeds
- ❋ 1 sprig fresh curry leaves
- ❋ 1 pound potatoes, peeled and cubed
- ❋ salt to taste
- ❋ 1/2 teaspoon ground red pepper
- ❋ 1/2 teaspoon ground cumin

Directions

- ➤ Heat the oil in a large skillet. Fry the dried red chile peppers, cumin seeds, urad dal, and mustard seeds in the hot oil until the seeds begin to splutter. Add the curry leaves and continue cookinganother 30 seconds.

- ➤ Stir the potatoes into the mixture. Season with salt. Cook and stir until the potatoes are tender, about 20 minutes. Sprinkle the red pepper and cumin powder over the potatoes; cook another 2 to 3 minutes.

Smashed Potatoes

Ingredients

- ❋ 1 1/2 pounds small yellow-fleshed potatoes
- ❋ 1/4 cup olive oil
- ❋ 1 teaspoon butter at room temperature
- ❋ 2 tablespoons balsamic vinegar

* 3 cloves garlic, minced
* 1 teaspoon dried rosemary
* 1/2 teaspoon dried sage
* 1/2 teaspoon ground thyme
* 1/2 teaspoon dried savory
* 1/2 teaspoon sea salt
* 1/2 teaspoon ground black pepper

Directions

> Place potatoes in a saucepan, fill with water to cover the potatoes, and bring to a boil. Reduce heat to a simmer, and cook the potatoes until tender but not mushy, about 20 minutes. Drain and allow potatoes to cool.

> While potatoes are cooking, combine olive oil, butter, balsamic vinegar, garlic, rosemary, sage, thyme, savory, sea salt and pepper in a bowl. Stir with a fork to combine well.Preheat an oven to 450 degrees F (230 degrees C).

> Line a baking sheet with parchment paper.Place the potatoes in a single layer on the prepared baking sheet, and lightly press down on the potatoes to partially crush them. Spoon the oil-herb mixture over each potato.

> Bake in the preheated oven until theedges of the potatoes arebeginning to crisp, about 25 minutes. Cool for about 5 minutes before serving.

Pork Tenderloins with Roasted Potatoes

Ingredients

* 1/4 cup olive or vegetable oil
* 2 garlic cloves, minced
* 1 1/2 teaspoons dried rosemary, crushed
* 1/2 teaspoon salt
* 1/4 teaspoon pepper
* 1 (3/4 pound) pork tenderloin
* 2 medium red potatoes, cut into chunks

Directions

- ➤ In a bowl, combine the oil, garlic, rosemary, salt and pepper. Place half of the marinade in each of two resealable plastic bags. Add pork to one bag and potatoes to the other bag. Seal bags and turn to coat; refrigerate for 8 hours or overnight.

- ➤ Drain and discard marinades. Place meat and potatoes in a greased 11-in. x 7-in. x 2-in. baking dish. Bake,uncovered, at 425 degrees F for 20-25 minutes or until potatoes are almost tender. Broil 5 in.

- ➤ from heat for 4-5 minutes or until potatoes are tender and a meat thermometer inserted in the pork reads 160 degrees F. Let stand for5 minutes before slicing.

Meatball Potato Supper

Ingredients

- ❀ 2 eggs
- ❀ 1/2 cup dry bread crumbs
- ❀ 1 envelope onion soup mix
- ❀ 1 1/2 pounds lean ground beef
- ❀ 2 tablespoons all-purpose flour
- ❀ 6 medium potatoes, peeled and thinly sliced
- ❀ 1 (10.75 ounce) can condensed cream of celery soup, undiluted
- ❀ 1 cup milk
- ❀ Paprika

Directions

- ➤ In a bowl, combine theeggs, bread crumbs and soup mix. Crumblebeef over mixture and mix well. Shape into 1-in. balls. In a largeskillet, brown meatballs in small batches over medium heat; drain.

- ➤ Sprinkle with flour; gently roll to coat.Place half of the potatoes in a greased 2-1/2-qt. baking dish. Top with meatballs and remaining potatoes.

> In a bowl, combine soup and milk until blended; pour over potatoes. Sprinkle with paprika ifdesired. Cover and bake at 350 degrees F for 60-65 minutes or until the potatoes are tender.

Garlic-Chive Mashed Potatoes

Ingredients

- ❀ 3 1/2 pounds russet potatoes, peeled and quartered
- ❀ 3 cloves garlic, peeled
- ❀ 1/8 teaspoon paprika
- ❀ 1 1/2 cups fat-free sour cream
- ❀ 1 cup reduced-sodium chicken broth, warmed
- ❀ 2 tablespoons minced chives
- ❀ 1 teaspoon salt
- ❀ 1/4 teaspoon pepper

Directions

> Place the potatoes, garlic and paprika in a large saucepan or Dutch oven; cover with water. Bring to a boil. Reduce heat; cover andcook for 15-20 minute or until potatoes are tender.

> Drain. In a largemixing bowl, beat the potatoes and garlic. Add sour cream, broth, chives, salt and pepper; beat until smooth.

Broccoli Potato Soup

Ingredients

- ❀ 2 cups broccoli florets
- ❀ 1 onion, sliced
- ❀ 1 tablespoon margarine

- 1 (10.75 ounce) can condensed cream of potato soup
- 1 cup milk
- 1/2 cup water
- 3/4 teaspoon chopped fresh basil
- 1/4 teaspoon ground black
- pepper
- 1/3 cup shredded Cheddar cheese

Directions

> In a large saucepan over medium heat, saut E the broccoli and onion in the butter or margarine, about 5 minutes, or until tender.

> Stir in the soup, milk, water, basil and pepper.Mix well and heat through, about 15 minutes. Add cheese and stir until melted.

Crunch Top Potatoes

Ingredients

- 1/4 cup melted butter
- 2 (15 ounce) cans sliced potatoes, drained
- 1 cup shredded Cheddar cheese
- 1 cup cornflakes cereal, crushed
- 1 teaspoon paprika

Directions

> Preheat oven to 375 degrees F (190 degrees C). Pour butter into a 9x13 inch pan.Arrange potato slices in a single layer over the butter. Combine thecheese, cornflakes and paprika in a bowl and sprinkle the mixture over the potatoes.

> Bake in a preheated 350 degrees F (175 degrees C) oven for 20 minutes or until heated through.

Potato Salad Deviled Eggs

Ingredients

- 8 eggs
- 1 large potato, coarsely chopped
- 2 teaspoons pickle relish
- 2 teaspoons mustard
- 4 teaspoons creamy salad dressing (such as Miracle Whip®) salt to taste
- ground black pepper to tastepaprika for garnish

Directions

- Place theeggs into a saucepan in a single layer and fill with water to cover theeggs by 1 inch. Cover the saucepan and bring the water to a boil over high heat. Once the water is boiling, remove from theheat and let theeggs stand in the hot water for 15 minutes.

- Pour out the hot water, then cool theeggs under cold running water in thesink. Peel once cold. Slice the cooled eggs in half lengthwise, and scoop out and reserve the yolks.

- While theeggs are cooking, place the cut-up potato into a saucepan with water to cover, bring to a boil, reduce heat, and simmer until the potato pieces are tender, 10 to 15 minutes. Drain the potato, and let cool.

- In a bowl, mash the reserved egg yolks with pickle relish, mustard, creamy dressing, salt, and pepper until well combined. Place thepotato into a bowl, and coarsely mash with a fork.

- Lightly combinethe potato with the yolk mixture. Stuff each egg half generously with potato salad, and sprinkle with paprika. Cover and chill until ready to serve, at least 20 minutes.

Potato Chocolate Cake

Ingredients

- ❀ 1 cup margarine
- ❀ 2 cups white sugar
- ❀ 4 eggs
- ❀ 2 (1 ounce) squares unsweetened chocolate, melted
- ❀ 1 teaspoon vanilla extract
- ❀ 1 cup prepared instant mashed potatoes
- ❀ 2 cups sifted all-purpose flour
- ❀ 1 teaspoon baking soda
- ❀ 1 teaspoon salt
- ❀ 3/4 cup buttermilk

Directions

➢ Preheat oven to 375 degrees F (190 degrees C). Grease and flour a 9x13 inch pan. Sift together the flour, baking soda and salt. Set aside.

➢ In a large bowl, cream together the margarine and sugar until light and fluffy. Beat in theeggs one at a time. Stir in the meltedchocolate, vanilla and mashed potatoes.

➢ Beat in the flour mixturealternately with the buttermilk, mixing just until incorporated.Pour batter into prepared pan. Bake in the preheated oven for 45 minutes, or until a toothpick inserted into the center of the cake comes out clean. Allow to cool.

Sweet Potato And Prune Casserole

Ingredients

- ❀ 6 sweet potatoes
- ❀ 1 (16 ounce) jar stewed prunes
- ❀ 3/4 cup honey
- ❀ 3/4 teaspoon ground cinnamon
- ❀ 1 teaspoon salt
- ❀ 1 fluid ounce prune juice

- 2 tablespoons lemon juice
- 1/4 cup pareve margarine, melted

Directions

> Pierce sweet potatoes, and place on a baking sheet. Bake in a preheated 425 degrees F (220 degrees C) for 1 hour, or until tender. Cool until sweet potatoes can beeasily handled. Peel, and cut into 1/4 inch thick slices.

> In a small bowl, combine honey, cinnamon, salt, lemon and prunejuice, and melted margarine.Cut prunes in half, and remove pits. In a casserole dish, arrangealternating layers of potatoes and prunes.

> Spoon honey mixtureover each layer.Bake at 350 degrees F (175 degrees C) for 45 minutes, basting occasionally with liquid in casserole dish.

Pork Chops with Scalloped Potatoes

Ingredients

- 6 (1/2 inch thick) boneless pork chops
- 6 medium red potatoes, thinly sliced
- 1 medium onion, thinly sliced
- 2 teaspoons dried thyme
- 1 teaspoon pepper
- 1/4 cup butter
- 1 teaspoon beef bouillon
- 1 cup hot water
- 1/4 cup all-purpose flour
- 1/4 cup water

Directions

> Preheat the oven to 350 degrees F (175 degrees C).
Heat a skillet over medium-high heat and coat with nonstick cooking spray. Brown the pork chops on each side, about 2 minutes, then set aside.

- Layer half of the potato slices, and half of the onion slices in thebottom of a lightly greased 9x13 inch baking dish. Season with half of the thyme and half of the pepper. Dot with 2 tablespoons of thebutter.

- Arrange pork chops on top of the potatoes, then cover with the remaining potatoes, onion, seasonings, and butter. Dissolve thebouillon cube in hot water, and pour evenly over the casserole. Cover with a lid or aluminum foil.

- Bake for 1 hour in the preheated oven. Remove the pork and potatoes to a serving dish with a slotted spoon. Pour the drippings into a skillet. In a small bowl or cup, whisk together the flour and water using a fork.

- Whisk into the drippings, and cook over medium heat until thickened and bubbly. Serve gravy with pork chops and potatoes.

Au Gratin Potatoes II

Ingredients

- 1 cup sour cream
- 1 (10.75 ounce) can condensed cream of celery soup
- 4 1/2 cups peeled and shredded potatoes
- 2 cups shredded Cheddar cheese
- 1/2 cup chopped green onions
- 1 cup cornflakes cereal
- 1/2 cup unsalted butter, melted
- 1 tablespoon chopped fresh parsley (optional)

Directions

- Preheat oven to 350 degrees F (175 degrees C). Spray one 8 inch square baking dish with vegetable cooking spray.In a large bowl, stir together the sour cream and soup. Add grated potatoes, cheese, and onions. Mix well, and pour into the prepared baking dish.

- Cover the dish with a lid or aluminum foil.Bake for 45 minutes in the preheated oven. In a small bowl, mix together the melted butter and cornflakes. Sprinkle over the top of the potatoes, and return to the oven.

> Bake uncovered, for an additional 20 minutes or until bubbly and corn flakes are golden brown. Remove from the oven and sprinklewith chopped parsley.

Mashed Potatoes with Horseradish

Ingredients

- ❁ 5 potatoes, peeled and quartered
- ❁ 2 tablespoons butter, divided ground black pepper to taste
- ❁ 1/2 cup sour cream
- ❁ 1 tablespoon prepared horseradish
- ❁ 2 teaspoons minced parsley

Directions

> Bring a large pot of salted water to a boil. Add potatoes and cook until tender but still firm, about 15 minutes. Drain, and mash with 1 tablespoon butter and black pepper.

> Stir in sour cream,horseradish and parsley. Whip potatoes and place in medium serving bowl.Melt remaining 1 tablespoon butter and pour over potatoes. Serveimmediately.

Baked Potato Soup II

Ingredients

- ❁ 1/3 cup butter
- ❁ 1/3 cup all-purpose flour
- ❁ 4 cups skim milk
- ❁ 6 large baking potatoes, scrubbed

* 1 cup sour cream

Directions

> Microwave potatoes until done. While potatoes are cooking make a roux over low to medium heat. Mix butter, margarine, or light olive oil, and flour. DO NOT BURN THE ROUX.

> When roux is thickened a bit, gradually blend in milk. Continue cooking over low to medium heat while preparing potatoes.

> Peel and cut up potatoes. You may want to mash some of thepotatoes also. Add potatoes to the milk mixture. Blend in sour cream. Soup is ready to be served.

Meat Shell Potato Pie

Ingredients

* 1 pound ground chuck or lean ground beef
* 1 (10.75 ounce) can condensed cream of mushroom soup,
* undiluted, divided
* 1/4 cup chopped onion
* 1 egg
* 1/4 cup dry bread crumbs
* 2 tablespoons chopped fresh parsley
* 1/4 teaspoon salt
* 1 pinch pepper
* 2 cups mashed potatoes
* 4 bacon strips, cooked and crumbled
* 1/2 cup shredded Cheddar cheese

Directions

> In a large bowl, combine beef, 1/2 cup soup, onion, egg, bread crumbs,parsley, salt and pepper; mix well. Press onto the bottom and up the sides of a 9-in. pie plate. Bake at 350 degrees F for 25 minutes; drain.

> Combine potatoes and remaining soup in a bowl; mix until fluffy. Spread over meat crust. Sprinkle with bacon and cheese. Bake at 350 degrees F for 15 minutes. Let stand for a few minutes. Cut into wedges.

Sweet Potato Souffle I

Ingredients

* 3 cups mashed sweet potatoes
* 3/4 cup white sugar
* 1/3 cup butter, softened
* 2 eggs
* 1 teaspoon vanilla extract
* 1/2 cup milk
* 1 cup flaked coconut
* 1/3 cup all-purpose flour
* 1 cup packed brown sugar
* 1 cup chopped walnuts
* 1/3 cup melted butter

Directions

> Preheat oven to 350 degrees F (175 degrees C).Combinethe mashed sweet potatoes with the white sugar, soft butter or margarine, beaten eggs, vanilla and milk. Spoon into a 2 quart oven proof baking dish.

> Combine the coconut, flour, brown sugar, chopped nuts and melted butter. Sprinkle over the top of the sweet potatoes.Bake at 350 degrees F (175 degrees C) for 30 to 35 minutes.

Polish Meat and Potatoes

Ingredients

- 🏵 4 potatoes, peeled and cut into 1 inch cubes
- 🏵 1 onion, chopped
- 🏵 2 green bell peppers, cut into 1 inch pieces
- 🏵 1/2 teaspoon onion powder
- 🏵 1/2 teaspoon garlic powder
- 🏵 1/2 teaspoon salt
- 🏵 1/4 teaspoon black pepper
- 🏵 1/4 cup vegetable oil
- 🏵 1 (16 ounce) package kielbasa sausage, cut into 1 inch pieces

Directions

- ➢ Heat oil in a large skillet over medium-high heat. Cook onions and potatoes for 15 minutes, stirring occasionally.

- ➢ Reduce flame to med and stir in bell pepper, onion powder, garlic powder, salt and pepper.

- ➢ Cover, and cook 5 minutes. Stir in kielbasa, cover, and cook for 15 minutes, or until onions are caramelized.

Famous Potatoes

Ingredients

- 🏵 6 large potatoes, cubed
- 🏵 1/2 cup butter, cubed
- 🏵 1 tablespoon garlic salt
- 🏵 1 tablespoon pepper
- 🏵 1/4 (2 pound) loaf processed cheese, cubed

Directions

> Preheat oven to 375 degrees F (190 degrees C). In a 9x13 inch casserole dish combine potatoes, butter, garlic salt and pepper.

> Bake in preheated oven for 45 minutes, stirring occasionally. Stir in processed cheese and stir to melt.

Herbed Twice-Baked Potatoes

Ingredients

* 2 medium baking potatoes
* 1 1/2 ounces reduced-fat cream cheese, cubed
* 1 tablespoon snipped chives
* 1/4 teaspoon salt
* 1/4 teaspoon dried basil dash cayenne pepper
* 3 tablespoons fat-free milk
* 3 teaspoons butter, melted and divided
* 1 dash garlic powder
* 1 dash paprika

Directions

> Scrub and pierce potatoes. Bake at 375 degrees F for 1 hour or until tender. Cool for 10 minutes. Cut potatoes in half. Scoop out pulp, leaving a thin shell.

> In a bowl, mash the pulp with cream cheese, chives, salt, basil and cayenne. Add milk and 1-1/2 teaspoons butter; mash. Spoon into potato shells.

> Drizzle with remaining butter; sprinkle with garlic
powder and paprika. Place on an ungreased baking sheet. Bake for 15-20 minutes or until heated through.

Sweet Potato Casserole V

Ingredients

- ❀ 3 cups cooked and mashed sweet potatoes
- ❀ 1/3 cup packed brown sugar
- ❀ 1/3 cup eggnog
- ❀ 2 tablespoons margarine, melted
- ❀ 1 teaspoon vanilla extract
- ❀ 1/2 teaspoon salt
- ❀ 2 egg whites
- ❀ 1/2 cup packed brown sugar
- ❀ 1/4 cup all-purpose flour
- ❀ 2 tablespoons butter

Directions

- ➢ Preheat the oven to 350 degrees F (175 degrees C). Coat one 2 quart baking dish with non-stick cooking spray.Combine the mashed sweet potatoes, 1/3 cup brown sugar, eggnog, melted margarine, vanilla extract, salt and egg whites.

- ➢ Spoon mixture into the prepared baking dish.Combine the 1/2 cup brown sugar and flour. Cut in the chilled 2 tablespoons margarine until the mixture resembles coarse crumbs.

- ➢ Sprinkle over the sweet potato mixture.Bake at 350 degrees F (175 degrees C) for 30 minutes.

Restaurant-Style Potato Skins

Ingredients

- ❀ 6 potatoes
- ❀ 1 cup vegetable oil
- ❀ 8 ounces shredded Cheddar cheese

- 1/8 cup bacon bits
- 1 (16 ounce) container sour cream

Directions

> Preheat oven to 375 degrees F (190 degrees C). Lightly grease a 9x13 inch baking pan.Pierce potatoes with a fork. Microwave the potatoes on high until they are soft; approximately 10 to 12 minutes.

> Cut the potatoes in half vertically. Scoop the inside out of thepotatoes, until 1/4 inch of the potato shell remains.Heat oil to 365 degrees F (180 degrees C) in a deep fryer or a deep saucepan.

> Place the potatoes in hot oil, fry for 5 minutes. Drain potatoes on paper towels.Fill the potato shells with cheese and bacon bits.

> Arrange them in the prepared baking pan.Bake for 7 minutes, or until the cheese is melted. Serve hot with sour cream.

Gingered Sweet Potatoes

Ingredients

- 2 tablespoons butter or margarine
- 2 tablespoons olive or vegetableoil
- 1/3 cup packed brown sugar
- 1 tablespoon honey
- 1 teaspoon ground cinnamon
- 1/2 teaspoon salt
- 1/2 teaspoon ground ginger
- 1/4 teaspoon pepper
- 1 medium sweet potato, peeled and cut into wedges

Directions

> In a skillet, heat butter and oil over medium heat. Stir in the brown sugar, honey, cinnamon, salt, ginger and pepper. Add the sweet potato wedges; toss to coat.

> Cover and cook over low heat for 20-30 minutes or until potatoes are tender, stirring occasionally.

Sweet Potato Cooked in Ginger Syrup

Ingredients

- ❋ 1 pound sweet potatoes, peeled and cut into chunks
- ❋ 1 quart water
- ❋ 1 (1/2 inch) piece ginger, peeled and sliced
- ❋ 1 cup palm sugar

Directions

> Combine the sweet potatoes with the water in a pot and soak for 30 minutes.Remove the potatoes from the water. Bring the water to a boil and return the potatoes to the boiling water with the ginger slices.

> Cook the potatoes at a boil until fork-tender, 20 to 25 minutes. Stir thesugar into the water until completely dissolved. Remove thesweet potatoes to individual bowls and spoon the ginger syrup over thepotatoes to serve.

Kielbasa with Peppers and Potatoes

Ingredients

- ❋ 1 tablespoon vegetable oil
- ❋ 1 (16 ounce) packagesmoked kielbasa sausage, diced
- ❋ 6 medium red potatoes, diced
- ❋ 1 red bell pepper, sliced
- ❋ 1 yellow bell pepper, sliced

Directions

- ➤ Heat the oil in a saucepan over medium heat. Place kielbasa and potatoes in thesaucepan. Cover, and cook 25 minutes, stirring occasionally, until potatoes are tender.

- ➤ Mix red bell pepper and yellow bell pepper into the saucepan, and continue cooking 5 minutes, until peppers are just tender.

Potato-Topped Meat Pie

Ingredients

- ❁ 1 pound ground beef
- ❁ 1 medium onion, chopped
- ❁ 3 garlic cloves, minced
- ❁ 1 egg
- ❁ 2tablespoons Worcestershiresauce
- ❁ 1 cup dry bread crumbs salt and pepper to taste
- ❁ 1 (10 ounce) package frozen corn, thawed
- ❁ 1 (10 ounce) package frozen peas, thawed
- ❁ 1 (10.75 ounce) can condensed cream of mushroom soup,undiluted
- ❁ 1/2 cup milk
- ❁ 3 cups mashed potatoes (prepared with milk and butter)

Directions

- ➤ In a large skillet, cook the beef, onion and garlic over medium heat until meat is no longer pink; drain. Cool for 5 minutes. In a bowl, combine theegg, Worcestershire sauce, bread crumbs, salt and pepper.

- ➤ Stir in meat mixture.Transfer to a greased 13-in x 9-in. x 2-in. baking dish. In a bowl, combine the corn, peas, soup and milk. Spread over meat mixture.

- ➤ Top with mashed potatoes. Bake, uncovered, at 375 degrees F for35 minutes or until lightly browned.

Sweet and Spicy Sweet Potatoes

Ingredients

- 2 large sweet potatoes, peeled and cubed
- 3 tablespoons olive oil
- 2 teaspoons packed brown sugar
- 1 1/2 tablespoons paprika
- 1/2 teaspoon ground black pepper
- 1/2 teaspoon onion powder
- 1/2 teaspoon garlic powder
- 1/2 teaspoon poultry seasoning
- 1/2 teaspoon chili powder
- 1 pinch cayenne pepper

Directions

- Preheat an oven to 425 degrees F (220 degrees C).Place the sweet potato chunks into a large mixing bowl. Drizzle with the olive oil, then sprinklethe brown sugar, paprika, black pepper, onion powder, garlic powder, poultry seasoning, chili powder, and cayenne pepper overtop.

- Toss until the potatoes areevenly coated with the seasoning. Spread onto a baking sheet.Bake in the preheated oven for 15 minutes, then turn the potatoes over with a spatula, and continue baking until the sweet potatoes are golden and tender, 10 to 15 minutes more.

Hawaiian Sweet Potato Casserole

Ingredients

- 1 cup light brown sugar

- ❀ 1 teaspoon ground cinnamon
- ❀ 6 large sweet potatoes
- ❀ 1 tablespoon cold butter, cut into pieces
- ❀ 2 teaspoons salt
- ❀ 6 firm bananas, sliced
- ❀ 2 (8 ounce) cans crushed pineapple
- ❀ 1 cup pineapple juice
- ❀ 1 teaspoon lemon juice
- ❀ 2 tablespoons honey

Directions

> ➢ Preheat an oven to 350 degrees F (175 degrees C). Butter a 9x13-inch baking dish. Stir together the brown sugar and cinnamon until evenly blended; set aside.

> ➢ Place the sweet potatoes into a large pot and cover with salted water. Bring to a boil over high heat; reduce heat to medium-low, cover, and simmer until just tender, 15 to 20 minutes. Drain and allow to steam dry for a minute or two; peel and cut into 1/2 inch slices.

> ➢ Layer the potatoes into the prepared baking dish, dot with butter, and sprinkle with salt. Arrange thebananas over the potatoes and sprinkleevenly with thebrown sugar mixture. Top with the crushed pineapple.

> ➢ Whisk together the pineapple juice, lemon juice, andhoney until the honey has dissolved. Pour over the casserole.Bake in the preheated oven until hot and browned on top, about 40 minutes.

German Potato Cheese Soup

Ingredients

- ❀ 4 cups water
- ❀ 2 1/2 cups chicken broth
- ❀ 4 tablespoons chicken soup base

- ❀ 1/2 teaspoon ground black
- ❀ pepper
- ❀ 2 large carrots, finely chopped
- ❀ 4 potatoes, peeled and diced
- ❀ 1 large onion, diced
- ❀ 2 stalks celery, finely chopped
- ❀ 1 red bell pepper, diced
- ❀ 1 cup mayonnaise
- ❀ 8 ounces processed cheese food (eg. Velveeta)
- ❀ 1 cup shredded sharp Cheddar cheese
- ❀ 1/2 cup shredded Swiss cheese
- ❀ 1/4 cup dry potato flakes

Directions

- ➤ In a large stock pot, combine water, chicken broth, chicken soup base, black pepper, carrots, diced potatoes, and onions. Bring to a boil, and then reduce heat. Simmer 15 minutes, or until vegetables are tender, stirring occasionally.

- ➤ Add celery and red bell pepper, and simmer for 5 minutes.Gradually add mayonnaise to hot soup, whisking until smooth. Reduce heat to medium low. Gradually stir in processed cheese, sharp Cheddar cheese, and Swiss cheese; continue stirring until cheese melts, about 5 minutes.

- ➤ Mix in potato flakes. Remove from heat, and let sit for 15 minutes before serving.

Whipped Sweet Potatoes with Pears

Ingredients

- ❀ 8 sweet potatoes
- ❀ 4 pears - peeled, cored and chopped
- ❀ 1 cup evaporated milk
- ❀ 2 teaspoons vanilla extract

* 1/2 cup packed brown sugar

* 4 tablespoons butter

* 1/2 teaspoon ground cinnamon

* 1 pinch freshly grated nutmeg

* 2 tablespoons orange juice

* 1 cup chopped pecans

Directions

> Preheat oven to 350 degrees F (175 degrees C).Prick the sweet potatoes with a fork and bake in the preheated oven1 hour, or until tender.

> Peel the baked sweet potatoes. Place in a medium bowl and whip until smooth.In a medium saucepan over medium heat, gently cook the pears 10 minutes, or until tender.

> Process the pears in a food processor until smooth.In a medium saucepan over medium heat, mix theevaporated milk, vanilla, brown sugar and butter. Heat until scalded. Blend into thesweet potatoes.

> Mix the pear puree, cinnamon, nutmeg, orange juice and pecans into the sweet potato mixture. Transfer to a large baking dish. Bake in the preheated oven 15 minutes, or until lightly browned.

Comfy Potato Soup

Ingredients

* 5 beer bratwursts

* 2 cups water

* 2 large carrots, chopped

* 1/4 large onion, chopped

* 2 (10.75 ounce) cans condensed cream of potato soup

* 2 cups milk

Directions

- ➢ Place the bratwursts and water into a large skillet, and set over medium heat. Bring to a boil, then cover and simmer for 10 minutes. Turn brats, and add more water if needed. Add carrots to the water. Cover and simmer for 10 more minutes.

- ➢ Drain, and slice thebratwurst.While the bratwurst is cooking, pour the milk and potato soup into a saucepan, and set over medium heat.

- ➢ Simmer until the bratwurst are cooked.Stir in the onion, and add the carrots and bratwurst. Cook, stirring occasionally for about 10 minutes.

Grilled Potatoes and Onion

Ingredients

- ❀ 4 potatoes, sliced
- ❀ 1 red onion, sliced
- ❀ 1 teaspoon salt
- ❀ 1 teaspoon ground black pepper
- ❀ 4 tablespoons butter

Directions

- ➢ Preheat grill for medium heat.For each packet, measure out 2 or 3 squares of aluminum foil largeenough to easily wrap the vegetables, and layer one on top of theother.

- ➢ Place some of the potatoes and onion in the center, sprinklewith salt and pepper, and dot with butter. Wrap into a flattenedsquare, and seal theedges.

- ➢ Repeat with remaining potatoes and onion.Place aluminum wrapped packageover indirect heat, and cover.Cook for approximately 30 minutes, turning once. Serve hot off thegrill.

Cheese Potato Puff

Ingredients

- 12 medium potatoes, peeled and cubed
- 2 cups shredded Cheddar or Swiss cheese, divided
- 1 1/4 cups milk
- 1/3 cup butter or margarine, softened
- 1 teaspoon salt
- 2 eggs, beaten

Directions

> Place the potatoes in a saucepan and cover with water; cover and bring to a boil. Cook until tender, about 15-20 minutes. Drain and mash. Add 1-3/4 cups cheese. milk, butter and salt; cook and stir over low heat until cheese and butter are melted. Fold in eggs.

> Spread into a greased 13-in. x 9-in. x 2-in. baking dish. Bake, uncovered, at 350 degrees F for 25-30minutes. Sprinkle with theremaining cheese. Bake 5 minutes longer or until golden brown.

Christian's Crazy Sherpa Potatoes

Ingredients

- 2 tablespoons butter
- 1 clove garlic, chopped
- 1/2 large potato, diced
- 1/4 cup green peas
- 1/4 cup chopped broccoli
- 1/4 cup chopped carrot
- 1/4 cup chopped zucchini

- 1/4 cup chopped green bell pepper
- 1/4 cup shredded Cheddar cheese

Directions

➢ Melt butter over medium heat and saute garlic. Stir in potato, peas, broccoli, carrot, zucchini and bell pepper.

➢ Stirring occasionally,
cook until potatoes start to brown, about 15 minutes. Serve with shredded cheese.

Underground Baked Chicken and Potatoes

Ingredients

- 4 (6 ounce) skinless, boneless chicken breast halves
- 2 tablespoons vegetable oil
- 2 teaspoons garlic salt
- 1/2 teaspoon black pepper
- 2 teaspoons dried oregano
- 4 medium baking potatoes

Directions

➢ Dig a hole about 1 foot into the ground. Place a layer of hot coals on the bottom, and cover with a 1/2 inch layer of dirt.

➢ Rub the chicken breasts with oil, then season with garlic salt, pepper, and oregano. Wrap eachbreast securely in aluminum foil and place into thehole.Cover the hole with about 6 inches of dirt and allow the chicken to cook for 3 to 4 hours.

➢ About 45 minutes before you are ready to eat, wrap the potatoes individually in aluminum foil, and place them in the coals of a campfire to cook. When the potatoes are ready, dig up the chicken and serve with potatoes.

Sour Cream Potato Rolls

Ingredients

- 1/2 cup sour cream
- 1/2 cup water (70 to 80 degrees F)
- 1/2 cup mashed potatoes
- (prepared with milk and butter)
- 1/4 cup butter or margarine, softened
- 2 tablespoons sugar
- 1 teaspoon salt
- 1/2 teaspoon baking soda
- 1/8 teaspoon ground mace
- 3 cups bread flour
- 3 teaspoons active dry yeast

Directions

- In bread machine pan, place all ingredients in order suggested by manufacturer. Select dough setting (check dough after 5 minutes of mixing; add 1 to 2 tablespoons of water or flour if needed).

- When cycle is completed, turn dough onto a lightly floured surface. Punch dough down. Divide into 18 portions; roll each into a ball.

- Place on greased baking sheets. Cover and let rise in a warm placeuntil doubled, about 30 minutes. Bake at 375 degrees F for 10-15 minutes or until golden brown. Serve warm.

Cheesy Breakfast Potatoes

Ingredients

- 1 tablespoon garlic-flavored oil

- 4 1/2 cups cubed potatoes
- 1 cup Canadian bacon, cut into 1/2-inch dice
- 3/4 cup chopped red bell pepper
- 1/4 cup chopped chives or green onions
- 2 cloves garlic, minced
- 1 teaspoon dried basil leaves
- 2 cups Sargento® Shredded Reduced Fat Mild Cheddar Cheese, divided
- Salt and pepper, to taste

Directions

- ➢   Heat oil over medium heat in large skillet. Add potatoes; cook 10 minutes, or until potatoes arebrowned and tender, stirringfrequently.

- ➢ Stir in bacon, red pepper, chives, garlic and basil. Cook 3 minutes, until red pepper is crisp-tender, stirring frequently.

- ➢ Add 1 cupcheese; stir until melted. Season to taste with salt and pepper. Top with remaining cheese.

Potato and Bacon Salad

Ingredients

- 5 eggs
- 4 slices bacon
- 2 tablespoons Dijon mustard, or to taste
- 1 cup mayonnaise
- 3 stalks celery, minced
- 2 pounds small potatoes
- 2 tablespoons chopped fresh parsley
- salt and pepper to taste

Directions

>   Place the potatoes in a pot with enough water to cover, and bring to a boil. Cook for about 20 minutes, or until tender. Drain and cool.Meanwhile, placeeggs in a saucepan and cover with cold water.

> Bring water to a boil and immediately remove from heat. Cover, and let eggs stand in hot water for 10 to 12 minutes. Remove from hot water, and place in a bowl of cold water to cool. Peel theeggs, and place 3 of them into a large bowl.

> Reserve therest for later. Mash theeggs in the bowl with a fork. Stir in themustard, mayonnaise, celery, salt and pepper. Set aside.

> Cook bacon slices in themicrowave for about 4 minutes, until crisp, or fry in a skillet over medium-high heat. Crumble 2 of the baconslices into the mayonnaise mixture.

> Reserve the rest for garnish.Peel and chop the potatoes, and stir into the bowl until evenly coated. Slice the 2 remaining eggs, and place on top of the salad. Crumble theremaining bacon over theeggs, then sprinkle parsley over the top.

Cheesy Ranch New Red Potatoes

Ingredients

- ❀ 12 small new red potatoes, scrubbed and halved
- ❀ 1 cup Ranch-style salad dressing
- ❀ 1 (8 ounce) package shredded Colby-Monterey Jack cheese
- ❀ 1 teaspoon freshly ground black pepper

Directions

> Preheat oven to 350 degrees F (175 degrees C).Place potatoes in a large saucepan over medium heat, and cover with water. Bring to a boil, and cook 10 minutes, or until tender; drain.

> Place cooked potatoes on an ungreased cookie sheet with the cut side up. Spread a spoonful of dressing on thetop of each potato half. Sprinkle with cheese, and lightly dust with pepper. Bake in the preheated oven for 5

minutes, or until cheese is melted.

Ranch Potatoes

Ingredients

- 5 pounds peeled and cubed potatoes
- 1 (8 ounce) package cream cheese,softened
- 1 (1 ounce) package ranch dressing mix
- 4 tablespoons heavy cream (optional)
- 1 pinch salt

Directions

➤ Bring a pot of salted water to a boil. Add potatoes; cook until tender but still firm. Drain, and transfer to a large bowl.

➤ Before mashing potatoes, add the cream cheese, salad dressing, cream and salt.Beat with a mixer until smooth. Serveimmediately.

Hot German Potato Salad I

Ingredients

- 6 potatoes
- 4 largeeggs
- 1 pound bacon
- 1 medium head escarole
- 1/4 cup apple cider vinegar

Directions

> Bring a large pot of salted water to a boil. Add potatoes and cook until tender but still firm, about 15 minutes. Drain, cool and chop.

> Placeeggs in a saucepan and cover with cold water. Bring water to a boil; cover, remove from heat, and let eggs stand in hot water for10 to 12 minutes. Remove from hot water, cool, peel and chop.

Place bacon in a large, deep skillet. Cook over medium high heat until evenly brown. Drain, crumble and set aside. Reserve bacon drippings.

> Place potatoes in skillet with reserved bacon dripping, fry until heated through. Add escarole, bacon, eggs and vinegar. Cook until escarole becomes wilted and serve warm.

Potato Pancakes III

Ingredients

- 3 large potatoes, peeled and quartered
- 1/4 cup milk
- 3 tablespoons butter
- 2 cloves garlic, minced
- 1/4 cup finely chopped cooked ham
- 1/4 cup shredded Cheddar cheese
- salt and pepper to taste
- 1/4 cup oil for frying

Directions

> Bring a large pot of salted water to a boil. Add potatoes, and cook until tender but still firm, about 15 minutes. Drain, cool and shred.In a medium saucepan over medium heat, mix milk, butter and garlic.

> Bring to a gentle boil, then mix in potatoes, ham and
Cheddar cheese. Season with salt and pepper, and cook, stirring occasionally, until the mixture reaches a dough-like consistency.

> Heat oil in a large skillet over medium high heat. Drop potato mixture by rounded spoonfuls into the oil, and cook, turning once, until lightly browned on both sides.

Chrysanthemum Sweet Potatoes

Ingredients

* ❀ 6 medium sweet potatoes, peeled and cubed
* ❀ 1/4 cup crushed pineapple,in juice
* ❀ 1/4 cup honey
* ❀ 3 tablespoons butter, melted
* ❀ 1/2 teaspoon grated lemon zest
* ❀ 1/2 cup chrysanthemum petals

Directions

> Preheat the oven to 350 degrees F (175 degrees C). Butter a 2 quart baking dish. Place the sweet potatoes into a large pot, and fill with enough water to cover. Bring to a boil, and cook until tender, about 15 minutes. Drain.

> Mash potatoes with pineapple, honey and butter using a whisk or electric mixer until smooth and creamy. Stir in the lemon zest and chrysanthemum petals. Transfer to the prepared baking dish. Bake for 20 to 30 minutes in the preheated oven, until hot and fragrant.

Fiery Red Pepper Potatoes

Ingredients

* ❀ 1 1/2 tablespoons soy sauce
* ❀ 1 pinch cayenne pepper, or to taste

- ❀ 1 1/2 tablespoons vegetable oil
- ❀ 3 potatoes, cut into bite sized pieces
- ❀ 4 green onions, chopped
- ❀ 1 large red bell pepper, chopped
- ❀ 2 teaspoons sesame seeds

Directions

- ➤ Whisk the soy sauce and cayenne pepper in a small bowl until the cayenne pepper is dissolved; set aside.Heat the vegetable oil in a large skillet over medium-high heat; cook the potatoes in the hot oil until golden brown, about 5 minutes.

- ➤ Stir in the onions, bell pepper, and sesame seeds; cook 1 minute more. Pour the soy sauce mixture over the potatoes; cook and stir untilthe liquid is completely absorbed, 1 to 2 minutes.

Chicken Potato Bake

Ingredients

- ❀ 1 (3 pound) broiler-fryer chicken, cut up
- ❀ 1 pound red potatoes, cut into chunks
- ❀ 1/2 cup prepared Italian dressing
- ❀ 1 tablespoon Italian seasoning
- ❀ 1/2 cup grated Parmesan cheese

Directions

- ➤ Place chicken in a greased 13-in. x 9-in. x 2-in. baking dish. Arrangepotatoes around chicken. Drizzle with dressing; sprinkle with Italian seasoning and Parmesan cheese.

- ➤ Cover and bake at 400 degrees F for 20 minutes. Uncover; bake 20-30 minutes longer or untilpotatoes are tender and chicken juices run clear.

Sweet Potato, Pear and Pineapple Bread Pudding

Ingredients

- 1 cup sour cream
- 3/4 cup whole milk
- 2/3 cup superfine sugar
- 3 eggs, beaten
- 1 tablespoon baking powder
- 1 teaspoon vanilla extract
- 1 teaspoon ground ginger
- 1 cup chopped canned pears
- 1 cup canned crushed pineapple, drained
- 1 (16 ounce) can sweet potatoes, drained and cut into chunks
- 4 cups French bread cubes
- 1/3 cup packed light brown sugar
- 1/4 cup all-purpose flour
- 1 teaspoon freshly grated orangezest
- 1/4 cup unsalted butter, melted
- 1 cup chopped pecans

Directions

- ➤ Preheat the oven to 375 degrees F (190 degrees C). Butter a 1 quart casserole dish.In a large bowl, whisk together thesour cream, milk, sugar, eggs, baking powder, ginger and vanilla.

- ➤ Stir in the pears, pineapple and sweet potatoes just to coat, then add the bread cubes and mix until evenly distributed. Pour into the prepared baking dish. Set aside.

> In a separate bowl, stir together the brown sugar, flour and orange zest. Briefly stir in the butter and pecans. Sprinkle over the top of the bread pudding. Bake for 30 minutes in the preheated oven, until evenly puffed up and browned.

Lebanese Chicken and Potatoes

Ingredients

- 8 cut up chicken pieces
- 8 medium potatoes, peeled and quartered
- salt to taste ground white pepper to taste
- 4 cloves garlic, crushed
- 1/2 cup extra virgin olive oil
- 1 cup fresh lemon juice

Directions

> Preheat oven to 425 degrees F (220 degrees C).Place chicken and potatoes in a large baking dish. Season generously with salt and white pepper.In a bowl, stir together garlic, olive oil, and lemon juice.

> Pour over chicken and potatoes. Cover dish with foil.Bake in preheated oven for 30 minutes. Remove foil, increase heat to 475 degrees F (245 degrees C), and cook until chicken and potatoes are golden, about 30 minutes.

Potato and Bean Enchiladas

Ingredients

- 1 pound potatoes, peeled and diced

* 1 teaspoon cumin
* 1 teaspoon chili powder
* 1 teaspoon salt
* 1 tablespoon ketchup
* 1 pound fresh tomatillos, husks removed
* 1 large onion, chopped
* 1 bunch fresh cilantro, coarsely chopped, divided
* 2 (12 ounce) packages corn tortilla
* 1 (15.5 ounce) can pinto beans, drained
* 1 (12 ounce) package queso fresco
* oil for frying

Directions

> Preheat oven to 400 degreesF (205 degrees C). In a bowl, toss diced potatoes together with cumin, chili powder, salt, and ketchup, and place in an oiled baking dish. Bake in the preheated oven for 20 to 25 minutes, or until tender.

> Meanwhile, boil tomatillos and chopped onion in water to cover for10 minutes. Set aside to cool. Once cooled, puree with half of thecilantro until smooth.

> Fry tortillas individually in a small amount of hot oil until soft.Mix potatoes together with pinto beans, 1/2 cheese, and 1/2 cilantro. Fill tortillas with potato mixture, and roll up.

> Place seam side down in an oiled 9x13 inch baking dish. Spoon tomatillo sauce
over enchiladas, and spread remaining cheese over sauce. Bake for20 minutes, or until hot and bubbly.

Creamy Potato and Leek Soup

Ingredients

- ❀ 6 potatoes, peeled and cubed
- ❀ 1 (14.5 ounce) can chicken broth
- ❀ 2 leeks, chopped
- ❀ 2 teaspoons margarine
- ❀ 1 1/2 cups heavy whipping cream

Directions

- ➤ In a medium pot over medium heat, combine the potatoes and broth and allow to simmer for 20 minutes, or until potatoes are tender.

- ➤ In a separate skillet over medium heat, saute the leeks in the butter or margarine for 5 to 10 minutes, or until tender.

- ➤ Add the leeks and the cream to the potatoes and stir well. (Note: This is the point I liketo take a potato masher and slightly thicken the soup.)

Mexicali Beef Potato Topper

Ingredients

- ❀ 1 pound ground beef
- ❀ 1 (10.75 ounce) can Campbell's® Condensed Cheddar CheeseSoup
- ❀ 1 cup Pace® Chunky Salsa
- ❀ 4 hot baked potatoes, split sour cream (optional)
- ❀ sliced pitted ripe olives (optional)

Directions

- Cook the beef in a 10-inch skillet over medium-high heat until well browned, stirring often to separate meat. Pour off any fat. Reduce the heat to medium.

- Stir the soup and salsa in the skillet and cook until the mixture is hot and bubbling. Spoon the beef mixture over the potatoes. Top with the sour cream and olives, if desired.

Cheesy Bacon Potatoes

Ingredients

- 4 cups hot mashed potatoes
- 8 ounces KNUDSEN Sour Cream
- 6 slices OSCAR MAYER Center Cut Bacon, crisply cooked, crumbled
- 1 cup shredded mild Cheddar cheese
- 2 green onions, sliced

Directions

- Mix all ingredients until well blended. Serve while hot

Whipped Cardamom Sweet Potatoes

Ingredients

- 5 pounds sweet potatoes
- 1/2 cup unsalted butter, softened
- 1/2 teaspoon ground cardamom salt and pepper to taste
- 1 quart vegetable oil for frying
- 3/4 pound thinly sliced shallots

Directions

- ➤ Preheat oven to 400 degrees F (200 degrees C).Prick sweet potatoes with a fork. Bake for 1 hour or until tender; reduce oven temperature to 250 degrees F (120 degrees C).

- ➤ Scoop potato flesh out of skins and place into a mixing bowl. Slowly beat in the butter and cardamom. Whip until potatoes aresmooth and fluffy; season with salt and white pepper. Keep warm in oven.

- ➤ In a large deep skillet, heat 1 inch of oil until shimmering. Add 1/2 of the shallots to oil and fry until crisp. Transfer the shallots, using a slotted spoon, to a paper towel; season with salt. Repeat theprocess until all the shallots are fried. Garnish top of potatoes with shallots.

Zesty Potato-Ham Casserole

Ingredients

- ❀ 2 1/2 cups Cook's® brand Bone-in Ham, leftovers or ham steak, cut into 1/2-inch cubes
- ❀ 9 medium potatoes, peeled and chopped *
- ❀ 1/2 medium onion, chopped
- ❀ 1 medium green pepper, seeds removed, chopped
- ❀ 1 1/2 teaspoons pepper
- ❀ 8 ounces sharp Cheddar cheese, grated
- ❀ 1 medium tomato, seeds removed, chopped

Directions

- ➤ Preheat grill (medium setting) **. Make foil packet by placing potatoes, onions and green peppers on the center of foil sheet.Sprinkle pepper over entire mixture and stir to mix well.

- ➤ Bring up foil sides and double fold top and sides to seal, leaving room for heat circulation inside. Place on grill for 20 minutes or until potatoes aretender.

> Remove from grill; add cubed ham, stirring slightly to mix. Reseal and return to grill for approximately 10 minutes. Remove from grill and sprinkle cheese& tomatoes over entire mixture.

> Return to grill, leaving the packet unsealed, but the grill lid closed, and cook for
approximately 5 minutes or until cheese is melted. Remove from grill and serve.

Meat and Potato Casserole

Ingredients

- ❀ 3 pounds top round, London Broil cut, cubed
- ❀ 5 potatoes - peeled and cubed
- ❀ 1 red onion, sliced
- ❀ 1 green bell pepper, chopped
- ❀ 1 1/2 pounds fresh mushrooms, sliced
- ❀ 16 ounces red wine and vinegar salad dressing

Directions

> Preheat oven to 350 degrees F (175 degrees C).
In a large skillet over medium high heat, saute thecubed meat until well browned on all sides. Place meat in a 10x15 inch baking dish.

> Next, place the potatoes, onion, green bell pepper and mushrooms over the meat. Top with the salad dressing and cover with foil. Bake at 350 degrees F (175 degrees C) for 1 hour, or until potatoes are tender.

Potato Casserole

Ingredients

- ❀ 1 (30 ounce) package frozen hash brown potatoes
- ❀ 2 cups shredded Cheddar cheese
- ❀ 1 (16 ounce) container sour cream
- ❀ 1 (10.75 ounce) can condensed cream of mushroom soup
- ❀ 1 onion, chopped
- ❀ 1 cup butter
- ❀ 3 cups crushed corn flakes

Directions

> Preheat oven to 425 degrees F (220 degrees C).
Pour the hash browns into a lightly greased 9x13 inch baking dish. In a large bowl, combine the cheese, sour cream and soup.

> In a large skillet over medium heat, combine the onion with 1 stick butter and saute for 5 minutes. Add this to the soup mixture and spread this over the potatoes in the dish.

> Next, arrange the crushed corn flakes over all in the dish. Melt theremaining stick of butter and pour this evenly over the corn flakes.Bake at 425 degrees F (220 degrees C) for 1 hour.

Argentinean Potato Salad

Ingredients
- ❀ 4 russet potatoes - peeled, boiled, and cubed
- ❀ 3 hard cooked eggs, chopped
- ❀ 1 (10 ounce) can mixed vegetables
- ❀ 1/2 cup mayonnaise
- ❀ 1/2 teaspoon black pepper

- ❀ 1/2 teaspoon ground mustard
- ❀ 1/2 tablespoon fresh lemon juice
- ❀ 1/2 teaspoon dried dill weed
- ❀ 5 tablespoons chopped pimiento-stuffed olives
- ❀ salt and black pepper to taste

Directions

- ➤ Bring a large pot of lightly salted water to a boil. Cook peeled potatoes until tender but still firm, about 15 minutes. Drain, cool, and cube.

- ➤ Placeeggs in a saucepan, and cover with cold water. Bring to a boil, and immediately remove from heat. Cover pan, and let eggsstand in hot water for 10 to 12 minutes.

- ➤ Remove from hot water and allow to cool. Peel and chop theeggs, and toss together with thepotatoes and vegetables in a large mixing or serving bowl.

- ➤ In a separate bowl, combine the mayonnaise, 1/2 teaspoon black pepper, ground mustard, lemon juice, dill weed, and green olives.

- ➤ Stir to blend. Pour dressing over the potato mixture, season with salt and pepper, and toss to coat. Cover, and refrigerate for 1 hour, or overnight.

Blue Green and Red Potato Salad

Ingredients
- ❀ 10 small red potatoes
- ❀ 4 ounces crumbled blue cheese
- ❀ 3 large Granny Smith apples -peeled, cored and sliced
- ❀ 3 green onions, sliced
- ❀ 1/2 cup sliced celery
- ❀ 1/2 cup sour cream
- ❀ 3/4 cup mayonnaise
- ❀ salt and pepper to taste

Directions

➢ Place the potatoes into a large pot and cover with salted water. Bring to a boil over high heat, then reduce heat to medium-low,cover, and simmer until tender, 15 to 20 minutes.

➢ Drain and allow to steam dry for a minute or two. Transfer potatoes to a large bowl and allow to cool to room temperature.

➢ Cut potatoes into bite size pieces and return to bowl. Stir in the bluecheese, apples, green onions, and celery. Mix in the sour cream and mayonnaise; season with salt and pepper to taste.

Swiss Scalloped Potatoes

Ingredients

❀ 5 medium potatoes, peeled and thinly sliced

❀ 1 small onion, thinly sliced

❀ 1 (4 ounce) jar diced pimientos, drained

❀ 3 garlic cloves, minced

❀ 2 cups shredded Swiss cheese, divided

❀ 3/4 teaspoon salt

❀ 1/4 teaspoon pepper

❀ 1 (14.5 ounce) can chicken broth

❀ 2 tablespoons butter or margarine

Directions

➢ In a greased shallow 3-qt. baking dish, layer a third of the potatoes, onion, pimientos, garlic and Swiss cheese; sprinkle with 1/4
teaspoon salt and a dash of pepper. Repeat layers once.

➢ Top with remaining potatoes, onion, pimientos, garlic, salt and pepper. Pour broth over the top; dot with butter. Bake, uncovered, at 375 degrees F for 1 hour.

> Sprinkle with remaining cheese. Bake 30 minutes longer or until liquid is absorbed and cheese is melted. Let stand for 10 minutes before serving.

Scalloped Potatoes 'n' Franks

Ingredients

- ❀ 2 tablespoons chopped onion
- ❀ 3 tablespoons butter or margarine1/4 cup all-purpose flour
- ❀ 1 1/2 teaspoons salt
- ❀ 1/8 teaspoon pepper
- ❀ 2 cups milk
- ❀ 1 cup shredded Swiss cheese
- ❀ 2 tablespoons minced fresh parsley
- ❀ 5 medium potatoes, peeled and thinly sliced
- ❀ 8 hot dogs, halved lengthwise and sliced

Directions

> In a saucepan, saute onion in butter until tender. Stir in flour, salt and pepper until blended. Gradually add milk. Bring to a boil over medium heat; cook and stir for 2 minutes.

> Remove from the heat;stir in cheese until melted. Add parsley. Place half of the potatoes in a greased 2-qt. baking dish; top with half of the sauce. Arrange hot dogs over the sauce. Top with remaining potatoes and sauce.

> Cover and bake at 350 degrees F for 1-1/2 hours or until bubbly. Uncover and bake 10 minutes longer or until lightly browned.

Creamy Smashed Potatoes

Ingredients

- 2 1/2 pounds potatoes, peeled and quartered
- 4 ounces reduced fat cream cheese
- 1/2 cup reduced-fat sour cream
- 1/2 teaspoon onion salt
- 1/2 teaspoon salt Dash pepper

Directions

- Place potatoes in a saucepan and cover with water. Bring to a boil. Reduce heat; cover and cook for 15-20 minutes or until tender.

- Drain and place in a large bowl; mash the potatoes. Add the remaining ingredients; mix well.Transfer to a greased 8-in. square baking dish. Bake, uncovered, at 350 degrees F for 30-35 minutes or until lightly browned.

Ultra Creamy Mashed Potatoes

Ingredients

- 3 1/2 cups SwansonВ® Chicken Broth (regular, Natural GoodnessВ „ў or Certified Organic)
- 5 large potatoes, cut into 1-inch pieces
- 1/2 cup light cream
- 2 tablespoons butter
- Generous dash ground black pepper

Directions

- Heat broth and potatoes in 3-quart saucepan over high heat to a boil.Reduce heat to medium. Cover and cook for 10 minutes or until potatoes are tender. Drain, reserving broth.

- Mash potatoes with 1/4 cup broth, cream, butter and black pepper. Add additional broth, if needed, until desired consistency.

- For an interesting twist: Stir 1/2 cup sour cream, 3 slices bacon cooked and crumbled (reserve some for garnish) and 1/4 cup chopped fresh chives into hot mashed potatoes. Sprinkle with remaining bacon.

Potato Yeast Bread

Ingredients

- ❊ 1 medium potato, peeled and cubed
- ❊ 1 1/2 cups water
- ❊ 1 tablespoon milk
- ❊ 5 tablespoons butter or margarine, softened, divided
- ❊ 5 cups all-purpose flour 3/4 cup sugar
- ❊ 1 (.25 ounce) package active dry yeast
- ❊ 1 1/2 teaspoons salt
- ❊ 1 teaspoon grated lemon peel
- ❊ 1/2 teaspoon ground nutmeg
- ❊ 3 eggs, lightly beaten cup water; cool to 120 degrees F-130 degrees F.

Directions

- Mash potato; measure 1/2 cup (discard any remaining potato). Add milk and 1 tablespoon butter to mashed potato (mixture will be soft).

- In a mixing bowl, combine 3 cups flour, sugar, yeast, salt, lemon peel and nutmeg. Melt remaining butter; cool to 120 degrees F-130 degrees F. Add the cooled potato water and melted butter to flour mixture; beat until moistened.

- Add eggs and mashed potatomixture; beat until smooth. Stir in enough remaining flour to form a firm dough. Turn onto a floured surface; knead until smooth and elastic, about 6-8 minutes. Place in a greased bowl, turning once to grease top.

> Cover and let rise in a warm place until doubled, about 1 hour.Punch dough down; turn onto a lightly floured surface. Shape into two loaves. Place in two greased 8-in. x 4-in. x 2-in.

> loaf pans.Cover and let rise until doubled, about 1 hour. Bake at 325 degrees F for 45-50 minutes or until golden brown. Remove from pans to wire racks to cool.

Cheesy Potatoes

Ingredients

- 4 large potatoes, peeled and sliced
- 1 small onion, finely chopped
- 1 1/2 cups shredded Cheddar cheese
- 1 teaspoon margarine
- salt and pepper to taste

Directions

> Layer the potatoes, onion, cheese, salt and pepper into a microwave safe casserole dish. Once finished layering, place 1 teaspoon of margarine on the top of the uppermost layer. Cover and cook in the microwave oven on HIGH for 10 minutes.

> Remove the dish from themicrowave and stir before cooking for another 10 minutes or until done. Stir well and serve.

Jalapeno Potatoes

Ingredients

- 4 boiling potatoes
- 2 cups milk

- 3 tablespoons flour
- 1 teaspoon salt
- 1/4 teaspoon ground black pepper
- 1/4 teaspoon garlic powder
- 1 cup shredded sharp Cheddar cheese
- 1 (4 ounce) can diced jalapeno peppers
- 1 (2 ounce) jar chopped pimentos, drained

Directions

- Preheat an oven to 350 degrees F (175 degrees C). Grease a 2-quart casserole dish.Bring a large pot of water to a boil; cook the potatoes in the boiling water until just tender, 15 to 18 minutes.

- Drain and allow to cool to the touch before peeling and slicing thin. Place the sliced potatoes in a large bowl.Pour the milk into a saucepan over medium heat; gradually whisk the flour, salt, pepper, and garlic powder into the warming milk until smooth.

- Continue heating and stirring until the liquid is boiling and thickened. Add the Cheddar cheese and jalapenopeppers; cook and stir until the cheese is completely melted. Pour the sauceover the potatoes. Scatter the pimentos over the mixture; pour into theprepared dish.Bake until the potatoes are completely tender, about 30 minutes.

Baked Potato Salad with Dill

Ingredients

- 4 baking potatoes
- 4 ounces fresh bean sprouts
- 1/4 cup coarsely chopped walnuts
- 4 celery, thinly sliced
- 4 radishes, sliced
- 3 tablespoons chopped fresh dill weed

- ❋ 2 tablespoons chopped fresh parsley
- ❋ 1/3 cup mayonnaise
- ❋ 2 tablespoons lemon juice
- ❋ 4 teaspoons Dijon-style prepared mustard
- ❋ 1/4 teaspoon curry powder

Directions

> Preheat over to 400 degrees F (200 degrees C). Pierce the potatoes with a fork, and bake in the preheated over for about an hour, oruntil tender.

> Remove from oven, let cool, and then chill until cold.Peel and cube the potatoes, and then add to a large bowl along with the bean sprouts, walnuts, celery, radishes, dill weed and parsley.

> Whisk together them mayonnaise, lemon juice, mustard and curry powder. Pour dressing over potato mixture; toss to coat. Cover and refrigerate until ready to serve.

Ham 'n' Cheese Potato Salad

Ingredients

- ❋ 2 1/2 pounds red potatoes
- ❋ 1 cup mayonnaise
- ❋ 1/2 cup sour cream
- ❋ 2 tablespoons Dijon mustard
- ❋ 1 teaspoon celery seed
- ❋ 1/2 teaspoon salt
- ❋ 1/4 teaspoon pepper
- ❋ 8 ounces Monterey Jack cheese, cubed
- ❋ 2 cups diced fully cooked ham
- ❋ 3/4 cup chopped fresh tomatoes
- ❋ 1/4 cup sliced green onions

* 1/4 cup minced fresh parsley

Directions

> ➤ Place potatoes in a large saucepan and cover with water. Bring to a boil. Reduce heat; cover and cook for 15-20 minutes or until tender. Drain.

> ➤ Meanwhile, in a large salad bowl, combine mayonnaise, sour cream, mustard, celery seed, salt and pepper; mix well. Cut potatoes into cubes.

> ➤ Add to mayonnaise mixture and toss to coat. Add remaining ingredients; mix well. Cover and refrigerate for at least 2 hours.

Faux Bombay Potatoes

Ingredients

* 3 turnips, diced
* 1/4 cup vegetable oil
* 1/2 teaspoon yellow mustard seed
* 1/2 teaspoon black mustard seed
* 1 1/2 teaspoons ground red pepper
* 1 teaspoon ground turmeric salt to taste

Directions

> ➤ Place the turnips into a large pot and cover with salted water. Bring to a boil over high heat, then reduce heat to medium-low, cover,and simmer until tender, 15 to 20 minutes. Drain and allow to steam dry for a minute or two.

> ➤ Heat the oil in a large skillet over medium-high heat. Fry the yellow mustard seeds, black mustard seeds, and turmeric in the oil until the mustard seeds begin to pop.

> ➤ Add the turnips to the skillet; cook and stir until the turnips are completely heated through, about 5minutes. Season with salt to serve.

Potato Squash Cakes

Ingredients

- ❀ 2 cups shredded potatoes
- ❀ 1 cup shredded yellow squash
- ❀ 1/2 cup chopped onion
- ❀ 1 egg
- ❀ 4 tablespoons self-rising flour
- ❀ 1/4 teaspoon garlic salt
- ❀ salt and pepper to taste
- ❀ 1/4 cup cooking oil

Directions

➤ In a large bowl, combine potatoes, squash, onion, egg, flour, garlic salt, salt, and pepper. If the batter is too thin, add more flour; if too thick, add milk. Form batter into 3-inch patties.

➤ Cover the bottom of a large skillet with just enough oil to cover thebottom of the pan, and heat over medium-high heat. Place patties in hot oil, and cook until golden brown on each side; drain on paper towels.

Benny's Potato Salad

Ingredients

- ❀ 2 1/2 pounds potatoes, cubed
- ❀ 4 hard-cooked eggs, peeled and chopped
- ❀ 1/3 cup chopped green olives
- ❀ 1/3 cup dill pickle relish
- ❀ 1/4 cup sweet pickle relish

- 1/4 cup chopped green onion
- 1/2 cup mayonnaise
- 3 teaspoons yellow mustard
- 3 teaspoons brown mustard
- 1 teaspoon white wine vinegar
- 1 teaspoon garlic powder
- 1 teaspoon ground black pepper
- 1 teaspoon ground white pepper
- 1/2 teaspoon salt
- 2 teaspoons celery seed
- 1/2 teaspoon dill seed
- 1 teaspoon chopped fresh dill

Directions

> Place potatoes in a large pot with enough water to cover. Bring to a boil, and cook for about 5 minutes, until tender but not mushy. Drain in a colander, and run under cold water to cool.

> Set aside. In a large serving bowl, Stir together the eggs, green olives, dill and sweet pickle relishes, green onion, mayonnaise, yellow and brown mustards, and wine vinegar.

> Season with garlic powder, blackpepper, white pepper, salt, celery seed, dill seed, and dill. Mix well, and stir in potatoes until coated. Chill for at least 2 hours to allow the flavors to blend.

Spicy Sweet Potato Soup

Ingredients

- 1/2 cup sour cream
- 1 teaspoon grated lime zest
- 2 large sweet potatoes, peeled and cubed

* 1 tablespoon butter
* 1 onion, sliced
* 2 cloves garlic, sliced
* 4 cups chicken stock
* 1/2 teaspoon ground cumin
* 1/4 teaspoon crushed red pepper flakes
* 2 tablespoons grated fresh ginger root
* 1/4 cup smooth peanut butter
* 1 lime, juiced
* 2 tablespoons chopped fresh cilantro
* salt to taste
* 1 large roma (plum) tomato, seeded and diced

Directions

> In a small bowl, stir together the sour cream and lime zest. Set aside in the refrigerator to allow the flavors to blend. Melt butter in a large pot over medium heat.

> Add onion and garlic, and cook for about 5 minutes, until softened. Add sweet potatoes, and chicken stock. Season with cumin, chili flakes and ginger. Bring to a boil. Reduce heat to low, cover, and simmer for 15 minutes, until potatoes are tender.

> Puree the soup using an immersion blender or regular blender. If using a counter top blender, puree in small batches, filling theblender just a bit past half way to avoid spillage. Whisk peanutbutter into the soup, and heat through. Stir in lime juice, and salt.

> Ladle into warm bowls, and top with a dollop of the reserved sour cream, a few pieces of diced tomato, and a sprinkle of cilantro.

Pumpkin, Sweet Potato, Leek and Coconut Milk

Ingredients

- ❀ 1 tablespoon vegetable oil
- ❀ 1 onion, finely chopped
- ❀ 1 leek, chopped
- ❀ 1 pound peeled and diced pumpkin
- ❀ 3/4 pound sweet potato, peeled and cubed
- ❀ 1 quart vegetable broth
- ❀ 1 1/4 cups light coconut milk

Directions

- ➤ Heat the oil in a soup pot over medium heat. Add the onion and leek, and cook for a few minutes, until soft. Stir in the pumpkin, sweet potato, and vegetable broth. Bring to a boil, then cover and reduce heat to low.

- ➤ Simmer for about 15 minutes, until vegetables are tender. Mash vegetables coarsely using a potato masher. Stir in the coconut milk, season with salt and pepper, and serve.

Twice Baked Sweet Potatoes with Ricotta Cheese

Ingredients

- ❀ 3 medium sweet potatoes
- ❀ 1 teaspoon olive oil
- ❀ 2 shallots, finely chopped
- ❀ 1/2 cup fat-free ricotta cheese
- ❀ 1/4 teaspoon salt
- ❀ 1/4 teaspoon ground black pepper

- 🏵 1/4 teaspoon ground ginger
- 🏵 1 tablespoon brown sugar
- 🏵 1/4 cup grated Parmesan cheese
- 🏵 2 1/2 tablespoons chopped fresh sage

Directions

> Preheat oven to 400 degrees F (200 degrees C). Pierce potatoes with a fork and bake until soft, about 1 hour. Remove from oven and cool until potatoes can behandled, about 20 minutes.

> Reduce oven temperature to 350 degrees F (175 degrees C). Grease a large baking sheet.Meanwhile, place olive oil in small skillet over medium heat.

> Add shallots and cook and stir until softened and beginning to brown, about 10 minutes. Set aside.Cut potatoes in half lengthwise and scoop out pulp, leaving a thin shell.

> Set shells aside. Place pulp into a blender or food processor and blend until smooth. Add ricotta, salt, pepper, ginger, and sugar to the blender; blend until smooth.

> Return potato mixture to a bowl; stir in shallots, Parmesan cheese, and sage. Spoon mixture back into potato skins. Place potatoes on prepared baking sheet. Bake until heated through, about 30 minutes.

Chicken Sauerkraut Potato Bake

Ingredients

- 🏵 2 cloves garlic, minced
- 🏵 1 tablespoon butter
- 🏵 1 (32 ounce) jar sauerkraut, drained
- 🏵 1 (2 1/2 pound) whole chicken, cut into pieces, skin removed
- 🏵 1 (15 ounce) can whole new potatoes, drained

Directions

➤ Preheat an oven to 350 degrees F (175 degrees C). Heat garlic and butter in a small skillet over medium heat. Cook and stir until garlic softens, about 2 minutes. Reserve.

➤ Spoon the sauerkraut into the bottom of a 9x13 inch baking dish; top with the chicken pieces. Scatter potatoes around the chicken, and sprinkle with the cooked garlic. Spoon some of the sauerkraut over the top of the chicken.

➤ Cover dish with aluminum foil. Bake in preheated oven until the chicken cooked through, and very tender, about 1 1/2 hours.

Orange Sweet Potatoes

Ingredients

❀ 8 sweet potatoes

❀ 2/3 cup packed brown sugar

❀ 4 teaspoons cornstarch

❀ 1/2 teaspoon salt

❀ 1/2 teaspoon ground cinnamon

❀ 1 cup orange juice

❀ 1/4 cup honey

❀ 3 tablespoons butter or margarine

❀ 2 tablespoons water

❀ 2 tablespoons grated orange peel

❀ 1/2 cup chopped walnuts

Directions

➤ Place sweet potatoes in a Dutch oven or soup kettle and cover with water. Bring to a boil. Reduce heat; cover and simmer for 25-30minutes or until tender. Drain. When potatoes are cool, peel and cut into 1/2-in. slices.

➤ Arrange in a greasedshallow 3-qt. baking dish; set aside. In a saucepan, combine the brown sugar, cornstarch, salt and cinnamon.

> Stir in the orange juice, honey, butter, water and orange peel. Bring to a boil; cook and stir for 2 minutes or until thickened.

> Stir in walnuts. Pour the mixture over the potatoes. Bake,uncovered, at 350 degrees F for 25 minutes or until heated through.

Cheesy Potatoes n Peppers

Ingredients

* 2 cups chopped onions
* 6 tablespoons butter or margarine
* 6 tablespoons all-purposeflour
* 1/2 teaspoon salt
* 1/2 teaspoon pepper
* 4 cups milk
* 2 cups shredded Swiss cheese
* 4 pounds potatoes, peeled and thinly sliced
* 2 (7 ounce) jars roasted red peppers, coarsely chopped

Directions

> In a large skillet, saute onion in butter until tender. Whisk in flour, salt and pepper until blended. Gradually add milk. Bring to a boil over medium heat. Cook and stir for 2 minutes or until sauce is thickened.

> Remove from the heat. Stir in cheese until smooth.Place half of the potatoes in two greased 11-in. x 7-in. x 2-in. baking dishes. Pour half of sauce over potatoes. Top with half to two-thirds of peppers and remaining potatoes.

> Pour remaining sauce over potatoes. Sprinkle with remaining peppers.Cover; bake at 350 degrees F for 1-1/4 hours. Uncover and bake 10-15 minutes longer or until potatoes are tender and sauce is thickened.

Tangy Potato Salad

Ingredients

- ❀ 12 medium red potatoes
- ❀ 1 medium onion, finely chopped
- ❀ 3 hard-cooked eggs, chopped
- ❀ 2 dill pickles, finely chopped
- ❀ 2 tablespoons snipped fresh parsley
- ❀ 3/4 cup chicken broth
- ❀ 3/4 cup mayonnaise or salad dressing
- ❀ 1 1/2 teaspoons salt
- ❀ 1/2 teaspoon pepper
- ❀ 1/4 teaspoon garlic powder
- ❀ 2 tomatoes, cubed
- ❀ 6 bacon strips, cooked and crumbled

Directions

- ➢ Cook potatoes in boiling salted water until tender. Drain; cool slightly. Peel and slice potatoes; combine with onion, eggs, pickles and parsley in a large salad bowl.

- ➢ Set aside. Heat chicken broth until warm; remove from the heat. Add mayonnaise, salt, pepper and garlic powder; mix until smooth.

- ➢ Pour over potato mixture and mix lightly. Cover and chill. Just before serving, gently stir in tomatoes and bacon.

Scalloped Cheese Potatoes

Ingredients

* 4 pounds potatoes, peeled and thinly sliced
* 2 (10.75 ounce) cans condensed cream of mushroom soup,
* undiluted
* 1/4 cup butter or margarine, divided
* 2 cups shredded sharp Cheddar cheese, divided

Directions

> In a large bowl, combine potatoes and soup. Layer half of themixture in a greased 13-in. x 9-in. x 2-in. baking dish. Dot with half of the butter and sprinkle with half of the cheese.

> Repeat layers. Bake, uncovered, at 350 degrees F for 60-70 minutes or until the potatoes are tender.

Norwegian Parsley Potatoes

Ingredients

* 2 pounds small red new potatoes
* 1/2 cup butter or margarine
* 1/4 cup chopped fresh parsley
* 1/4 teaspoon dried marjoram

Directions

> Cook potatoes in boiling salted water for 15 minutes or until tender. Cool slightly. With a sharp knife, remove one narrow strip of skin around the middle of each potato.

> In a large skillet, melt butter; add parsley and marjoram. Add the potatoes and stir gently until coated and heated through.

Cheesiest Potatoes Casserole

Ingredients

- ❋ 8 large potatoes, peeled and sliced
- ❋ 1/3 cup all-purpose flour, divided
- ❋ 1 (8 ounce) package Cheddar cheese, sliced
- ❋ salt and pepper to taste
- ❋ 1/2 teaspoon paprika
- ❋ 1 cup milk

Directions

> Preheat oven to 250 degrees F (120 degrees C).In a 2 quart casserole dish layer 1/3 of the potatoes, then 1/3 of theflour and 1/3 of the cheese.

> Repeat layering 2 more times, ending with cheese. Season with salt, pepper and paprika. Pour milk over top; use more or less, to reach 2/3 of height of casserole dish.Bake in preheated oven for 1 hour.

German Potato Salad

Ingredients

- ❋ 4 potatoes
- ❋ 4 slices bacon
- ❋ 1 tablespoon all-purpose flour
- ❋ 2 tablespoons white sugar
- ❋ 1/3 cup water

* 1/4 cup white wine vinegar
* 1/2 cup chopped green onions salt and pepper to taste

Directions

> Bring a large pot of salted water to a boil. Add potatoes; cook until tender but still firm, about 15 minutes. Drain, cool and chop.

> Place bacon in a large, deep skillet. Cook over medium high heat until evenly brown. Drain, crumble and set aside. Reserve bacon fat.

> Add the flour, sugar, water and vinegar to skillet and cook in reserved bacon fat over medium heat until dressing is thick.

> Add bacon, potatoes and green onions to skillet and stir until coated. Cook until heated and season with salt and pepper. Servewarm.

Pork Chop Potato Casserole

Ingredients

* 8 pork chops (1/2 inch thick)
* 1 teaspoon seasoned salt
* 1 tablespoon vegetable oil
* 1 (10.75 ounce) can condensed cream of celery soup, undiluted
* 2/3 cup milk
* 1/2 cup sour cream
* 1/2 teaspoon salt
* 1/4 teaspoon pepper
* 1 (26 ounce) packagefrozen shredded hash brown potatoes
* 1 cup shredded Cheddar cheese, divided
* 1 (2.8 ounce) can French-fried onions, divided

Directions

➤ Sprinkle pork chops with seasoned salt. In a skillet, brown chops on both sides in oil.In a large bowl, combine the soup, milk, sour cream, salt and pepper; stir in hash browns, 3/4 cup cheese and half of the onions.

➤ Spread into a greased 13-in. x 9-in. x 2-in. baking dish. Arrangepork chops on top.Cover and bake at 350 degrees for 40 minutes.

➤ Uncover; sprinkle with the remaining cheese and onions. Bake, uncovered, 5-10 minutes longer or until potatoes are tender, cheeseis melted and meat juices run clear.

Chicken and Potato Parcels

Ingredients

✿ 4 baking potatoes, peeled and cubed

✿ 2 skinless, boneless chicken breast halves - diced

✿ 2 medium red bell peppers, chopped

✿ 1 large white onion, chopped

✿ 3 celery ribs, chopped

✿ 2 cups favorite barbeque sauce

Directions

➤ Make four foil packets by the following method, using 1-foot squares of heavy duty aluminum foil: fold square in half and smooth flat. Seal each of the narrow ends by folding over each edge threetimes to make a 1/4-inch border, smoothing flat after every fold.

➤ You should now have a foil packet that is open on one long side. Repeat to form four packets.In a bowl or resealable plastic bag, combine the potatoes, chicken cubes, red peppers, onion, celery, and barbequesauce; mix well.

➤ Evenly divide the mixture among the foil packets. Roll up the open end of the packets to seal.

> Place packets on a grill over the coals of a fire. Cook until the potatoes are tender and the chicken is fully cooked, about 25 minutes, depending on the intensity of the heat.

Potato Ginger Soup

Ingredients

* 3 large potatoes, sliced
* 4 cups chicken broth
* 1 pound fresh mushrooms, chopped
* 3 tablespoons grated fresh ginger root
* pepper to taste
* 1/4 cup chopped green onion

Directions

> In a large pot, combine the potatoes, chicken broth, mushrooms and ginger. Bring to a boil, and cook for about 20 minutes. Season with pepper.

> Puree in batches using a blender, or in the pan using an immersion blender. Serve hot, garnished with green onions.

Sweet Potato Souffle III

Ingredients

* 6 sweet potatoes
* 1 cup white sugar
* 1/2 cup milk
* 1/2 cup melted butter

* 1 teaspoon vanilla extract

* 2 eggs, beaten

* 1/2 teaspoon salt

* 1 cup dark brown sugar

* 1/3 cup all-purpose flour

* 1/3 cup melted butter

* 1 cup chopped pecans

Directions

> In a large stockpot, cover sweet potatoes with 1 inch of water; boil for 20 minutes, or until fork tender. Drain, allow to cool and removeskins.Preheat oven to 350 degrees F (175 degrees C).

> Grease or butter one 2 quart casserole dish.Place potatoes in a mixing bowl and with an electric mixer, beat on low speed until potatoes begin to break up. Increase speed to medium high and blend until smooth.

> Reduce speed to low and addsugar, milk, butter, vanilla, eggs and salt. Mix well. Allow any potato 'fibers' to remain on the beater and remove. Pour sweet potato mixture into the casserole dish.

> Prepare the topping in a small bowl by whisking together the brown sugar, flour, butter and pecans. Sprinkle mixture over potatomixture and bake for 40 minutes.

Sweet Potato Pecan Pie

Ingredients

* 1 (9 inch) unbaked pie crust

* 2 cups cooked and mashed sweet potatoes

* 2 eggs

* 3/4 cup white sugar

* 1/2 teaspoon salt

* 1 teaspoon ground cinnamon

- ❀ 1/2 teaspoon ground ginger
- ❀ 1/4 teaspoon ground cloves
- ❀ 1 2/3 cups light cream
- ❀ 3 tablespoons butter, softened
- ❀ 2/3 cup packed brown sugar
- ❀ 2/3 cup chopped pecans

Directions

- ➤ Bake sweet potatoes until tender, peel and mash. Make sure all lumps are removed, straining if necessary.Lightly beat eggs. Blend together eggs and sweet potatoes. Stir in sugar, salt, cinnamon, ginger, and cloves.

- ➤ Blend in cream. Pour into pie shell.Bake in preheated oven at 400 degrees F (205 degrees C) 45-55 minutes or until knife inserted halfway between center and edge of pie comes out clean. Cool completely on rack.

- ➤ To make Caramelized Pecan Topping: Combine butter or margarine, brown sugar, and pecans. Gently drop by spoonfuls over cooled pie to cover top. Broil 5 inches below heat until mixture begins to bubble, about 3 minutes. Watch carefully, if cooked too long, top will turn syrupy. Cool on rack.

Steak and Potato Salad

Ingredients

- ❀ 2 pounds boneless sirloin steak(1 inch thick)
- ❀ 1/2 cup cider or red wine vinegar
- ❀ 1/4 cup olive or vegetable oil
- ❀ 1/4 cup soy sauce
- ❀ 6 cups cubed cooked potatoes
- ❀ 1 cup diced green pepper
- ❀ 1/3 cup chopped green onions
- ❀ 1/4 cup minced fresh parsley

* 1/2 cup Caesar salad dressing Lettuce Leaves

Directions

➢ Place steak in a large resealable plastic bag or shallow glass container. Combine vinegar, oil and soy sauce; pour over the steak. Cover and refrigerate for 1 hour or overnight. drain, discarding marinade.

➢ Grill or broil steak for 8-10 minutes on each side or until meat reaches desired doneness (for medium-rare, a meat thermometer should read 145 degrees F; medium, 160 degrees F; well-done, 170 degrees F).

➢ Slice into thin strips across the grain and place in a bowl. Add potatoes, green pepper, onions, parsley and dressing; toss to coat. Serve on lettuce if desired.

Hash Brown Potato Salad

Ingredients

* 5 bacon strips, diced
* 6 green onions, sliced
* 1 (16 ounce) package frozen cubed hash brown potatoes
* 1/4 cup white wine vinegar or cider vinegar
* 1/2 teaspoon celery salt

Directions

➢ Place bacon in a 1-1/2-qt. microwave-safe bowl. Cover and microwave on high for 5-6 minutes or until bacon is crisp. Removewith a slotted spoon to paper towels to drain. Add onions to thedrippings; cover and microwave on high for 1 minute.

➢ Add the potatoes; cover and cook on high for 10 minutes, stirring several times. Add vinegar, celery salt and bacon; toss.

Restaurant-Quality Baked Potato Soup

Ingredients

- ❀ 2 potatoes
- ❀ 3 tablespoons margarine
- ❀ 2 cups chopped whiteonion
- ❀ 2 tablespoons all-purpose flour
- ❀ 4 cups chicken stock
- ❀ 2 cups water
- ❀ 1/4 cup cornstarch
- ❀ 1 1/2 cups instant mashed potato flakes
- ❀ 1 teaspoon salt
- ❀ 3/4 teaspoon ground black pepper
- ❀ 1/2 teaspoon dried basil
- ❀ 1/8 teaspoon dried thyme
- ❀ 1 cup half-and-half
- ❀ 1/2 cup shredded Cheddar cheese
- ❀ 8 ounces bacon - cooked and crumbled
- ❀ 2 green onions, chopped

Directions

- ➢ Preheat oven to 400 degrees F (200 degrees C). Bake potatoes for 1 hour, or until done. Set aside to cool.Melt butter in a 3 quart saucepan over medium heat.

- ➢ Saute onions until tender and golden brown. Stir in flour, and cook 5 minutes to make a roux. Pour in chicken stock and water. Add cornstarch and mashed potato flakes. Season with salt, pepper, basil and thyme.

- ➢ Bring to a boil, reduce heat, and simmer for 5 minutes.Remove the skin from the cooled potatoes, and discard. Dice thepotatoes into 1/2 inch cubes, and stir into soup, along with the half-and-half.

- ➢ Simmer for 15 to 20 minutes, or until thick. Spoon intobowls, and garnish with shredded cheese, bacon and chopped green onion.

Sweet Potato Balls

Ingredients

- ❀ 1 (40 ounce) can sweet potatoes, drained
- ❀ 1/4 cup butter salt to taste
- ❀ 3 cups crushed cornflakes cereal
- ❀ 3/4 cup real maple syrup
- ❀ 10 large marshmallows

Directions

- ➢ Drain sweet potatoes and put into large mixing bowl. Mash the potatoes with butter or margarine. Salt to taste.

- ➢ Hand pat mixture into 3 inch diameter balls. Roll in crushed corn flakes and put into 9x12 inch greased baking dish. Pour maple syrup evenly over all balls.

- ➢ Bake at 325 degrees F (165 degrees C) for 40 minutes. The last fifteen minutes put a marshmallow over each ball.

Roasted Potatoes with Tomatoes, Basil, and Garlic

Ingredients

- ❀ 2 pounds red potatoes, chopped
- ❀ 1 1/2 cups chopped fresh tomatoes
- ❀ 3/4 cup fresh basil, chopped
- ❀ 3 cloves garlic, pressed
- ❀ 3 tablespoons extra virgin olive oil

* 1 teaspoon chopped fresh rosemary

Directions

> Preheat oven to 400 degrees F (200 degrees C).In the prepared baking dish, toss the potatoes, tomatoes, basil, and garlic with the olive oil.

> Sprinkle with the rosemary. Bake 20 to 30 minutes in the preheated oven, turning occasionally, until tender.

Veggie Potato Salad for a Crowd

Ingredients

* 3 pounds small red potatoes, unpeeled
* 2 cups chopped red onions
* 12 ounces fresh green beans, trimmed, cooked al dente
* 3 1/2 cups roughly chopped red cabbage
* 1 pint grape tomatoes, halved
* 3 tablespoons capers, drained
* 2 ounces basil leaves, trimmed and torn in large pieces
* salt and freshly ground black pepper to taste

* Mustard Dressing:
* 2/3 cup extra virgin olive oil
* 3 tablespoons white balsamic or rice vinegar
* 1 teaspoon salt
* 1 1/2 teaspoons Dijon mustard
* 3 cloves garlic, crushed

Directions

- In a large pot, cook whole potatoes until done. Cool. Cut into bite-sized pieces. In a very large bowl, combine all ingredients frompotatoes through basil.

- Whisk together dressing ingredients. Toss with vegetables, and add salt and pepper to taste. Chill. Serve.

Scalloped Sweet Potatoes and Apples

Ingredients

- ❀ 6 sweet potatoes
- ❀ 1 1/2 cups peeled, cored and sliced apples
- ❀ 1/2 cup brown sugar
- ❀ 1/2 teaspoon salt
- ❀ 1 teaspoon ground mace
- ❀ 1/4 cup butter

Directions

- Place sweet potatoes in a large pot with enough water to cover, and bring to a boil. Boil until tender, then cool, peel, and cut into 1/4inch slices.

- Preheat oven to 350 degrees F (175 degrees C). Grease a 9x13 inch baking dish.Arrange half the sweet potatoes in the bottom of the prepared baking dish. Layer half of the apples over the sweet potatoes.

- In a small bowl, mix together brown sugar, salt, and mace, then sprinklehalf of the mixture over the apple layer. Dot with half the butter. Repeat layers of sweet potato and apple, and top with remaining brown sugar mixture and butter.

- Bake in the preheated oven for 50 minutes, until apples are tender and top is golden brown.

Pumpkin, Sweet Potato, and Leek Soup

Ingredients

- 3 tablespoons olive oil
- 2 leeks, chopped
- 1 small white onion, chopped
- 1 stalk celery, chopped
- 1 small carrot, chopped
- 2 sweet potatoes, peeled and diced
- 1 medium sugar pumpkin, seeded and cubed
- 2 tablespoons chopped garlic
- 1 quart chicken stock
- 1 cup heavy whipping cream
- 1 bay leaf
- 1 tablespoon chopped fresh sage
- 1 pinch ground cloves
- 1 pinch ground nutmeg
- 1 pinch ground cinnamon salt to taste
- ground black pepper to taste

Directions

➤ Heat oil in a heavy-bottom pot. Add leeks, onion, celery, carrot, sweet potatoes, pumpkin, and garlic, and saute until they start to brown.

➤ Add bay leaf, stock, and cream; bring to a boil. Reduce to a simmer and cook until all vegetables are tender. Add sage, cloves, nutmeg, cinnamon, and salt and pepper to taste. Remove bay leaf, and puree. Serve hot.

Pot O' Gold Potato Soup

Ingredients

- 3/4 cup chopped celery
- 3/4 cup chopped onion
- 1/4 cup butter or margarine
- 2 (14.5 ounce) cans chicken broth
- 2 1/3 cups mashed potato flakes
- 1 1/2 cups milk
- 1/2 cup cubed process American cheese
- 3/4 teaspoon garlic salt
- 1/8 teaspoon chili powder
- 1/2 cup sour cream

Directions

- In a 3-qt. saucepan, saute celery and onion in butter for 2-3 minutes. stir in broth; bring to boil. Reduce heat. Add potato flakes; cook and stir for 5-7 minutes.

- Add milk, cheese, garlic salt and chili powder. Cook and stir until cheese is melted. Just before serving, add sour cream and heat through (do not boil).

Speedy Sweet Potatoes

Ingredients

- 2 (16 ounce) cans sweet potatoes, drained
- 1/2 teaspoon salt
- 1 (8 ounce) can crushed pineapple, drained
- 1/4 cup coarsely chopped pecans
- 1 tablespoon brown sugar
- 1 cup miniaturemarsh-mallows, dividedground nutmeg

Directions

- In a 1-1/2-qt. microwave-safe dish, layer sweet potatoes, salt, pineapple, pecans, brown sugar and 1/2 cup marshmallows.

- Cover and microwave on high for 5-7 minutes or until bubbly around theedges. Top with the remaining marshmallows. Heat, uncovered, on high for 1-2 minutes or until marshmallows puff. Sprinkle with nutmeg.

All-Time Favorite Sweet Potato Pudding

Ingredients

- 1 (29 ounce) can sweet potatoes
- 2 eggs, lightly beaten
- 1 cup packed brown sugar
- 1 cup milk
- 1/4 cup melted butter
- 2 teaspoons lemon juice
- 1/4 teaspoon ground ginger
- 1/4 teaspoon ground cloves
- 1/2 teaspoon ground cinnamon
- 1/2 teaspoon salt

Directions

- Preheat an oven to 350 degrees F (175 degrees C). Grease a 1 1/2 quart baking dish. Combine sweet potatoes and eggs in a medium bowl. Beat in the brown sugar, milk, butter, lemon juice, ginger, cloves, cinnamon, salt. Pour into prepared dish. Bake in preheated oven until hot and golden brown on top, about30 minutes.

No-Fuss Sweet Potato Pumpkin Mousse

Ingredients

- 1 (15 ounce) can cut sweet potatoes in syrup, drained (1/4 cup syrup reserved)
- 1 (15 ounce) can 100% purepumpkin puree
- 1/4 cup honey

- ❋ 1/2 teaspoon pumpkin piespice
- ❋ 1/2 teaspoon ground cinnamon
- ❋ 2 cups sweetened* whipped cream or whipped dessert topping

Directions

➢ Puree sweet potatoes and reserved syrup in a food processor. Add pumpkin, honey, pie spice, and cinnamon, and process untilblended and smooth. Scrape into a large bowl.

➢ Fold in the whipped cream (don't over mix) and serve, or store mousse tightly covered in the refrigerator for up to 24 hours.

Garlic Thyme Potatoes

Ingredients

- ❋ 2 pounds small red potatoes
- ❋ 4 garlic cloves, minced
- ❋ 1 tablespoon olive or canola oil
- ❋ 1 tablespoon minced fresh thyme
- ❋ 1/2 teaspoon grated lemon peel
- ❋ 1/4 teaspoon salt
- ❋ 1/4 teaspoon pepper

Directions

➢ Peel a narrow strip of skin around the center of each potato. Place potatoes in a steamer basket; place in a saucepan over 1 in. ofwater. Bring to a boil.

➢ Cover and steam for 20-30 minutes or until tender. In a serving bowl, combine the remaining ingredients. Add potatoes and toss gently to coat

---

Potato and Spinach Croquettes

Ingredients

- ✤ 1 pound baking potatoes, peeled and diced
- ✤ 1 pinch ground nutmeg
- ✤ 4 teaspoons butter
- ✤ 1 egg yolk
- ✤ 1 cup vegetable oil for frying
- ✤ 1/3 cup freshly grated Parmesan cheese
- ✤ 1/3 cup frozen chopped spinach, thawed and drained
- ✤ 1/2 cup all-purpose flour
- ✤ 3 eggs, beaten
- ✤ 1 tablespoon peanut oil
- ✤ 1 1/3 cups dry bread crumbs

Directions

- ➢ Place the potatoes into a saucepan and fill with enough water to cover. Bring to a boil, then reduce the heat and simmer until tender enough to easily pierce with a fork.

- ➢ Drain and toss gently over low heat for a minute to completley dry out. Press them through a sieveor just mash with a potato masher until smooth. Season with salt,pepper and nutmeg. Mix in the butter and egg yolk, then spread out on a tray to cool.

- ➢ Preheat the oil in a deep-fryer to 365 degrees F (180 degrees C). The oil is the proper temperature when a cube of bread browns in about 15 seconds.

- ➢ In a large bowl, mix together the Parmesan cheese and spinach. Blend in the mashed potatoes. On a floured surface, using floured hands, roll small handfuls of the mixture into cylinders about 3/4 inch thick and 2 1/2 inches long. Tap theends to flatten.

- ➢ Season 1/2 cup of flour with salt and pepper and place on a tray. In a shallow bowl, whisk together theeggs and peanut oil. Place the bread crumbs into a separate shallow bowl. Roll the croquettes in seasoned flour, then dip into theegg and then coat with breadcrumbs.

- ➢ Fry the croquettes a few at a time, so they have some room in between, until golden brown, 5 to 6 minutes. Carefully remove from the oil using a slotted spoon and drain on crumpled paper towels.

Sweet Potato Salad

Ingredients

- ❀ 3 pounds red potatoes
- ❀ 2 1/2 pounds sweet potatoes
- ❀ 1/4 cup white wine vinegar
- ❀ 1/4 cup olive oil
- ❀ 1 clove garlic, minced
- ❀ 1/4 cup dill pickle relish
- ❀ 1/2 cup chopped red onion
- ❀ 1/3 cup mayonnaise
- ❀ 1 pinch ground black pepper
- ❀ 1/3 cup sour cream
- ❀ 1/2 cup chopped parsley

Directions

➢ Bring a large pot of salted water to a boil. Add potatoes; cook until tender but still firm, about 15 minutes. Drain, cool and slice.

➢ In a large bowl, combine the vinegar, olive oil, garlic, dill pickle relish and onion. Mix and cover with sliced potatoes.Whisk together mayonnaise, pepper, sour cream and parsley. Pour over potatoes and chill at least 8 hours.

Ice Cream Baked Potatoes

Ingredients

- ❀ 1 pint vanilla ice cream
- ❀ 1 (1 ounce) envelope instant cocoa
- ❀ 4 tablespoons sweetened whipped cream

Directions

- ➢ Scoop out 4 balls of ice cream roughly the size and shape of small potatoes. Roll in the hot cocoa mix until coated.

- ➢ Place on a plateand top with a dollop of whipped cream. The ice cream will look likebaked potatoes with sour cream on top. Eat and enjoy.

Mashed Maple Sweet Potatoes

Ingredients

- ❀ 4 large sweet potatoes
- ❀ 1/2 cup softened butter
- ❀ 1 cup heavy cream
- ❀ 2 tablespoons vanilla extract
- ❀ 1/2 cup packed light brown sugar
- ❀ 1 teaspoon salt
- ❀ 1/2 cup maple syrup
- ❀ 1 cup chopped pecans
- ❀ 2 eggs, beaten
- ❀ 2 tablespoons maple syrup
- ❀ 1/4 cup chopped pecans

Directions

- ➢ Preheat oven to 375 degrees F (190 degrees C). Line a baking sheet with aluminum foil. Place sweet potatoes onto the prepared baking sheet, and bake in preheated oven until soft, 45 minutes to 1 hour. Remove from the oven and allow to cool slightly before peeling and placing into a large bowl.

- ➢ Preheat oven to 350 degrees F (175 degrees C). Butter a 2 quart casserole dish. Mash the warm potatoes along with butter, cream, vanilla extract, brown sugar, salt, 1/2 cup maple syrup, 1 cup chopped pecans, and eggs.

> Spread mashedsweet potato into the prepared bakingdish, and sprinkle with the remaining 2 tablespoons of maple syrup, and 1/4 cup of pecans. Bake sweet potatoes in preheated oven until thoroughly hot, 30 to35 minutes.

Ham, Potato and Broccoli Casserole

Ingredients

- 1 (16 ounce) package frozen French fries
- 1 (16 ounce) package frozen chopped broccoli
- 1 1/2 cups cooked, cubed ham
- 1 (10.75 ounce) can condensed cream of mushroom soup
- 1 (10.75 ounce) can milk
- 1/4 cup mayonnaise
- 1 cup grated Parmesan cheese

Directions

> Preheat oven to 375 degrees F (190 degrees C).Spray a 9x13 inch baking dish with cooking spray. Cover bottom of dish with layer of French fries.

> Add a layer of broccoli, then sprinkleham evenly over broccoli. In a small bowl mix together soup, milk and mayonnaise.

> Pour mixtureevenly over ingredients in bakingdish and sprinkle with cheese. Bake uncovered in preheated oven for 40 minutes.

Golden Rice Cakes with Sweet Potato-Ginger

Ingredients

- 3 tablespoons canola oil

- ❀ 2 cloves garlic, minced
- ❀ 2 cups dry jasmine rice
- ❀ 2 1/2 cups water
- ❀ 1 teaspoon salt
- ❀ 1 sweet potato
- ❀ 1 (14 ounce) can coconut milk
- ❀ 1/2 cup orange juice
- ❀ 1 tablespoon minced fresh ginger root
- ❀ salt and pepper to taste
- ❀ 1 carrot, coarsely chopped
- ❀ 1/2 red bell pepper, chopped
- ❀ 4 green onions, chopped
- ❀ 2 eggs, beaten
- ❀ 2 green onions, thinly sliced

Directions

➢ In a saucepan with a tight-fitting lid heat 1 tablespoon of the canola oil with the garlic over medium heat for 1 minute, stirring constantly.

➢ Add the jasmine rice and stir constantly for 1 minute more. Add the 2-1/2 cups water and 1 teaspoon salt.

➢ Bring rice to a boil, then reduce the heat to low, cover the pan, and cook the rice for 15 minutes. Transfer the rice to a large bowl, and let it cool for 15 minutes While the rice cooks, cut the sweet potato into thirds.

➢ Place the pieces in a pot, and cover them with cold water. Bring the potatoes to a boil, and cook them until they are tender, about 20 minutes. Drain and let them cool.

➢ In a saucepan bring the coconut milk, the water or orange juice, and the minced ginger almost to a boil, then turn the heat to low and cook for 5 minutes. Remove the pan from the heat.

➢ Peel the skin off the cooled sweet potato. Puree the sweet potato flesh with the coconut-ginger liquid in a blender or food processor. Pour the sweet-potato puree back into the saucepan and add salt and pepper.

- ➢ Mince the carrot, the red pepper, and the coarsely chopped scallions in a food processor. Add 1/2 of the jasmine rice and the 2beaten eggs; run the machine in spurts until the mixture has a mealyconsistency

- ➢ .Put this mixture back into the bowl with the rest of thejasmine rice and mix well. Put half of this mixture into a clean bowl.Heat two skillets or a large griddle over medium-high heat. Divide the remaining canola oil between the skillets or spread it on thegriddle.

- ➢ Divide the rice mixture in each bowl into thirds. Form each of the six parts into a ball then placeeach ball in a skillet or on thegriddle. Pat the ball down to form a cake about 1 1/2 inches thick. Fry the cakes for 3 to 4 minutes per side, or until they are golden brown.

- ➢ Reheat the sauce, and ladle it into plates. Place a rice cake on each plate, and top with the finely chopped scallions.

Parmesan Potato Soup

Ingredients

- ❋ 4 potatoes, cubed
- ❋ 3/4 cup chopped onion
- ❋ 1/2 cup all-purpose flour
- ❋ 1/2 teaspoon seasoning salt
- ❋ 1/4 teaspoon sage
- ❋ 4 1/2 cups chicken broth
- ❋ 1 cup grated Parmesan cheese
- ❋ 1/2 cup margarine
- ❋ 1/2 teaspoon dried basil
- ❋ 1/4 teaspoon celery salt
- ❋ 1/4 teaspoon onion salt
- ❋ 1/4 teaspoon ground black pepper
- ❋ 1/4 teaspoon dried thyme
- ❋ 6 cups milk

12 slices crisp cooked bacon, crumbled

Directions

- Cook the potatoes in boiling water until tender. In a soup kettle, saute onion in butter or margarine until tender.

- Stir in flour and spices. Gradually add broth, stirring constantly. Bring to a boil; cook and stir for 2 minutes.

- Add potatoes, and return to a boil. Reduce heat, cover, and simmer for 10 minutes. Stir in milk and cheese. Heat through. Stir in bacon.

Pat's Potato Salad

Ingredients

  12 medium red potatoes, cooked, peeled and cubed
  1 medium red onion, chopped
  1 cup chopped fresh parsley
  1 1/2 cups mayonnaise
  1 cup sour cream
  1/4 cup sugar
  1/4 cup vinegar
  4 teaspoons ground mustard
  1 teaspoon salt

Directions

- In a large bowl, combine potatoes, onion and parsley. In a small bowl, combine remaining ingre-dients. Pour over potatoes and mix well. Refrigerate at least 1 hour before serving. Salad can beprepared a day ahead.

Chicken and Potato Soup

Ingredients

- ❀ 2 tablespoons butter

- ❀ 2 1/2 pounds skinless, boneless chicken breast halves - diced

- ❀ 1 large onion, diced

- ❀ 6 medium potatoes, diced

- ❀ 1 (15 ounce) can carrots, drained

- ❀ 1 (10 ounce) can peas, drained

- ❀ 1 (11 ounce) can corn, drained

- ❀ 1 cup milk

- ❀ 2 cups water, or as needed hot pepper sauce to taste salt to taste

- ❀ ground black pepper to taste

Directions

- ➢ Melt the butter in a large pot over medium heat, and cook thechicken 10 minutes, or until evenly browned and juices run clear.

- ➢ Mix the onion into pot with the chicken. Mix in potatoes, carrots, peas, and corn. Pour in milk an enough water to cover allingredients.

- ➢ Season with hot sauce, salt, and pepper. Bring to a boil. Reduce heat to low, and continue cooking 30 minutes, stirringoccasionally, until potatoes are tender.

No-Fry Spicy Potato Skins

Ingredients

- ❀ 4 large russet potatoes

- ❀ 1/4 cup olive oil

- ❀ 1 teaspoon salt

- ❀ 1/2 teaspoon ground black pepper

- ❀ 1 1/2 teaspoons chili powder

- ❀ 1 1/2 teaspoons curry powder

- ❀ 1 1/2 teaspoons ground coriander seed

Directions

- ➤ Preheat the oven to 400 degrees F (200 degrees C).Bake the potatoes for 1 hour. Remove the potatoes from the oven, but keep the oven on.

- ➤ Slice the potatoes in half lengthwise, and let them cool for 10 mins. Scoop out most of the potato flesh, leaving about 1/4 inch of flesh against the potato skin (you can save the potato flesh for another use, like mashed potatoes)

- ➤ Cut each potato half crosswise into 3 pieces. Place the olive oil in a small cup. Dip each potato piece into the olive oil and place it on a baking sheet. Repeat this with the remaining potato pieces

- ➤ Combine the salt and the spices and sprinkle the mixture over the potatoes. Bake the potato skins for 15 minutes or until they are crispy and brown. Serve them immediately.

Make-Ahead Potatoes

Ingredients

- ❀ 10 large potatoes, peeled and quartered
- ❀ 1 cup sour cream
- ❀ 1 (8 ounce) package cream cheese, softened
- ❀ 6 tablespoons butter, divided
- ❀ 2 tablespoons dried minced onion
- ❀ 1/2 teaspoon salt
- ❀ Paprika

Directions

- ➤ Place potatoes in a Dutch oven or large kettle; cover with water and bring to a boil. Reduce heat; cover and cook for 20-25 minutes or until potatoes are tender.

- ➤ Drain potatoes and place in a bowl; mash. Add sour cream, cream cheese, 4 tablespoons butter, onion and salt; stir until smooth and the cream cheese and butter are melted. Spread in a greased 13-in. x 9-in. x 2-in. baking dish.

➢ Melt the remaining butter; drizzle over the potatoes. Sprinkle with paprika. Refrigerate or bake immediately, covered, at 350 degrees F for 40 minutes; uncover and bake 20 minutes longer.

➢ If potatoes aremade ahead and refrigerated, let stand at room temperature for 30 minutes before baking.

CPSIA information can be obtained
at www.ICGtesting.com
Printed in the USA
BVHW010336080521
606756BV00008B/1872

9 781802 673821